FROM TRANSFORMATION TO
TRANSFORMACTION

FROM TRANSFORMATION TO TRANSFORMACTION

Methods and Practices

David Gutmann

Routledge
Taylor & Francis Group

LONDON AND NEW YORK

First published 2009 by Karnac Books Ltd.

2 Park Square, Milton Park, Abingdon, Oxfordshire OX14 4RN
52 Vanderbilt Avenue, New York, NY 10017

Routledge is an imprint of the Taylor & Francis Group, an informa business

First issued in paperback 2019

British Library Cataloguing in Publication Data

A C.I.P. for this book is available from the British Library

   ISBN 978-1-85575-615-1 (pbk)
   ISBN 978-0-367-32464-3 (hbk)

Translated and reviewed by Marie-Claude Confida-Dufeigneux

Edited, designed, and produced by The Studio Publishing Services Ltd, www.publishingservicesuk.co.uk
e-mail: studio@publishingservicesuk.co.uk

CONTENTS

To my late mother, Sarah Myriam (1922–2006), and my very lively wife Annie and my sons, Michaël, Raphaël, and Benjamin

David Gutmann was born in Paris in 1950. A graduate of the Institute of Political Studies in Paris, with also a Masters in Public Law and an MSc in Political Sciences, he was the mentee of Maurice Duverger but also the disciple of Wilfred Bion. He is currently the President and CEO for Praxis International (Conseillers de Synthese/Advisers in Leadership), a company that he founded with Jacqueline Ternier-David in 1989. He also is the Executive Vice-President of the International Forum for Social Innovation and directs the Third Programme Leading Consultation (jointly organized with Hull University, The Business School, UK, and IFSI) which leads to MPhil and PhD. Adviser to numerous leaders of companies or other institutions in France as well as abroad, he is *Maître de Conferences* at l'Ecole Nationale d'Administration (ENA), Visiting Professor in the Business School, Hull University, and External Professor at the University of Glamorgan (Business School), Board Member of the International Association for Group Psychotherapy and Group Processes (IAGP) and past President of its section "Organizational Consultation". He also initiates and directs international conferences on the theme of Transformation.

Miriam Berger is a clinical psychologist, member of Besod'Siach and Chief Psychologist of Amcha, an organization for the psychological support of the survivors of the Shoah and their descendants.

Avi Bergman is a clinical psychologist, and a consultant in organization. He is one of the founders of Besod Siach, the Israeli Association for the progress of dialogue between groups in conflicts. He teaches at Tel Aviv University.

Emmanuel d'André is Honorary President, Group 3 Suisses-Cofidis, President of the Royaumont Foundation.

Yehuda Lancry was Israel's Ambassador to France from 1992 to 1995. A former Deputy Speaker of the Knesset and Chairman of the Ethic Committee (1996–1999), he was appointed ambassador of the United Nations in 1999, serving until 2002.

Beverley Malone PhD, RN, FAAN, is the CEO of the National League for Nursing, USA, a Member of IFSI, France, and AKRI, USA, a Fellow of the A. K. Rice Institute, USA, and a faculty member of Leading Consultation, France.

Ronan Pierre has been assigned temporarily to The International Forum for Social Innovation by the French Navy during his national military service.

Laurence Ponthieu was an intern at Praxis International.

Pascale Ravot-Loucheux was born in 1969. She graduated from Sciences PO in Paris and has a Masters in marketing and research. Pascale is responsible for one of the four departments in the global Fast Moving Consumer Goods Unit in TNS Sofres France—a worldwide research company. She has been working in market research since 1997 and joined TNS in 2000 after experience in an advertising company.

Catherine Sandler, MD, has over twenty years' experience of consulting to individuals and organizations. A doctor at Sandler Lanz, she is one of the UK's leading executive coaches, working with business leaders and top teams at Board level. Catherine has taught at London Business School, INSEAD, and the Tavistock Clinic.

Jacqueline Ternier-David is President of the International Forum for Social Innovation, Paris; CEO of Praxis International (Conseillers de Synthèse/Advisers in Leadership); Academic Adviser, the Leadership and Consultation Group, Hull University, Business School; External Fellow of the University of Glamorgan.

Christophe Verrier, MD, is Treasurer of The International Forum for Social Innovation; Academic Adviser, the Leadership and Consultation Group, Hull University, Business School; External Fellow of the University of Glamorgan; Adviser in Leadership, Praxis International, Paris.

Pierre Zecchini was President, Group 3 Suisses International, between 2002 and 2008.

PREFACE ONE

For the past twenty years I have used the services of an Adviser in Leadership, and I can unequivocally affirm that his is an arduous career.

It is, in fact, a profession in which the Adviser in Leadership is expected not to give advice to his partner—such an evocative and rich word. Sometimes, he must even expect to receive and accept counsel.

It is a profession in which one must convert convictions into working hypotheses and present them unassumingly, in order not to exert exaggerated influence on the "Other" present in his partner.

It is a profession in which one must continually reveal immanent paradox and be aware of inevitable distinctions from one's working partner, in order to lead him or her to emerge from habitual ways of reasoning and synthesis.

It is a profession in which the consultant is so well allied with his working partner and so well integrated into the culture of his partner's enterprise that, at times of institutional duress, he might even become the system's first choice for a scapegoat.

And last, it is a profession in which it is essential for the consultant to avoid the projections coming from his partner and those around him, all the while attending to them with keen sensitivity.

But, in concrete terms, what is the usefulness of an Adviser in Leadership?

First, and unlike the working relationship needed for psycho-analysis, the consulting process consists in two human beings of flesh and blood, who carry out unrestricted face-to-face dialogues and who, in spite of the winding paths that those same dialogues pursue, seek to attain a clear purpose. That purpose is to bring forth a more effective manager or corporate participant.

For this to develop, the principal requirement is a substantial and mutual trust in the relationship with the Adviser in Leadership. The leader's or manager's position is always a lonely and solitary one. The mutual trust built with the consultant might be the corpo-rate manager's only reliable companion, permitting him to confi-dently express doubts within this shared relationship, enabling him to comprehend his habitual patterns of thought, and presenting him with yet other new or transformed possibilities for thought and decision. In short, the dialogues shared with the Adviser in Leadership serve to expand the manager's awareness of the rich variety of personal and institutional "Otherness" that is extant and discoverable.

But it must be clear that the Adviser in Leadership essentially focuses on his partner's professional role, even as both participants cannot but also be aware of other, human dimensions.

Thus, little by little, within this space for being unguarded and for re-creating, the partner increases the freedom and depth of his capacity for reflection. He deepens his awareness of himself, notably in regard to his relationships with the enterprise of which he is in charge. He better understands the resistances that he endures or provokes, once they are reflected back to him in images distorted in the mirror that the Adviser in Leadership considerately holds up for his view.

Each person is unique and so different that his or her personal experience in this process is not very interesting to anyone else. Thus, I doubt that I will inspire much passion when I say that David Gutmann and I have explored the matter of omnipotence, as well as the distinctions between power and authority and between want and desire.

I would like to underscore the relevance of the notion of passage in this process of transformation. If one allows himself to be entrapped in the experience of passage, it can often be extremely painful. However, it can also become a benign encounter if one recalls at the right moment that a passage consists essentially in a given period of time preceding a transformation that one wants and anticipates to be positive or beneficial.

Now, twenty years after beginning this passage, I have changed, as has the entire world. Certainly not all for the better, but surely a little better, thanks to the Adviser in Leadership's close and benevolent companionship.

David Gutmann and I continue to address each other with both our first and last names, in order to ensure intimacy and respect, of equal necessity in enabling one to better follow Blaise Pascal's maxim: "Work towards thinking well . . . this is the principle of ethics". So that there should be no ambiguity about the practical role of the Adviser in Leadership, I will add: "And work towards doing well . . . in order to continually improve our performance of affairs."

Emmanuel d'André
Honorary President, Group 3 Suisses, Cofidis; President,
Royaumont Foundation
January 2009

PREFACE TWO

One of the most engaging aspects of the work of David Gutmann—the "good man" promised by his family name—is undeniably his deep involvement with language and his pursuit of its sources and dynamics.

Whether through recurrent references to etymology, destined to polish a word and restore its original brilliance, or in the distillation of abridged or blended words not found in any dictionary, the full measure of David Gutmann's genius shines in his inventiveness and intrepid exploration of novel linguistic territories.

What extraordinary linkages are revealed in the meaning of words! Simply recall, for example, that the French word *safran* (saffron, in English), the treasured spice, refers also to a ship's rudder, and, by association, to the notion of government and its modern translation as "management".

Consider for a moment the subtle shift that David Gutmann brings about in a brief reflection on a series of words: *la vie*, *la survie*, *la frénévie* ("life, survival, hyperlife," in English). The notion of subsistence, through progressive refinement of the words and their roots, undergoes a metamorphosis into *sous-vie* or "under-life" (or even "underlying life" in English).

One would have to be completely deaf to the linguistic subtlety generated by the radical shift in prepositional prefixes from *sur* ("on, "over," or "sur-", in English) to *sous* ("beneath" or "under", in English), in order to miss out on the new patch of reality thus clarified and set free from the meanings customarily assumed in everyday discourse.

Likewise with *frénévie*, a neologism that "we invented several years ago", according to David Gutmann's commentary. Although the reader may intuitively look up the word "frenzy" or "frenetic" in the dictionary, the new word has been transmuted by the effects of its fusion and association with the French word *vie* ("life", in English). Words or meanings blended and hybridized in this way are imbued with the power to stimulate new intellectual, emotional, and linguistic growth.

Thus, solely by uttering *frénévie*, one opens access to an avalanche of meanings, with many angles that are ordinarily buried in the steady erosion of language. In the process set in motion by the creation of *frénévie*, one opens up forbidden or forgotten areas of linguistic enquiry, long hidden in the sediment of routine usage. Something absent has been added back into one facet of life's meaning. Anew, one becomes aware of the profound alienation born of our unthinking "race against time" and our "pre-programmed escape" in the spurious obliteration of "lack and loss, essential even today for desire to emerge". Lack and loss give birth to desire, and all four ingredients are vital for life itself.

For David Gutmann, to take action upon language is also to change reality. In the melding of two words, transformation and action, he establishes a single new concept of *Transformaction*, in which the very idea of change is brought to the fore and accentuated. Transformaction is not a slick makeover for commercial purposes, nor is it conceived and distorted by institutional or marketing heavyweights. Rather, it deals with a shift by which the simple insertion of the letter *c* initiates for the individual a burst of further possibilities and opens for the collective unaccustomed avenues for sharing exploration of life's myriad expressions of the "other".

David Gutmann's diverse fields of activity and interest attest to his art: linguistics, psychoanalysis, philosophy, political science, and organizational and institutional psychology. For him, they all champion the cardinal objective: the sovereign good of individuals in their passage through the world.

For this passage, with its numerous crossroads and complex byways, over peak and abyss, he presents an indispensable and particularly inspired guide for the voyager astray in us.

Yehuda Lancry

PREFACE THREE

In almost thirty years of sharing and close contact with Praxis International, can I say that my role as manager and leader has been "transformed"? Is my role performance more effective because of the consultations? With practice, have I been able to bring into harmony my inner nature and my outer life?

How shall I respond to these questions?

The response is not self-evident. Indeed, it seems to me that only through some mysterious alchemy do the tools used by the consultants give rise to realizations or insights that themselves mobilize transformation.

The tools used are many and varied. They are proposed, tried out, embraced, assimilated, and forgotten. They encompass black boxes, glass boxes, zig-zags of movement forward and back, the flow of progress and regression, insights, inputs, and outputs. In sum, all these often abstruse and tough-to-enunciate constructs acquire coherence mainly through experience and afterwards through attempts at verbalization while one passes through transformation from one state to another.

In my time with Praxis International, there were moments of challenging hands-on experience in order to bring out sundry conscious and unconscious anxieties present in my relationships with the institution, taken to mean my boss, my colleagues, and my co-workers.

There were also calls on my intellectual faculties to find solutions that, all things considered, would be acceptable and sensible. There was debate and there was dissent, as well as rich contributions to the dynamics of guiding the evolution of socio-technical systems and of those who bring them to life.

I hold precious three discoveries or constructs that have been valuable in the course of my evolution as manager.

First, the concept of a "working hypothesis". Embedded in the dialectics helpful in moving any human transaction forward, the simple formulation of a working hypothesis carries awesome force. My earlier reasoning was almost binary: I had the solution or I did not. Now, with the same self-confidence, I can formulate diverse working hypotheses, without the risks of being judged or of being judgemental.

Each person, while playing the same score and rhythm as others in the system, digs out and uses notes from his own unconscious in order to make sense of the unfolding scene. This way of approaching dialogue and discussion is a veritable antidote to being overrun by an overbearing ego, because, while involved in forming a working hypothesis, one continually adapts to the reality perceived, enters into fantasy and make-believe, relives key moments (what if . . .? what if I . . .?), and re-enters the rhythm of the performance, eventually synthesizing a fresh take on beliefs that were formerly unquestioned or unimaginable. All the parties involved come together with transformed perspectives, channel their energies, and confer. A consensus may reveal itself, in the moment or somewhat later. And so, one begins to move forward.

Second, the concept of the "here and now" has been for me a true revelation. It is true that the concept is nothing new, but what for me is certain is that the here and now was deeply ingrained in my core after a particularly trenchant exercise during professional training focused on authority and leadership. The crux of the matter lay in the fact that I found that none of my personal resources, whether physical or psychological, succeeded in providing a solution for the poignant situation with which I was confronted. There and then, I met my absolute limits. Yet, in that predicament, simply attending to my immediate experience set in motion a genuine act of transformation that redeemed me. And, since then, nothing has been the same. I have, in fact, acquired a reflexive appeal to the power of the here and now, which, all these many years later, is still an unquestionable aid and comfort in difficult circumstances. And so, one continues to move forward.

Last, I want to keep present in my awareness two regulatory mechanisms described by Freud: the reality principle and the pleasure principle. Here again, no surprise, but rather a personal adaptation and adoption, because this incursion into psychoanalysis via the application to professional affairs of the sentiment of infantile omnipotence is of considerable help in disentangling and side-stepping the institutional or personal blockages with which this fantasy is associated. While not exactly wanting to slip into caricature, I ask myself what have I not missed in earlier discussions by confusing reality with pleasure! By mistaking "I can" for "I want". In the consultation with an Adviser in Leadership, objective analysis allows me to sort out poorly conceived behaviours and to replace them with more reasonable postures.

It is well to engage in experimentation from which one can take some learning for present and future use. But full consciousness of learning, the "ah-ha!" moment of recognition, is not possible without the painful, disconcerting confrontation between a novel experience and what one has previously accepted as certain and true. Learning from experience in this way leads to adaptation and adoption of new awareness, which is expressed through transformation. And so, such is the far-reaching value of insightful dialogue with an Adviser in Leadership. Hence, one continues steadily forward.

Certainly, an assortment of implements is effective in contributing to our growth. Their regular or occasional practice contributes to immediate bursts of learning as well as to more gradual maturation of our understanding. Finally, there are probably no hard and fast rules. Everything depends on the readiness and fertility of the individual terrain.

But, how do we accomplish those transformations that we fervently hope for, without knowing very well how to do so? Or, more to the point, how have I been able to transform a course of action in my own life by using these resources?

Using my own experience, it is clear to me that all Praxis

International's effort is directed to setting in motion vital forces, so that they in turn spark transformations and stir revelations. By delving into the leader's impulses, strivings, and/or desires, the powers of the unconscious begin to surface and lead to discernment and insight, and thus to actions transformed. The transformative power liberated in moving from one state to another begins to "move" a leader when the intense forcefulness of his or her unconscious is no longer indiscriminately active, but is instead present in conscious form.

The consultant works towards revelation and acts as midwife and intermediary for it. Secure in his own self-possession and acumen, the consultant enables the leader or manager to elicit whatever lies inside, now outside of consciousness, and afterwards accompanies him in discovering that his own array of resources, including personal conditioning, beliefs, absolute certainties, and strengths, may quite naturally lead him to suddenly abandon a preplanned solution, because the way to salvation lies within what is immediate and yet new. This immediate yet new is what permits the sensitive modification of a present state. It is as if this passage is conceived inside us, and so we must continually give birth to renewals through transformation in order to enhance our own life and the life of the institutions for which we are temporarily responsible.

Provocative and fruitful working hypotheses that jar homeostasis and are directly involved in transformation—they, I believe, are what has most effectively influenced and stirred me in my personal and professional life; all this through the alchemy of regular encounters, confrontations, practical experiences, advances and retreats, progress and regression, of which the Adviser in Leadership is a master builder.

The ego is the worst enemy of these kinds of transformation, because the ego is at the centre of perception and evaluation of conscious operations. Deliberate setting out to transform any situation or perspective obligates the active participation of the ego, whereas veritable transformation, which leads to profound modification, relies upon appeal to internal strengths, unique to each individual and corresponding to the individual's basic or inner nature.

The credit for our ability to engage transformation is due to the marvellous instruments that are part of the consultant's work: the reflections on institutions, on dialogues held and conversations contested, on insights and other challenges to mental and emotional transformation, on lessons taken from theories and real-life situations.

In short, my experience has been that every input from Praxis International works to get us off to a good start, channelling our personal energies in a direction that is solely our own: a path that is the true and awesome path of all life: our individual journey to Becoming and Being.

Pierre Zecchini

FOREWORD

This book describes a journey of discovery from transformation to transformaCtion that extends and enhances the life of the organization. The journey occurs on the seas of anxiety and passion, which threaten to sweep an organization towards either paralysis and depression or a hyperlife of perpetual hysterical motion. On this journey, the consultant serves as the chief advisory navigator, helping to guide the ship to circumvent the dangerous rocks as the organization zigs and zags though the waters. While at times the organization may find itself circling in a vortex, trapped in cyclical duplication and potential disappearance, there exists the underlying assurance that transformation is occurring, has occurred, and will continue throughout the journey to transformaCtion.

David Gutmann points out that this is a never-ending journey for the organization, even after the work of the consultants has ended. He and his colleagues note that the consultant accompanies the institution in its transformation work, both expecting and allowing for pauses in the rhythm of the work, recognizing the forces that attempt to thwart and drown transformation under waves of anxiety and passion. "But the seeds of the transformation are already planted" within the organization's being, and the institution will rise from the depths to continue on its journey towards transformation. The author describes the ultimate destination as continually moving, as a dynamic organization changes its people, customers, and environment. Professor Gutmann proclaims, "There is no final victory." And, just as clearly, the reader will come to discover that there is no defeat, but only a continual process of discovery and surprise.

This book serves as an exploration of transformation from its relation with chaos and the beginning to its currency with power and authority. It highlights a pathway for both the training of leaders, managers, and consultants, and the continuing development of those who aspire to lead and work with corporations and other institutions. There are significant case studies and exemplars that help to create pictures in the mind of this work, providing not only the conceptual description of transformation, but also the zig-zag reality that confronts every leader, manager, and consultant. This book should be an essential part of the curriculum for students learning to become consultants, as well as for any professional who wishes to lead and work with or within organizations. Continue to read and discover this gift to leadership, a gift of more ZIGS than ZAGS in your professional and non-professional organizational life. Bon voyage.

Beverly Malone, PhD, RN, FAAN
CEO National League for Nursing; Member of IFSI; International Permanent Faculty, Leading Consultation; Member, Praxis Network; AK Rice Fellow; Midwest AK Rice member.

Introduction

David Gutmann

The theme of Transformation is the thread of my reflection in this book.

In my first book with Oscar Iarussi (1999), already published in four languages, I expressed what transformation means for me. A man of passion for my work and, more broadly, for life in general, I did not describe a new theory, but a very specific and useful approach to an existing one.

The most important is that my way of thinking and reflecting is not to be conceptual, but to integrate the experience of life (including emotions, feelings, sensations, etc.), first as a source of meditation, reflection, and discernment for action, but also for learning, shared learning, or learning to share with others.

At the crossroads of the political, psychic, and spiritual dimensions, I am able to underline some basic processes that belong to human beings, whether these apply to single individuals or to collective, institutional, or social organizations.

How can life be transformed? How can human beings transform their life, conditions, and roles, as well as institutions and their environment? What is the link between mental and psychic transformation, or unconscious processes, and transformation of/in the real? What is the very essence of these processes that affect each of us along our way from birth to death?

In a later book (2005), I and some of my colleagues explored these basic issues in relation to disillusionment (seen as a liberating process), desire, and its corollary, lack, especially the links with what makes us human: the necessity of dialogue.

From Transformation To TransformaCtion may constitute the follow-up to this reflection. It evokes the practical consequences of this approach, and relates several interventions and reflections made by myself and my colleagues, travelling all over the world and discovering other experiences, other countries, other cultures, and revealing our curiosity to discover what human beings are made of.

This book is another "journal" of my apparently continuous journey all around the world. It is a handbook, a *vade mecum*, almost a manual of instruction for anyone who wants to deal with transformation (which is nothing other than our basic daily experience!).

This book presents a quest for evidence that (institutional) transformation is possible under certain conditions that must be taken into account. It shows how the approach of transformation has been applied to a diversity of situations, institutions, and people through various working processes. Each time, it is a new adventure, but also new learning.

Here, there is a splitting process, which is deeply denied, pushing a peace process in an unending cycle of immobility and repeated failures; there, the tremendous admiration of the members of a hi-tech company for their leader blocks not only their creativity, but any kind of desire in an institution hurled into processes of envy. In yet another place, people are the prisoners of their history, personal history linked to the history of their country, until the Other is able to show how these processes exist only in their minds. More broadly, a very recent experience shows how a "simple" working conference can open new perspectives on the political future of a whole country. Finally, the last chapter tries to present how anxiety and passion, depression and generativity are inevitable when we want to be alive.

Everywhere, it is not only the individuals or the systems that carry their conscious and unconscious history; following Jacques Lacan, I believe that words can be seen also as pieces of the chain of the unconscious.

Thus, although it appears to be a book about practice from practitioners, this collection of texts has not been written only for the managers or the people of any working institution. It is about life and liberation, it is about liberty and libido, it is about passion and desire. It is written to accompany each one, concretely, in the process of building and transforming his or her own life.

CHAPTER ONE

Groups and transformation[1]

David Gutmann, with Laurence Ponthieu,
Jacqueline Ternier-David, and Christophe Verrier

S mall groups, like any system, evolve and transform themselves continuously. Processes of transformation can be seen as going through recognizable stages. Awareness of these stages allows for better understanding of the processes and even their regulation. We will explore these conceptual stages here, using a case from our experience as consultants.

Before analysing this example of a process of transformation engaged in by a group, a few elements of methodology used regularly in our practice are presented.

Every group is a *system* open to forces of transformation that are transmitted from the inside and from the outside. But an aptitude for integrating these forces does not mean that the group is capable of transforming itself easily. On the contrary, each group is moved by a homeostatic principle that is more or less powerful and that is directly stimulated by forces of transformation. It opposes these forces in order to conserve the group in its original state as best it can.

These *resistances* to the transformation of the group are individual and collective. They can be carried or expressed by persons whose habits or routine are disturbed, or they can manifest

1

themselves in the group's difficulty in moving from one organization—distribution of power, authority and roles—to another.

These resistances can take on the form of repetition, or, in a
slightly more favourable case, that of reproduction with a certain
limited renewal. (In the case of sexual reproduction, the element
reproduced is not exactly identical to its genitors.) By repeating the
same things, the group bans creating, innovating, and, therefore,
transforming itself.

We propose to define the TRANS-FORMATION of a group as
the passage, or voyage, of the group from one state to another, or
from one form to another.

This passage is neither regular nor continuous: it is chaotic,
erratic, and discontinuous. Because it comes up against irregular
resistances, the movement of transformation adopts a path composed of *zig-zags*, progressions and regressions, constructions and
destructions. We even think that the presence of these resistances,
and therefore of this zig-zagging path, are clues confirming the
authenticity of a process of transformation in progress that distinguishes itself from a simple measure of superficial regulation.

Generally, this sinuous passage comprises blurred phases that
are strange, if not incomprehensible. It seems lost in the obscurity
of a *black box*. It is on this black box that the *manager* of the group
on the one hand, and the *consultant* on the other, concentrate their
attention in order to perceive, identify, and better understand the
path of the transformation at the instant it is constructed. In fact, it
is the only way to influence this path later on, even, in the best of
cases, to regulate it.

We will now relate one of our recent experiences, in which a
group of twenty-four people, comprising the all-male management
team of a French service company of 75,000 employees, engaged
in a process of transformation. This transformation was observed
at its inauguration for the duration of a day and a half, at the end
of which the results were notable without, of course, proving a
definitive success.

In the preceding four years, this company had been subject to an
important modification of its structures, with, notably, the reduction of the number of its hierarchical territorial layers from three to
two. The transformation of the institution could take place only
thanks to the determined political will of the Managing Director, A.

In fact, parallel to the transformation of A's role, this process demanded the transformation of the role of B, the Deputy Managing Director, and a duplication process for the transformation in order to involve the other company employees.

Our role first consisted in conducting a long study (for more than eighteen months, with a team of eight consultants) in order to make a diagnosis of the state of the transformation progress, which was the subject of a report. In it, we described the different modes of resistance the institution had towards transformation. In particular, we showed how A's charisma and the admiration that he aroused in the personnel could be interpreted as the institution's best system of resistance. The stakes of the transformation were focused on this brilliant Managing Director who, pushed to a preaching process rather than to delegation, could engage less in the duplication process of this transformation from then on. We also emphasized the poor functioning of the management team. By accepting decisions taken in a separate, small, and informal committee without really discussing them, this team effectively became a recording—if not an admiration—studio.

With A's agreement, this report remained confidential for one year, until B, the former Deputy Managing Director, having become Managing Director, decided to present the report to his team in a day and a half seminar. Actually, the aim of this meeting was not only to present our diagnosis, but also to question the functioning of the management team in order to really transform it. In fact, the moment was well timed. The group—that is, the management team—was already destabilized, notably, from the affective point of view, by the change of Managing Director. It was caught up in its own doubts and interrogations about the still present souvenir of its former director. Would the team recognize B and trust him? Would it accept that this seminar truly marked the investiture of B as Managing Director? The other favourable, and even indispensable, element was the trust that B accorded to the principles and the structure of this meeting as well as to our team. No process of transformation can really succeed in a group without the adhesion, or even the impetus, of its leader. Three of our consultants, a woman and two men, took part in this seminar.

The first morning, in which neither B nor C, his new deputy, participated, was devoted to work in two sub-groups (the composition of the groups was determined according to objective criteria that resulted in the management team being divided into two categories: operating and functional). Each sub-group was given the task of establishing its own diagnosis of the situation, the management of the enterprise, the results of the transformation, and their own role in the company. A space for reflection was open to members of the management team so that they could conduct work in a way appreciably different from their usual approach. They were asked to distance themselves and their individual and collective acts. In addition, they were involved in a work of analysis instead of passively attending the presentation of our work. The consultants' role during that morning consisted of observing what happened in the sub-groups, then in progressively inviting them to ask spontaneous questions while discouraging the "natural" tendencies to look to others for the origin of their own dysfunction.

For each of the two sub-groups, this exercise was, in reality, an occasion to express their frustration concerning the Managing Director. Sometimes taking on a tone of vindication, these managers stigmatized their lack of autonomy, the absence of recognition by the system, and the small amount of influence they had in decision-making processes. The sub-group of operations managers went so far as to evoke great differences (in reality, very small) in remuneration within the management team.

By adopting such a negative and contesting position, a position that appeared to us to be in the area of regression, they seemed to handle themselves like veritable subordinates, and thus reinforce the rules of the system. They appeared to submit to their own role and rule out the possibility of inventing new ways of functioning for themselves. Any creativity in escaping the usual framework that they had known until then seemed to be prohibited.

However, we felt that the expression of this discontent was important. On the one hand, finding a public and collective occasion for expression was in itself new; on the other hand, this episode allowed everybody to share the same established fact concerning the team's dysfunctioning.

The afternoon was devoted to reports by each sub-group, followed by a presentation in the form of dialogue in which we communicated our own diagnosis. Thanks to the work of the morning, this diagnosis was, from then on, a shared representation of reality. It had been brought into circulation, and this reality had thereby become less frightening: it could be stated without being challenged or rejected.

The evening, a decisive moment, offered the possibility of a voluntary and very open discussion bringing together more than half of the group. It was an opportunity to register reactions that were fairly favourable to our conclusions, despite the realism and the absence of compromise with which we disclosed them. The evening was an informal moment in which disorder and de-structuring seemed to permeate the group without its being submerged by anxiety. On the contrary, the "chaos" was calm, almost benevolent, as if full of a peaceful trust. It was in this incomplete group that the first indications of a process of innovation sprang up. A determining question emerged and was addressed to the consultants: "You who have 'studied' us for so long, can you tell us how one can transform one's own role? In addition, is this possible?" This question seemed to mark the expression of a more or less collective wish for transformation. To encourage this process, another question was asked by the consultants: what part were the members of this management team able to give to *surprise* (in their functioning, in their roles, in their capacities, and in their results) from now on?

The end of the evening was devoted to a meeting between the Managing Director, his deputy, and the consultants. Certain points were clarified (such as that of the difference in salaries). In addition, the creation of an anecdotic surprise was planned for the next day; work habits were to be slightly changed. We decided to work without tables by forming a large circle composed of twenty-seven chairs on one side of the room. The climate of trust that had been established could allow this formal but symbolic destabilization.

The next day, the process continued. Of course, the arrangement of the room was highly unusual for the members of a management team such as this: it broke with the rites of work while putting each participant in a new, almost uncomfortable position. With only a few exceptions, they placed themselves next to their colleagues while respecting previous differentiations, as if, confronted with a relative uncertainty and a certain amount of insecurity, the sub-groups spontaneously reconstructed themselves. The sentiment of uncertainty was also a result of the deliberate absence of a clearly defined task. Would the morning be devoted to a mere brainstorming?

How to conclude it? This uncertainty was reinforced by the Managing Director, who had decided to intervene very little, deliberately letting the group steer its work. B was content to deliver some of his impressions, avoiding any definitive conclusion, and leaving his deputy in charge of regulating the discussion. By choosing to act this way, he freed his team from practices inherited from the past that were repeated, and even excessively ritualized.

Among the hypotheses that we had proposed the night before, one was often taken up: that of *mourning*. The enterprise, beginning with its management team, had to mourn not only the former structure, now transformed, but also A, the former Managing Director. Had the work of this double mourning really been accomplished? It was increasingly clear that, by giving his team the opportunity to participate in a seminar such as this, B clearly marked taking up his role and opening a new era. Beyond the highly explicit discussions on the subject of mourning, two metaphors emerged separately and spontaneously, to be associated later on by one of the participants to the *coffin*, and then to the *cradle*.

Anxiety rose. It took the form of fear that was felt and verbally expressed by the Deputy Managing Director, C. This anxiety rose to its zenith in a brief and violent dispute between a participant and a consultant. The consultant reproached the participant with being irrelevant, and using a technocratic way of speaking, thereby preventing them from discovering, or even simply discussing, what was in question, that is, the functioning of the team and its responsibilities. The remarks became more and more vehement until a violent attempt to leave the seminar was made by the participant involved in this quarrel. The attempt was curtailed thanks to an intervention by some of his colleagues.

Then, suddenly, like a loosened spring, the atmosphere transformed itself. Various propositions for the reorganization of the team's functioning and its internal and external relationships emerged. One participant traced a schema on a flip chart; the form of expression remained traditional, but it expressed a truly innovative content. Another participant extended the design of the schema with a new colour. Representations quickly followed one after another, and collective reflection was established in a veritable fever of creativity. It was not very surprising to note that the members of the sub-group who, the night before, had been the most reticent, emerged among the most creative, without hesitating to take the leadership in expressing proposals. At the end of the work session, a consultant suggested prolonging personal involvement into reflection and action coming from each participant. It was decided that the following week each participant would produce a document of a few pages summarizing his impressions, ideas, and wishes; the follow-up to this work would be elaborated afterwards. It goes without saying that the Managing Director did not formulate a definitive conclusion to the work session.

Thus, the reflection of a managing team was engaged around its own functioning. Of course, the contours of new structures and new relations were drawn, but it was even more evident that, to reach this result, the group had to engage in a process of transformation. It had had to move from the juxtaposition of individuals to integration to a real team capable of collective reflection and creation. A collective wish for such integration had also to emerge. Obviously, at this precise moment, the transformation still remained virtual, partial, and therefore fragile. But its base had been stated; a crucial step had just been taken.

We now present various points concerning the process of transformation. In our example, we think that resistances expressed themselves several times. As of the first morning of work (in subgroups), the managers adopted regressive behaviour with a tone of vindication. Thus, they carefully avoided questioning themselves about their own role and could even less transform it. The fact of being in a group—and, more particularly, in a long-standing group with an extensive history in common—considerably reinforced this type of resistance, as if the group were a source of solidarity among persons engaged in the work of resistance.

Other resistances manifested themselves by the repetition of technocratic speeches that prevented the discussion from taking shape. In other cases, elements exterior to the discussion were used, almost by chance, to crystallize resistances to transformation. An interpretation was made about the place where the seminar was held (a historical castle of the French monarchy), whose symbolic content served as a substrate to feed the fantasies about the despotic nature of the company's management.

Other resistances were anticipated and thwarted by the Managing Director when he decided to adopt a different form of behaviour in order to innovate and escape the vicious circle of repetition.

Sometimes resistances accumulate, become more radical and tense, and lead to delicate, dangerous moments that the group must go through (and beyond). Deep hesitations and temptations to retreat or to reach a shady compromise with the obstacle were intertwined. We observed this in the dispute between one of the consultants and a participant. Symbolically, the resolution of this crisis allowed the demolition of some of the last cores of resistance. In effect, when one feels an arc tighten, the rupture of the line of resistance is, in general, brutal and indivisible. This recalls the fall of the Berlin Wall in November 1989, as well as the Jericho Walls during the summer of 1993. Resistances are not conquered progressively; they yield all at once and leave room for surprise, for an unknown, sometimes devastated space that must be reconstructed. Thus, the management team was able to arrive at a point where it really began to create collectively.

On the other hand, we think that the appearance of *regressions* is inherent to processes of transformation. When they do not become irreversible, these regressions are often useful in future *progressions*. Thus, the work carried out at the beginning of the seminar gave fairly deceptive results, in any case, for the managers at this hierarchic level. But, by allowing the entire group to agree on a shared perception of reality, this regression was indispensable for launching the creativity that appeared that evening and, above all, the next day.

The emergence of numerous feelings and affects within the group is associated with this chaotic passage of transformation: fear and courage, suffering and pleasure, uncertainty, faith and doubt, enthusiasm or depression, patience and impatience. Our example is an illustration of this. Another indication of transformation is also the increase in anxiety, a corollary of this type of process, which results as much from the established power play in the group during moments of stability as in the uncertainty born of the invention and implementation of processes that are still unknown.

The anxiety of the group is therefore delicate to handle, because, in times of stability, the group—like many other types of institutions—is kept by its very structure in a traditional role of defence against anxiety. The success of a transformation often depends on the regulation of this anxiety.

The work of the consultant, therefore, consists primarily in identifying and interpreting the affects that emerge in the group in order
to better understand the evolution of the process of transformation.
In the present case, the climate noted on the evening of the first day
was favourable. The criticisms formulated during the day by the
managers or consultants were severe, but rarely destructive. The
trust awarded by the Managing Director did not weaken. There was
no deep-rooted contention disputing the principle of the seminar.
On the contrary, a desire for transformation was expressed, a desire
that was, of course, up to the consultants to highlight and accompany. All these clues—intuitively perceived during the seminar and
clearly identified *a posteriori*—allowed for relative confidence in the
aftermath of the process once it was engaged.

The work of the consultants also consists of accompanying the
group's manager in regulating the transformation. In the case of a
group, the breadth, the number, the frequency, the turbulence, and
the duration of zig-zags that form the path of the process of transformation are closely related to the human (and sometimes financial) cost of its transformation. In addition, without suitable
regulation, the process of transformation can flounder and lead the
group to an extreme situation where the magnitude and frequency
of zig-zags increase more and more. Anxiety then spreads to the
point of drowning all or part of the group; chaos becomes predominant; destructions and regressions win over steps in the direction
of construction and progression. The whole group thus evolves
either towards madness—that is, an explosive/implosive situation
where anxiety, no longer contained, submerges persons in the institution—or towards bursting, disintegration, or atomization.

How can this unfavourable outcome be avoided, and what
capacity for action or influence can the group develop concerning
its own transformation?

The path of this transformation can be interpreted at will *a posteriori*, as we have done through the example presented at the beginning of this chapter. Nevertheless, it is more important to delimit it
in the best possible way at the moment of the transformation (here
and now), as it unfolds. Therefore, the goal is first to identify these
steps as best and as quickly as possible in order to define the most
suitable itinerary during the process. This is true for leader(s) of the
group, each of its members, and, eventually, for the consultant.

In effect, transformation goes trough a *black box*, whose obscurity contains segments of the passage taken by the group. By definition, these segments are neither seen, known, nor understood. On the contrary, other segments, as if they overran the black box, are identified and apprehended by certain members of the group. These points emerge like tips of an iceberg above water: they necessarily imply the existence of a hidden mass that is even larger, beyond what is apparent and its appearance. To abandon the metaphor, in reality it is a question of an unknown itinerary that is long and tangled, lost in the darkness of the black box. In addition, the emerged segments do not, alone, allow the reconstituting of the complete path, or even the forming of a view of the whole.

Other steps along this path are visible, but *a priori* untouchable: they seem out of reach or outside the capacity for action, influence, and regulation by the members of the group; these elements can be found in a transparent *glass box* that itself contains the black box (Figure 1).

From then on, understanding of the transformation of the group must pass by the following moments that are, of course, non-consecutive, but complementary and mutually enriching. The first consists of partially reducing the volume of the black box by unveiling more of the segments that are contained on the path taken by the group. This process needs the interpretation of objective and subjective data that traverse and build the group throughout its evolution. The intervention of a consultant exterior to the group, whose role consists in unveiling, in revealing a part of the contents of the black box, is sometimes decisive.

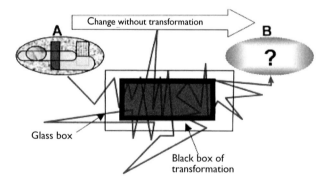

Figure 1. Path and transformation.

For each member of the group (beginning with its manager or its leader) the second step consists of developing one's own capacity for interpreting and regulating this path. In other words, once extricated from the black box, whose dimensions have been reduced thanks to the clarification phase, certain segments become visible but still seem unable to be influenced: one then finds them in the glass box. For this, one possibility, sometimes with the help of a consultant, is to distinguish reality from fantasy, that is, to determine the elements on which the members of the group *really* have no grip in relation to those on which they *believe* they have no hold. It is particularly important to identify the *boosters* and the *buffers* at the heart of the process of transformation. The *boosters* are the elements (roles, persons, systems, or sub-systems, structures, the environment of the group) that accelerate and encourage the process in the direction of progression. The *buffers* are, in contrast, the elements explicitly or implicitly related to resistances created by transformation that hold it back or stop it, and sometimes even encourage regressions.

Thus, this work allows members of the group to better apprehend the contours of the passage and the steps that the group traverses in the course of its transformation. Hence, the phases of progression and regression are better identified even if clarification is always incomplete, the black box never being able to be reduced completely, and it is possible at the same time to further progression and to admit that regressions are necessary for future advances.

Therefore, the regulation of transformation consists of identifying and treating the difficulties of the passage in order to encourage the "zigs" and limit the "zags", thanks to the capacity for interpretation and action that has been developed. Regulation also supposes favouring certain leads by launching deliberate accelerations and by placing *pawns* or *blockers* at other places when the time comes, that is, by launching mechanisms destined to support the road already taken by preventing returns that are too long-lasting.

Systems other than groups, up to large organizations or even nations, can meet this process of transformation, and also the roles of persons in institutions. These transformations have numerous points in common, among which are the advance in zig-zags, the sequence of progressions and regressions, and the presence of a black box as a metaphor for the difficulty in clearly perceiving the path of the transformation at the moment when it occurs. Transformation, then, represents an essential process of being, towards life and desire. Suffering, and even the violence that it necessarily implies, is a very small price to pay in terms of the meaning that transformation gives.

Note

1.   This article was published in 1995 by the Danish review *Udevidste Processer: Organisation og Ledelse*, pp. 171–181.

CHAPTER TWO

Transformation

David Gutmann, with Christophe Verrier

Our praxis of the work of adviser in leadership enables us to observe institutions regularly, often in great depth. They transform according to particular processes in which we have noticed certain analogies with biological mechanisms.

Thus, in order to describe our own representation of the transformation of institutions, we will lean on a biological metaphor, while remaining cautious with the use of such a process. A biological metaphor, while proving to be a useful framework in our demonstration, still remains somewhat limited. We will, therefore, attempt to overcome those limits by drawing on the political and psychic dimensions of these processes, making links to the role that managers and consultants can take up in these transformations.

Transformation and chaos

In the beginning there was chaos.

In almost every mythology, the world is born out of a transformation of chaos where elements progressively differentiate from one another.

From the very beginning of the world, chaos and transformation are intimately linked. Afterwards, chaos does not disappear completely: it remains present in one form or another. It consistently stands as one of the many possible futures, in particular in cases where the current transformation might be swept away by one of the regressions it carries in its very core.

Thus, the pursuit of transformations, since the creation of the world and then the birth of man, can be perceived as a perpetual struggle against and with chaos. In fact, chaos is used as one of the indispensable and recurrent stages of transformation processes: out of every transformation a part of chaos emerges; or, to put it another way, every transformation includes a reconnection with a part of the original chaos.

We must now clarify what we mean by transformation.

By definition, the idea of *transformation* links back to a fundamental life process and its perennial dimension. Biologists make a distinction between phenomena of *repetition* and those of *reproduction*, the study of which is genetics. While repetition produces something identical, reproduction introduces the idea of some kind of renewal: the item reproduced is not completely identical to the original one. Reproduction implies an element of novelty.

REPETITION	CREATION
REPRODUCTION	INNOVATION

Biology also describes the concept of *homeostasis*, that is to say, the full range of processes aimed at maintaining an organism in its normal and functioning state, a state referred to as physiological. A homeostatic system therefore generates a certain amount of processes aimed at correcting variations produced by this or that influence that an organism is subjected to by its environment (physical, bacterial, or viral aggression, for example). That system therefore enables the organism to resist the transformations that its environment is attempting to impose.

For historians, the idea of change is sometimes explored through the concept of *revolution*. However, this word also means "a return to the point of departure during a periodical movement" (see also Gramsci, 1920, p. 26).

As for the word *reform*, it emphasizes the new form that a system takes at the end of its evolution and ignores the journey involved in this process.

Let us go beyond these analogies and return to the issue of institutions and their transformation. For it is indeed the term that we feel is most appropriate.

Transformation

For us, the *transformation* of an institution is the *journey* of this institution from one state to another, or, rather, from one *formation* to another (see Figure 1, in the previous chapter). This journey is clearly different from change without transformation ("everything must change so that nothing changes", di Lampedusa, 1958, p. 180). The idea of change, strongly held in people's minds, intuitively represents a process in which an institution would move from one state to the other using a regular, continuous, even perhaps harmonious trajectory. Change without transformation is a largely idealized representation of evolution processes in which the presence of chaos, in one form or another, is negated. This representation also implies that the initial objectives set by managers must precisely be those reached by the institution at the end of the process.

In our work, such a concept of evolution betrays a very superficial vision of these processes. Not only does it question the capacity for action of managers, but it also refutes the inherent complexity of life.

Thus, with institutions, transformation must be thought of as different from a simplifying regulation. It is, for us, the goal of any intervention (managing, training, consulting, etc.), each of them being thought of through the perspective of a journey (*trans-. . .*).

Zig-zags and resistances

In all cases of transformation, the homeostasis metaphor is useful to describe certain reactions, always present, of the system transforming itself. The latter produces *resistances* to the process of transformation. These resistances are very varied in form. They are also expressed more or less overtly. Sometimes, the stakeholders in an institution in transformation try to recreate the procedures or relationships that transformation necessitates abandoning. This resistance by *repetition*—which is the expression of a deeply buried tendency within each of us—can be hidden or disguised in a manner more or less conscious. In any case, it stands in direct opposition to principles of *creation* and *innovation* induced by the transformation process:

> To innovate, to create is for everyone's unconscious to leave the road laid down by our parents: it is therefore in a certain way a judgement that this model is insufficient or must be DEPASSE. [Rueff & Moreau, 1987, quoted in Mendel, 1992]

This extract highlights how much processes of creation are antagonistic to the strong tendency for repetition held in our heritage.

Collusion, idealization of a manager, apparent difficulty in communicating, are yet other examples of resistances.

In our experience, resistances are a clear indication of the depth of the current transformation, so much so that an absence of resistance indicates an absence of real transformation.

These resistances in part explain the journey of institutions along their transformation process. This journey is a zig-zag (see Figure 3), a chaotic succession of progressions and regressions, of construction and deconstruction.

ACTIONS

PROGRESSION	REGRESSION
CONSTRUCTION	DESTRUCTION

This characteristic leads us to formulate the hypothesis that the emergence of phases of regression is inevitable in processes of transformation. In fact, in practice, these regressions very often announce a progression to come. Conversely, a progression is never final and must not weaken the manager's vigilance, since a regression will always erupt at one time or another.

Resistances come up in an irregular manner, sometimes accumulate, become more radical, and, in an increasingly pressing way, lead to extremely delicate, uncertain, and often very dangerous moments that must be overcome in a context made even more delicate by the emergence of strong feelings and emotions generated by the zig-zags.

The trajectory of a transformation from A to B is therefore much more complex than that of a simple change. Even more so since B, the objective set by the manager, is mostly virtual, for the result in reality, as one emerges from strange and unpredictable zig-zags, can differ quite substantially from it. Therefore B, which evolves during the process, is only a possible representation of the result; a representation that, offered to the institution in order to kick-start and sustain the process, becomes useful as *transitional object*.

This is why we can state that in a process of transformation the road travelled, the journey, is more important that the goal.

Affects and anxiety

In the institutions in which they operate, transformations lead to the emergence of many feelings or affects. We present them here as indissociable—perhaps even dialectical—couples, in order to emphasize the fact that their very presence is as much revealing of the processes at work as the meaning that they seem, at first glance, to indicate.

Thus, transformations trigger fear and demand courage; they also require patience, inflict pain, or offer pleasure.

The list we present in Table 1 is not exhaustive. Certain affects or feelings have yet to be clearly identified, others depend on the circumstances in which each transformation operates, others still belong to the people within these institutions and, although they are a result of the transformation at work, they are not always expressed.

Another clue, a mark of any transformation process, is the *anxiety* that results from the disruption to the power dynamics that had been established during times when stability was the rule. Any institution in transformation accepts and conveys a certain amount of anxiety, in direct relationship to the zig-zag journey it is involved in, that is necessary for the invention of its future.

Table 1.   Affects associated with transformation.

Enthusiasm	Depression
Patience	Impatience
Pleasure	Suffering
Desire	Lack
Certainty	Uncertainty
Courage	Fear
?	?
Love	Hate
Faith	Doubt

However, one of the issues that the managers of the institution must resolve is that of the regulation of anxiety and, more generally, that of the transformation process itself.

Black box and glass box

Not only do institutions transform along a sinuous, erratic path, made up of zig-zags, but they also follow a trajectory that is not always identifiable. Moreover, and that is the second form that chaos takes, some of these stages are obscure, incomprehensible, invisible even, at least to begin with: it is as if they were drowned in the darkness of a tunnel without light or encased within a *black box*. This black box contains segments of the trajectory followed by the institution in the course of its transformation that are not seen, known, or understood by the institution's members.

As with a black box in an aeroplane, one must open it in order to truly get to know and understand what happened during the flight—in particular the trajectory followed by the plane.

Other stages of this itinerary are visible—therefore located outside of the black box—but seemingly untouchable: they appear to be out of reach, outside of the capacity for action, influence, or regulation of managers; these stages are visible but are not analysed; they seem held within a *glass box*, a transparent box.

Both black box and glass box invite managers to question their own room for manoeuvre and, of course, to question any fantasy of omniscience or omnipotence.

The role of consultant

The range, the number, the frequency, the turbulence, and the duration of the zig-zags are directly linked to the human (and financial)
cost of the transformation. The role of managers in the institution
therefore consists of looking for the most appropriate itinerary, and
then regulating it through encouraging the "zigs" and limiting the
"zags".

In the absence of an adequate regulation, the future of the transformation process is very open: the possibility of an entropic regression, leading to the ruin of the institution, cannot be ruled out. In
other cases, the transformation can skid and lead to an extreme situation in which the range and frequency of zig-zags forever increase.
Then, anxiety spreads to the point of drowning part, or all, of the
institution, chaos becomes permanent and omnipresent, destructiveness and regressions get the upper hand over forces of construction and progression. In that case, management panics and the
whole process evolves towards madness (depression or hysteria),
that is to say, an explosive or implosive situation where anxiety is
no longer contained but, rather, dominates people and sub-systems
within the institution.

The role of the consultant is to accompany the managers of the
institution along the transformation process by helping them to
choose, and engage the institution in, the best possible itinerary. To
be more precise, the consultant contributes, through his interpretations and the process of revelation, to the clarification of several
elements.

- The consultant contributes to reduce partially the volume of
  the black box through unveiling some of the segments of the
  institution's trajectory contained within it.
- The consultant helps managers to recover their capacity for
  regulation of elements of this trajectory contained within the
  glass box: one possibility in this respect is that of distinguish-
  ing reality from fantasy, that is to say, differentiating the
  elements on which the manager actually has no hold from
  those on which he thinks he has no hold.
- Finally, the consultant contributes to seek and identify, with
  the managers, the *boosters* and *buffers*. Boosters are elements

(roles, people, systems, or sub-systems, arrangements, etc.) that accelerate and encourage the transformation process through progression. Buffers, in contrast, are elements that belong explicitly or implicitly to the resistance to transformation that slows the transformation down or encourages regressions. (To avoid misunderstanding, we should explain that the word "buffers" is used here to describe inhibitors, rather than to mean "cushions", or shock-absorbers.)

Thus, this work enables the consultant and the leaders of the institution to better gauge the shape of the path and the stages that the institution passes through in the course of its transformation. Phases of *progression* and *regression* become better identified and it becomes possible to encourage progressions and to admit that regressions are often necessary for future progressions.

This regulation also implies the encouragement of movement going in the right direction through launching, when the time is right, planned accelerations, and placing appropriate blockers to prevent setbacks that would be too great. (We have borrowed the term "blockers" from the financial world, in which context they are computer programmes that block aspects of stocks and shares investment management, in particular sales. These programmes are automatically activated to prevent the beginning or worsening of a stockmarket crash in which sales tend to mechanically and artificially trigger other sales.)

However, even the best regulation does not enable the destruction of all resistances. At best, it can go around them or soften them. Sometimes, when deep hesitation is mixed with the temptation to reverse, to give up, to compromise, we can feel the bow tighten. Resistances accumulate, forming a barrier that seems insurmountable.

Then, the only things that matter are determination, faith, and knowledge, both intellectual and experiential, of this type of process, even if they will not suppress either the surprise or the hesitation. To proceed, it is then necessary to implement ethics, aesthetics, and methodology.

The breakdown of the most fundamental line of resistance is brutal, indivisible. It reminds one of the fall of the Berlin Wall on 9 November 1989. Essential resistances are not won over progressively:

they give way suddenly, leaving room for an unknown, sometimes devastated space, which must be rebuilt through innovation.

Thus, the zig-zag trajectory of transformation and the other marks of resistance, affects, guilt, anxiety, and the mystery and opacity of the breakthrough, are so many manifestations of the part of chaos contained in the process.

In all cases, transformation is a breakthrough, difficult and uncertain. It generates as much happiness as sadness, as much anxiety as euphoria.

Transformation, indeed, is nothing more than one of the aspects of life.

CHAPTER THREE

Chaos and transformation: the primary scene[1]

David Gutmann, with Christophe Verrier

I n this chapter, we would like to present some ideas about the way to facilitate handling the issue of chaos, to use it, to work with it: this way is transformation.

Chaos. My first encounter with "the English chaos" was in Leicester, when, at that time being unfamiliar with different British accents, I mistook the word for "cow", and wondered briefly what these quiet animals were doing in a very serious seminar!

Chaos is a word derived from Greek mythology. It describes the global confusion of elements of matter before the formation of the world. It is the emptiness that pre-exists creation, ready to become the matrix of the world.

Thus, chaos has a double meaning:

- emptiness, the confusion existing before creation (which becomes a process of differentiation and transformation);
- disorder (although disorder is the opposite of order, and not of chaos).

Since chaos is not organized (and since it existed before man), the human spirit can neither describe it nor visualize it.

Myths

Reminding us how we passed from disorder to order, the founding myth of the primary scene justifies the existing order, including its political dimension, and provides comfort. Thus, the fear of chaos, which is maintained, contributes to the principle of homeostasis of groups and society.

More generally, the myth delivers answers rather than seeking the relevant questions. It is reassuring and gives a unique and final answer that negates existential anguish. Indispensable for the creation of a group, the myth aims to unify thoughts and behaviour, and to lead to action. But, as the fundamental principle of a group, it also engenders distrust of disorder, rebellion, and innovation (*Encyclopedia Universalis*, 1990). In this way, the myth seems to belong to the *conservative* part of any group.

Only a certain level of scepticism *vis-à-vis* myths creates the uncertainty necessary to transform a group or a society. Conversely, complete acceptance leads to fanatical attitudes or totalitarian regimes.

Greek mythology

Myths were created to impart a meaning to our life and roots. Today, they still influence us, even if only unconsciously. For instance, the Greek myths inspire the journey of transformation; they can also trap us in our fears or, on the contrary, push us to take risks.

In Greek mythology, the long, step-by-step transformation of Chaos (as the infinite and empty space that existed before creation was known) leads to the coexistence of several generations that are very different from each other. However, attempts to regress are multiple, and impart a zig-zag trajectory to the transformation process.

Chaos coexisted with Nyx, her daughter, and Erebus, her son. Nyx was the goddess of night (the eternal, biblical night, rather than the "simple" night as opposed to day), while Erebe represented the infernal darkness that pre-exists the creation of the universe.

The Earth (Ge, or Gaia) sprang from Chaos, and herself gave birth to Ouranos (or Uranus), the Heavens, and Pontus, the Sea. Gaia and Ouranos together begat numerous offspring, including the one-eyed Cyclopes, the Hundred-handed Giants, and the twelve Titans.

However, although each generation shows tremendous progress in giving rise to a more differentiated new generation, it also immediately adopts regressive behaviour in order to prevent this new generation from existing fully, as explained below.

Ouranos's reign

Ouranos imprisons his rebellious sons, the Cyclopes, in Tartarus (a region of the Underworld). In doing so, he threatens the progress of the transformation. But Gaia persuades the Titans to rise against their father, led by Cronos, the youngest. Ouranos is deposed, and the Cyclopes are freed, but, once Cronos has won, he again consigns the Cyclopes to Tartarus, together with the Hundred-handed Giants, who had helped him to free the Cyclopes.

After having been defeated by Cronos, Ouranos plots to destroy Cronos and his brothers in order to effect a regression to the previous position, that of his and Gaia's reign. The Titans triumph, however.

The Titans' reign

Thus, the Titans dominate the world, but the question then arises as to whom the power should be given: the eldest brother, or Cronos, the youngest, who had demonstrated his authority and leadership? The Titans decide that Cronos will reign, but that the descendants of the eldest Titan will succeed him. (Ouranos had cursed Cronos, stating that he, too, would be deposed by his own son.)

To respect this decision and avoid the curse, Cronos swallows each of his children (by his sister Rhea) at birth. However, when Zeus, the youngest child, is born to Rhea, she gives Cronos a stone wrapped in a baby's blanket to swallow, together with Hera, Zeus's twin sister. Zeus is then hidden in Crete, brought up by the Curetes (Rhea's priests), and fed by Amalthea, the goat, who was rewarded by being placed among the stars as Capricorn, while one of her horns became the Cornucopia, or Horn of Plenty.

Once he is an adult, following the advice of his aunt Metis (whose name means *intelligence, intuition*), Zeus enters Cronos's service. With his mother Rhea's help, Zeus gives Cronos an emetic that causes him to disgorge the stone and all the other children (Hestia, Demeter, Hera, Hades, and Poseidon), who join Zeus in making war on Cronos. This war lasts for ten years, until Gaia promises Zeus victory if he frees the Cyclopes and the Hundred-handed Giants from Tartarus. This he does, helped by his brothers Hades and Poseidon, and thus overcomes Cronos. Then he marries his twin sister, Hera, and establishes the reign of the Gods (Olympians).

The Olympians' reign

Men are created by the Titan Prometheus, on Zeus's instruction. As soon as they are created, however, Zeus fears that they believe themselves equal to Gods. He tempts them (with Pandora's Box), then tries to drown them in a deluge that Poseidon triggers at Zeus's request. (Interestingly, most myths [Greek, Biblical, and Nordic, but not Chinese] tell the story of a deluge, and meteorologists confirm that an ice age ended around the year 5000 BC, provoking a transitory rise in the level of oceans.) Only a couple of people survived, giving rise to the risk of regression to the former situation.

In these myths, the chaotic periods of wars, violence, massacres, etc. alternate with periods of harmony. Thus, the creation of the world appears to be a succession of transitory progression and regression. The myths also help us to see connections between chaos, creation, and transformation.

Incest and parricide evoke the (con)fusion that is opposed to the process of differentiation. Regression, destruction, and inversions (consider Rhea–Hera) alternate with progression. The birth of Cronos (Time), at the third generation, leads to patience (and makes it appear).

The Nordic myths[2]

In Nordic mythology, there are two kinds of gods. One is the *Aesir*, of whom Odin, god of poets, kings, warriors, and magic, and Thor, god of war, asked to fight the Giants, deadly enemy of the gods, are examples. The other is the *Vanir*. According to Georges Dumézil (1959) the Vanir originally held an inferior position, but they ascended to the highest rank after a time of rivalry. However, in contrast to the Aesir's rules, marriage between brothers and sisters is not forbidden among Vanir.

The Vanir's genealogy

This genealogy, like that of Greek mythology, evokes incestuous relationships between brothers and sisters. But here, such relationships are only suspected (with malevolence) in the second generation, between Freyr (god of fertility) and Freyja (goddess of fertility, love, beauty, and war).

The Giants

They appear in the Nordic myths as well as in Greek mythology, and in rather similar roles.

The Völuspà

The *Völuspà* is a poem, part of the *Poetic Edda* (a collection of Old Norse poems), which tells of the prophecy of a *völva* (a wise woman, or priestess) questioned by Odin (the "All-Father"). She says that first there was primeval chaos, when nothing existed but the Ginnungagap (the yawning void) and the frost giant, Ymir. Creator gods, known as the sons of Bur, then created Earth and the Midgard (central space, or middle earth), and the gods differentiated the day, the night, and the years, and lived in total felicity in the Idavoll (the central plain of Asgard, the home of the Aesir) until a disaster happened that was announced by three monstrous female Giants.

The same story exists in Snorri Sturluson's *Prose Edda* (1179–1241): born from a stone, Burri generates Bor, who has three children, Odin, Vili, and Ve. They kill the giant Ymir and spill his blood.

The blood provokes a deluge and drowns Ymir's descendants (obtained by parthenogenesis) except for the Giant Bergelmir, who had embarked in a lùdr (a kind of box).

Then, Odin and his brothers make the world from Ymir's body: the sea with his blood, the mountains with his bones, the trees with his hair, fortifications with his eyelashes, the clouds with his brain, and the sky with his skull.

The singing of the Rig (Rigsmal)

Snorri Sturluson's *Prose Edda* also tells of the rise of the social classes from the tribulations of Rig (the creator of three races of men, also known as Heimdall). This myth suggests that all the human beings have a divine origin, but are not equal.

The end of the world, the Ragnarok

The Ragnarok is a huge and inevitable disaster in which the gods are destroyed. Nevertheless, they face this ultimate battle with tremendous courage.

This disaster is announced by a winter that lasts three years (the *fimbulvetr*: the fantastic winter). It brings natural cataclysms and terrible fights among human beings, splitting families. The analogy with the Judeo-Christian myth of the Apocalypse is striking.

If the Ragnarok ends the reign of the old gods, it cannot be interpreted as an absolute end. Poetic *Edda*, as well as Snorri's *Prose Edda*, describe another beginning of a new world. This rejuvenation would lead to a golden age. There again, just one human couple would survive and give birth to a new human race.

We find there a good representation of the zig-zags of transformation: creation, life, destruction, and re-creation without knowing what follows.

Chaos and transformation

In mythologies, the creation of the world comes from a transformation of chaos during which elements differentiate one after the other. Nevertheless, chaos does not disappear totally: it always remains in a certain form. It can always be one of the possible futures, particularly if transformation is swept away by one of the regressions that inevitably occurs.

The processes of transformation, a consequence of which is the creation of men, and, thus, of groups, organizations, and institutions, look like a permanent fight against chaos. In other words, chaos is used as one of the inevitable and temporary stages of transformation.

From each transformation, a part of chaos emerges, or, any transformation takes up with part of the original chaos.

The zig-zag trajectory of the transformation and other signs of resistances, affects, guilt, anxiety, mystery, and the opacity of the passage (Erebe) are many expressions of this part of chaos. When absorbed by the fine regulation of the transformation of the institution that he or she leads, how can a manager handle and use this chaos?

The concept of transformation gives some answers to this question. It allows identification and, thus, recognition of the existence and the nature of chaos. Thus, it helps the manager to accept it and to identify the limits in blocking regression and destruction as soon as possible.

This approach demonstrates that a transformation consists, in part, of chaos, which means that a part of its process is, and will remain, unclear, not understandable, whatever is said or done. In other words, this approach helps the manager to overcome his fantasy of omnipotence and omniscience, which can lead him to think that the institution he leads and the transformation that happens in it hold no secrets for him.

While preserving the mystery of the chaos (the unthinkable chaos), this approach clarifies some of the processes of a transformation. For instance, it identifies how resistances and their consequences work, and also the role of anxiety. Thus, this approach tries to push as far as possible the limits of what cannot be described. It also shows how this part of chaos is necessary to creativity.

Beyond the mix that the idea of chaos suggests, and whose richness we can imagine intuitively, this zig-zag process increases the manager's anxiety. Maybe the lack of understanding (of readability) of the institution in transformation triggers the desire to create and develop a new form for the institution.

However, in the core of the zig-zag, the stake might be in the manager's (or his/her colleagues') capacity to *transform* this anxiety into creativity. Nevertheless, the consultant's role, whether it is carried out by a manager, another member of the institution, or a professional consultant, is also to attempt to reduce the chaos (the volume of the black box, and the existence of the glass box), although it is not possible to eradicate it totally (Figure 2).

Finally, the role of consultant is to prevent, as far as possible, an unfavourable evolution of the transformation, one in which the institution is overwhelmed by chaos. In helping the manager and the rest of the institution to accept the idea of chaos, but also stopping as soon as possible regression and destruction (blockers), the consultant helps the manager and the other members of the institution to *contain* chaos—which is very different from any attempt to *submit*, *handle*, or *control* chaos.

This is a paradox: this passage, consisting of progression and regression, destruction and construction, patience and impatience, depression and enthusiasm, doubt and faith, etc., creates chaos while simultaneously confronting it, and all the spiritual, psychic and political aspects of this passage bring chaos into the process of transformation.

In the best cases, keeping the idea of chaos in mind helps us to accept it, to reveal it, and even to create it. It also helps us to tolerate it, to contain, shape, and use it.

"You want to know what will happen after,
I don't know who could tell you it,

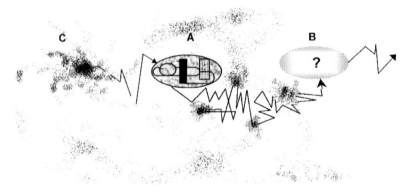

Figure 2.   The effect of a zig-zag: chaos and transformation.

because I have never heard anybody describing
the future of the world beyond these things.
Turn then to good account what you have learned!"
(Snorri Sturluson, Prose Edda)

This sentence reminds one of the principles derived from psychoanalysis, which could be stated as: "the present precipitates the past and holds and contains the future". Chaos and transformation.

Note

1. This is an edited and expanded version of a paper originally presented to the conference "Boundaries between Chaos and Order", Copenhagen, Denmark, in March 1994.

CHAPTER FOUR

The division into us–them as a universal social structure[1]

David Gutmann, with Miriam Berger and Avi Berman

Introduction

P eople tend to view their social, political, and in-group affili-
ations as an articulation of their chosen values, stemming
from ideological roots and expressing a carefully thought out
and rational worldview. At the same time, they are inclined to shun
other groups that espouse contrary values and ideals. This avoidance, too, is perceived as freely chosen and value-based.

As opposed to this common belief, and without underrating
the influence of value-based choice and ideological affiliation, we
claim that the division into opposing groups, cast as "us" and
"them", constitutes a basic structure of human social organization.
It is, in a sense, a projective way given of human nature (that people are disposed to deny). Conceived in this manner, this division
predates contents, opinions, and ideologies, and is impulsive and
unconscious in character.

It is this division that defines "us" as a source of closeness and
sharing and "them" as different, antithetical, negative, and, often,
a potential enemy. Ideologies and group history are built on the
foundation of this structural division.

This chapter describes in detail the observations and findings that demonstrate the division into "us" and "them", the process by which "them" is transformed into an enemy, the process of building an ideology on its basis, and the difficulties in maintaining a dialogue after it has taken place.

In the discussion that follows our description, we claim that it is possible to view the division into "us" and "them" as a kind of an inborn human instinct that is functional in consolidating the resources of the group and transforming it into a cohesive working team.

In addition, we suggest that there might be a more psychological rationale for this division: it functions as a group defence mechanism that offers an identity and a sense of belonging instead of the anxiety-provoking chaos that man faces when he is an individual in a nameless crowd.

The central idea of our thesis is that the division of people into opposing groups of "us" and "them" is a basic structure in the social organization of human beings; it is almost a basic fact of human nature. According to this idea, and without in any way detracting from the importance of the free choice of values and adherence to an ideology, this division precedes content, ideas, and ideologies; it is impulsive, irrepressible, unavoidable, and unconscious.

According to common belief, people tend to regard their membership of a group, whether social or political, as an expression of their choice of values; values that are perceived as based on ideological reasons. People are very invested in them and see them as thought out, rational products of their worldview. At the same time, they tend to set themselves apart from other groups that embrace opposing ideologies. This, too, is perceived as an expression of a free choice of values.

It is this division that defines "us" as a source of togetherness and partnership, while "them" is defined as different, opposing, and often a potential enemy. Ideologies and group history are formulated on the basis of this structural division. Spontaneous interactions between "us" and "them" (as well as within every group) are interpreted against the backdrop of this division and reinforce it time and again.

There are those (Bion, 1961; Freud, 1921c) who claim that the essential social organization is the primal horde. The primal horde is a group that has a leader, a group identity, and a sense of belonging on the part of the individuals in it.

As a continuation of the idea of the primal horde, we maintain that the primal horde seeks another, opposing horde, so that the two hordes can behave in the characteristic manner of "us" and "them". Each horde reinforces the sense of identity and belonging of its individual members; they consolidate and unify each other's motivation for action.

This social mechanism is part of the primal processes of identity creation, and is perhaps parallel to Winnicott's basic concept of the formation of "me" and "not me" (1960).

Our professional work in B'sod Siach (an association established by professionals in the social sciences to study the relationships between groups in conflict and to seek a way of creating and promoting a dialogue between them) has demonstrated that the above mechanisms of projection can explain similar phenomena in the inter-group domain as well; splitting and projections operate not only between individuals, but also between groups;

Since Freud (1925d), projection has been recognized as a primary defence mechanism capable of explaining a large number of situations in which the individual attributes positive elements to himself and negative elements to an "other". Thus, projections into "them" can be considered as a form of collective purification process.

Robins and Post (1997) suggest that ". . . we need our enemies. They provide a comforting explanation of what is wrong with ourselves" (pp. 302).

Volkan (1988) traces the origins of social conflict to the crib and argues that fear and hatred of the stranger is deeply rooted in the human psyche. He claims that the fear of the stranger and projection of hatred upon the other are the psychological foundation of the concept of enemy.

Having given this short introduction, we shall describe now in detail the phenomenon that led us formulate the above views.

Background

We initially observed the behaviours we have described at an experiential conference of B'sod Siach. B'sod Siach is an organization that brings together people of diametrically opposed political and social views, as well as of contrasting religious and ideological beliefs, for the purpose of holding joint activities and promoting dialogue between them. The group in this conference consisted of people from two clearly identifiable socio-political camps. Members of these groups have profoundly conflicting social and political world outlooks. These groups are conventionally termed "Right" and "Left". This terminology covers a wide range of differences.

- *Religious beliefs*. Most of the individuals on the Left are secular; most of the individuals on the Right are religious.
- *Attitude towards the occupied territories*. The Right regards the areas captured in the Six Day War as having reverted to their rightful owners; settling Judea, Samaria, and the Gaza Strip is perceived as a religious calling and a pioneering enterprise. The Left regards these areas as having been taken away from their rightful inhabitants, i.e., the Arab population. The Left views Jewish settlement in these areas as a dispossession of its inhabitants and a dangerous act of provocation.
- *Attitude towards the Arabs*. The Right tends to view the Arabs as potential enemies, and is doubtful about the prospects of a true and lasting peace with them. The Left believes in peace with the Arabs and sees in them the potential for good neighbourly relationships.
- *Values*. The Right regards *nationalism* as a supreme value. The Left regards *man* or the *individual* as having supreme value. The former distinguishes between members of its own nationality ("The Chosen People") and others. The latter distinguishes between those who accept universal humanitarian values and those who regard themselves as a unique, special nation that is above the rest.

The differences between these two groups are perceived as being very pronounced and deep. In most cases, these opposing identities are forged during childhood, within the nuclear family. As a result, the attitudes that are held are considered to be highly stable and lasting. Changes in attitude, not to mention reversals of attitude, are rare. People tend to adhere to these views and regard them as part of their adult personality and identity.

The differences in attitudes, as well as the differences between the people who hold them, are so pronounced and so deep that an encounter between them is a rare event, which society tends to regard sceptically, or even avoids altogether.

It would appear that the "us" *vs.* "them" motif in these diametrically opposed groups is well established, having been built up gradually in the individual over many years, and reinforced through education and socialization. One would expect that the members of these groups would cling to their deep personal, social, and political identities, and that these identities would prove stable and durable in the face of social pressure. For this very specific reason, in the course of the simulations to which we refer later in this chapter, it was striking to observe that the processes of splitting into "us" and "them" reactivate themselves so readily according to cues in the here and now, and cross the boundaries of deeply rooted, firmly fixed in mind identities.

We will now describe the conference, which brought together people from the above opposing groups. Since dialogue between these groups is rare, a simulation (based on an idea of David Gutmann's) designed to open up and facilitate channels of communication and promote a dialogue between people was conducted. An hour was allocated to the simulation, followed by an additional hour for processing and discussing the material that was generated during the simulation.

The participants were arbitrarily divided into three groups, designated "Right", "Left", and "Government". This division was completely random, using slips of paper that were given to participants as they entered the hall where the simulation was held. Four sites were set aside in the room, each with signs designating them as "Right", "Left", "Government", and "Town Square".

The task assigned to the participants was to ". . . explore the relationships that are formed between the groups in the room". The participants were informed that the site "Town Square" was intended for meetings between representatives of the groups.

The participants were not given explicit instructions to form into groups. They were also not told *which* groups to form. In fact, the conference participants could have divided themselves into many different, self-evident, or conventional groups, according to gender, age, social class, profession, etc. Divisions such as male and female,

Right wing (in origin) and Left wing (in origin), religious and secular, consultants and participants, various occupational categories, and so on could all be feasible possibilities.

As mentioned above, all participants were randomly presented with slips of paper and seated themselves in chairs spread throughout the room. The room had been prepared in the usual manner for a plenary session: participants sat in rows, and the staff sat up front. After the primary task was announced, the members of staff were supposed to assume the role of consultants and remain close to their assigned territory so as to be available to facilitate dialogue there, should the participants request it.

As the planners of the simulation, we assumed that the participants would feel a personal struggle, a conflict, between their long-standing individual identities and the prospect of changing their perspectives and viewing the world from the standpoint of the other group members. We felt that such a conflict might increase the receptiveness of the participants to the viewpoint of the opposing group.

However, to our surprise, there were almost no signs of conflict during the simulation. Instead, the participants displayed two other distinct forms of behaviour:

1. They took the slips of paper *literally* and created group membership on that basis.
2. They complied with the *content* of the lottery slips they had been issued. The groups that were thus randomly formed following the assignment became permanent and stable; each began constructing positions and viewpoints designed to delineate group boundaries and create common ground for all of its members.

Below is a description of the course of events.

After the assignment was announced, events in the room proceeded very rapidly. The participants immediately broke up into groups of Right and Left, *according to the slips of paper they had been issued, and not according to their real-life, long-standing identities*. In other words, about half of the participants in the right-wing group were "lefties" in real life, and about half the participants in the left-wing group were "righties" in real life. Participants moved their chairs to their allocated territories in the hall and immediately formed two closed circles. Each circle quickly became engrossed in itself.

Those who received the slips saying "Government" appeared much more hesitant. They sat in an open circle, looking bewildered and embarrassed, facing the other participants who were sitting in their closed circles. It took some time before they turned to each other and began discussing the possibility of forging a distinct identity and assuming a feasible role for themselves.

The Right and Left groups were preoccupied with themselves. From observing and listening to what was going on in their groups, the consultants discerned that participants were very busy finding common ground and building group identities. The atmosphere was cordial and attentive. The participants invested much effort in creating a sense of kinship. They endeavoured to find common denominators and smoothed over differences and areas of potential conflict. (In this sense, the process actually did achieve the aims of the conference: the participants within the small groups did, in fact, listen very attentively to one another, in spite of belonging to different ideological groups.)

Each group tended to obey the lottery slips and adopt the identity inscribed on them. Participants in the right-wing group sharpened their positions and attempted to help their members form a common right-wing identity. At the same time, the participants in the left-wing group, including those who in real life were identified with the Right, set out to formulate a leftist identity. The members were engaged in strengthening group cohesion. Participants introduced themselves and became acquainted with the others. The groups made an effort—even within the time span of less than a single meeting—to give each of the members a sense of belonging and were careful to create and maintain an atmosphere of acceptance.

Unlike the other two groups, the "Government" remained rather embarrassed and bewildered. Its members were unable to form a common stand, a plan of action or come up with a tentative role definition. After about half an hour, most of the participants in the "Government" left their assigned territory and joined the Right or Left groups, according to their personal preferences. A few minutes later, the remaining members of the Government also dispersed. *From that point onwards, there were only two groups of participants in the room, each seeing itself as "us" and the other as "them".*

Most of the time allocated for the simulation passed without any meetings between representatives of the groups taking place. The territory designated as the "Town Square" remained empty, and the consultants assigned to it had nothing to do. At this point, it was decided that the consultants would make a group (system) intervention; an announcement was read to the participants, reminding them of the primary task of the organizational event.

The participants showed little interest in the announcement. They expressed some frustration with the consultants' "intrusive" behaviour and complained that it interrupted important discussions taking place in the groups and interfered with the intimacy that was just beginning to form between members.

There were, however, a few participants who did show interest in the primary task and wanted to carry it out. One of them asked his group's permission to act as its representative, approach the other group, and then come back and report on it. His request was greeted with ambivalence (some opposed his request on the grounds that it was not yet the appropriate time); eventually, his request was granted, but with indifference and little enthusiasm.

Nevertheless, this participant got up and went over to the other group. As he approached them, all discussion ceased and all eyes turned to him. With a smile, he cordially explained his aim, reminding them of the primary task assigned to everyone.

The group received him with coolness and hostility. Some of the participants became excited, claimed that he was a spy, treated him as an enemy, and demanded that he "get out".

Others were more rational, and asked him to come back at another time, claiming that "this" was not the right time for his endeavour. They maintained that "We haven't finished getting to know ourselves yet, so we aren't ready to get to know the other group".

The messenger returned to his own group within three minutes.

When he returned to his group, here too all discussion ceased, and all eyes turned to him. He recounted, in a factual manner, what had transpired. The members of his group, who until then had been indifferent to his endeavour, reacted indignantly to the information he brought back. As far as they were concerned, the others had thrown him out. What had been his personal initiative until then had suddenly turned into a group enterprise, with him becoming their assigned delegate, and thus his return was considered a disgrace and a provocation. The atmosphere became charged with emotion and hostility, and the other group began to be perceived as enemy territory. At that point the members of his group became rather agitated. They decided to refuse to meet with the other group.

Such a meeting between the two groups never actually took place; the participants gave preference to their division into groups of "us" and "them" and rejected the assigned task of exploring the possibility of an inter-group dialogue.

The polarization in the room affected the consultants as well. Some of them deviated from their role as observers and moved physically in the direction of one of the groups, even though their task required them to remain in their assigned territory and not approach the participants. Other consultants remained seated in their neutral places.

This first simulation we have described was followed by others, constructed in the same format and conducted at similar conferences and workshops. The simulations were repeated in different settings, with different populations, with people from diverse cultures who speak different languages. We held these workshops for various groups in conflict, for behavioural sciences professionals as well as for non-professionals. We had no reason to suspect that limited education or intelligence or a different socio-cultural background had a decisive effect on the participants' behaviour.

Our initial observations about the nature of this process were confirmed time and again. After much experience with this format, we came to the conclusion that the structural division of "us" and "them" is a profound and basic force that has a powerful influence on human behaviour.

It is our impression that the division into "us" and "them" reflects a deep, *unconscious* need. This need exerts very powerful pressure to belong to "my group", to be "us" and to distance, to split, oneself from "the other group" or "them". It makes it difficult for people to remain neutral, pressuring them to belong and choose between two sides, rather than having multiple alternatives open to them. At the same time, the other group, the "them", gradually takes on the qualities and attributes of an enemy. These boundaries and the way they are defined can remain stable over time.

Our observations were enriched with other findings, some of which are presented below.

As soon as participants began to consider the other group in terms of "us" and "them", they spontaneously began to use rhetoric appropriate to such a division. The simulations made it possible for us to see that the scantiest information was sufficient for participants to create slogans, symbols, and metaphors. The brief and minimal instructions of the consultants (consisting of slips in different colours or with just one word inscribed on them) were sufficient to arouse a rich and extensive associative resonance on the part of the members in each group.

In all of the groups, as expected, the "us" was described in more positive terms than the "them". For example, in one of the simulations, a group described "us" and "them" as follows: "We are the activists, the rebels, while " they" are absolutely boring and depressing". At the same time, the other group took considerable pride in the "civilized" level of the conversation between two of its members; a conversation that lasted for most of the simulation. Members of this group did not make verbal comments about those who left them for the other group, and did not relate to them. However, their body language indicated their reservations, even contempt, for the noise and confusion that reigned in the other group (which, as mentioned, was proud of its participants' "activism").

In a number of simulations, we decided not to write anything on the slips of paper, and instead distributed slips of different colours. In these cases, too, the participants rapidly and obediently split into two groups according to the colour of their slips. Thus, lottery slips of different colours took on immense significance.

The participants began to formulate slogans and symbols related to them. The colour blue, for instance, became the symbol of gentility, tradition, or stability. The colour red came to symbolize humanitarianism, or the "working class".

At one simulation (conducted at an international conference for professionals), one of the participants noticed that the slips of the "them" had a word written on them, while the slips of the "us" had none. She told her group members excitedly: "They have something we don't have. They're the rich ones and we are the poor. We have nothing to lose." As a result of her remarks, the group began to perceive itself as being "the just ones" who are deprived and discriminated against and the "them" group was seen as exploitative.

We have noticed that the above process is gradual, rather than immediate. When a group crystallizes into "us" it differentiates itself from the rest of the world. The "us" is distinguished from the "not us" gradually. The process systematically begins with the denial of the existence of the other group.

The "them" group is discerned and not discerned at the same time. More precisely, it is deliberately and conspicuously ignored. In a number of the simulations we conducted, the two groups occupied crowded rooms, and sat in circles that were tangential to each other. Participants in each group sat with their backs to the participants in the "other" group, the backs of their chairs rubbing, obviously ill at ease. All this transpired without the groups exchanging a glance or a word, to say nothing of a dialogue between them, as had been proposed by the consultants in the primary task.

The participants appeared to be capable of maintaining such an atmosphere for quite some time. When the consultants intervened in this static situation, the response was almost invariably: "First we must get to know ourselves . . . First we will hold a discussion among ourselves and later, we'll see . . .". This "later", for the most part, never arrived, and when an inter-group encounter did take place, it was usually after the consultants had intervened.

It is, thus, little wonder that any suggestion that one group takes an interest in the other group is perceived as superfluous (if it comes from the "us" group), or hostile (if it comes from the "them" group). Any intervention, no matter how mild or polite, from the "them" group is almost always greeted with hostility and rejection. Such a response almost always engenders feelings of hurt, rejection, and hostility in return. From this point onwards, the mutual *avoidance* that started the process is transformed into mutual *animosity*.

Statements of great suspicion, devoid of any perspective or humour, often accompany such moments. One might say that the atmosphere hardens. Some members, sometimes the entire "us" group, now have a score to settle with the members of the "them" group. It is at this point that there are instances of emotional (and, hence, irrational) behaviour towards the "them" group. The prevailing affects expressed by the members are vengefulness, narcissistic vulnerability, and envy.

In simulations that offer a choice between co-operation and a competitive confrontation, the dominant inclination at this point is towards confrontation, attended by militant enthusiasm: expressions of cohesiveness are at their height. The groups are then often seen whispering and giggling happily. They are gathered in close physical proximity. Glances are occasionally shot at the "them" group. Impressions are immediately reported and carefully listened to.

Of the many simulations that we conducted, in only two instances did the participants voluntarily achieve inter-group dialogue. In several other instances, the groups that were formed conducted such a dialogue only after the consultants reminded them of the primary task.

Some exceptions

Most of the participants in the simulations we conducted behaved in a manner similar to that described above. Nevertheless, there were also a number of exceptions.

In one of the simulations, the participants chose to undertake the primary task and enter into an inter-group dialogue. Representatives from both groups were sent to the assigned meeting place and became engrossed in conversation, while the two groups continued to be involved in formulating their identity. During this time, two representatives of one of the groups withdrew from their group, declared themselves to be an independent group, and invited other participants to join them. They were joined by three other participants. This brought the number of groups in the room to four. The representatives of the two original groups that were to conduct an inter-group dialogue began moving around and offering ideas and suggestions. Group coherence appeared shaky and the ideas suggested by the representatives were not accepted. What transpired here appears to justify the claim made by the vast majority of the groups that refused to meet for an inter-group dialogue on the grounds that "we must first become a cohesive group ourselves". It appears that the process of establishing and consolidating group cohesion does indeed require time and effort, as they claimed, and is a safeguard against the danger of disintegration.

At one of the international conferences, inter-group unity was indeed achieved. After the groups were formed in the room (in that simulation, slips of three different colours were distributed and three groups were formed), they all joined together and paraded in a single colourful circle, singing and chanting slogans. The participants enjoyed themselves greatly, and the atmosphere was easy and cheerful. We noticed that during the parading all the participants gave up the territory assigned to their groups, and no longer returned to their seats.

At another simulation, conducted for behavioural sciences professionals, the participants refused to split into groups on the basis of the slips of paper they received, claiming that they knew "that trick". Nevertheless, to our surprise, they did split into two groups voluntarily, on the basis of criteria they themselves suggested, and from then on the simulation moved along a course having the same characteristics as described above.

A conceptualization of these observations

After collecting numerous observations in different settings, it appears that some typical behaviours repeat themselves throughout most of these simulations. As with the work done by David Gutmann and his team in an intervention with the Arab University of Jerusalem in July 1996, this approach of conceptualization is to make associations out of mere facts, images, and fantasies. This approach progressively gives a meaning to some behaviours and actions. This meaning is in no sense a truth, but the sense elaborated can be a "prerequisite" for the understanding of behaviours, especially when there are "hidden elements".

Division into two groups

The participants preferred to be divided into just two groups (except when three or more types of slips were issued, in which case the participants tended at first to comply with their slips).

Obedience

The participants tended to obey the slips they were issued, as if they were an order from high level to split into groups. They usually did this quickly, accurately, and without much protest.

Intra-group belonging

Processes of intra-group belonging began to develop within each of the groups. The atmosphere was accepting, pleasant, empathic, and conducive to feeling included and safe. Within each group, acceptance and tolerance of differences were displayed, as long as the participant wanted to belong.

Establishing the "us": loyalty and kinship

("First we'll get to know ourselves.")

In all groups, a sense of loyalty and kinship was established, first via the above mentioned interpersonal relationships, and later, verbalized and represented in the members' discourse. This was perceived as having precedence over, and being preferable to, any other possible task. We observed two elements in the process: on the one hand, we noticed that the group's effort to create cohesiveness was effective and did bring about cohesiveness, a common language and a more efficient way of making group decisions; on the other hand, the process of building a sense of loyalty and kinship, and maintaining it over time, is liable to become a never-ending task. The tendency and motivation for creating a cohesive "us" results in the rejection of proposals for inter-group encounters, regardless of whether they come from the "us" group or the "them" group.

Establishing the "them"

Processes of developing perceptions regarding the other group consist of several stages. First, its existence is denied; it is dismissed as either non-existent or unimportant. Then it is discerned as "them". Afterwards, it is perceived as a nuisance or as an unwanted, or even unjust, intrusion. Finally, it is perceived as an enemy.

Creating the enemy

At the stage when the group is putting effort into creating the "us", the existence of the "them" is discerned but denied. As previously mentioned, any approach by the "them" group to the "us" group is perceived as an intrusion. The "us" group reacts to their sense of being intruded upon by behaving in a rejecting and rude manner. Thus, it offends and angers the "them" group. The affect becomes laden with suspicion, narcissistic vulnerability, and a wish for revenge, to which both groups are party. From this moment on, the "them" group is perceived as having ill intentions and the "us" group as a victim. Self-defence is considered to be necessary and justified.

Formulation of an ideology

While energy is invested in creating an "us" identity, words that are said in the room arouse associations and become charged with group meaning. The members seem to be hunting for group metaphors. When they are found, they describe the uniqueness of "us".

During the observations we discerned the following phenomena:

1.   Various expressions are tossed into the air; some refer to the division of the groups.
2.   Of these expressions, some turn into metaphors and slogans involving splitting, especially of one group *vs.* the other group or groups.
3.   These metaphors are fleshed out into group narratives.
4.   They choose some of them as expressing their identity within the group and their belonging to it (they verbalize them by mutual consent, with a sense of pleasure).
5.   The sayings begin to become group "property", a kind of independently existing object. Thus, a sort of group ideology is born that defines the uniqueness of the group *vis à vis* the rest of the world, and an agreement with it becomes a criterion for membership.
6.   Such a criterion demands "binary" obedience (agrees/disagrees, belongs/does not belong) on the part of the group members.

Probing towards a group dialogue

We found that the splitting and the inter-group animosity can remain stable for some time. Only rarely did the groups achieve inter-group dialogue, and in most of these cases it occurred only after reminders by the consultants about the primary task (i.e., it was brought about by an outside party).

On the other hand, there were instances when the inter-group dialogue led to the fragmentation of the entire group into several nondescript sub-groups.

On some rare occasions, the groups were really interested in each other and became involved in an inter-group dialogue with apparent pleasure. Mostly, third-party interventions proved necessary to achieve this.

Discussion

We are using the term *social structure* to refer to a primal, basic, perhaps even inborn, social behaviour that characterizes human society, one that goes beyond nations and cultures. We are suggesting that the division into two groups—"us" and "them"—reflects such a social structure.

The division into "us" and "them" can be regarded as a major social mechanism, a form of social organization that has defensive, projective as well as developmental, structuring functions. We suggest perceiving this structure as a basic social instinct of human beings.

In our opinion, the forming of archaic collective identities and a sense of kinship precedes the modelling of an individual's personality. Only at a later stage, when we align ourselves with specific groups that correspond to a defined social context, can processes of personal development and individuation evolve.

We believe that the above illustrations in the simulations reflect a universal, unconscious, social process that occurs in human society on a broad scale: between groups, between organizations, between sub cultures, and between nations. We have chosen to refrain from referring to socio-political meanings that could be associated with these illustrations. The reader might—we hope—notice the various meanings that are hinted at in the illustrations, on his own.

It seems to us that we can understand the phenomena we have described in terms of purpose (what they exist for) and in terms of cause (why they exist in such a way). In terms of purpose, we believe that the division into "us" and "them" has a certain benefit: it becomes part of the processes leading to an individual self-definition and identity formation.

Moreover, the division into "us" and "them" promotes group cohesiveness. This cohesiveness combines motivations and inner resources of each individual into a collective pool. It is experienced by its members as a sense of togetherness, similarity, consensus, and acceptance. This positive experience enhances the participants' desire to give of themselves to the group, and to voluntarily reduce their own individuality, desires, and personal needs. In this way, the group can turn into a team, an organization—or even a nation— that is able to work towards mutual goals and use its resources for the benefit of its individual members and for the group as a whole. We believe that the process of consolidating a group identity and a sense of "us" includes a certain degree of closing off and hostility against "them". It appears that this attitude towards "them" increases at the beginning of the process and is likely to decrease gradually when the group identity is achieved and well established (promoting a sense of security and self worth). The decrease in the level of negative feelings towards "them" facilitates probing towards a group dialogue that can be successfully achieved at this stage. Nevertheless, there is marked difference between groups in the degree that they are closed off and hostile towards "them". A high level of negative feelings towards "them" is likely to prevent a dialogue between groups from developing altogether.

In our opinion, self-definition is a process that occurs through identification and separation. It has two main elements:

1. The element of similar to me.
2. The element of different from me.

It is our hypothesis that the process of differentiation requires both. It is impossible to formulate and delineate a distinct identity (individual and group) without each of these elements. The division into "us" and "them" can be regarded as a structure that provides dividing lines within the chaos and anchors them in social reality. Thus, the group that we term "us" attributes all of the *similar to us* aspects to itself, and ascribes all of the *different from us* elements to the other group. In other words, *"us"* represents a collective form of *"me"* and *"them"* represents a collective form of *"not me"*.

The division into "us" and "them" as a mechanism of defence

As we have mentioned before, the division into "us" and "them" may have emotional reasons. The absence of a sense of belonging to a group can create feelings of distress in the individual. This sense of distress is probably connected with man's fear of being alone, with the absence of a sense of kinship, and with the depression that accompanies living without others that are different from you.

All these issues are described in literature: we will mention some of the ideas that relate to them.

Fear

It appears that, in an undefined space, the individual becomes filled with anxiety and is flooded with fear of annihilation. Some authors in psychoanalytic literature describe such a state of extreme anxiety, and we suggest that their thinking can be applied to understand man's feelings in an anonymous crowd as well.

Bion (1962, 1977) refers to it as a "nameless dread"; Winnicott (1987, 1989) calls it "disintegration anxiety" regarding an "unthinkable" emotional state of "falling forever"; Klein (1946–1963) talks about the danger of "annihilation" as a derivative of an inborn death instinct (in the same article). Bollas (1995) says that an empty space fills up with evil, and the term "black hole" is widely used to describe a fear of annihilation and a sense of an existential catastrophe that man faces.

Depression

Winnicott (1950) claims that a global society leads to depression, whereas conflict extricates us from it. "If the whole world were our society, then it would need to be at times in a depressed mood . . . The concept of a global society brings with it the idea of a world suicide" (p. 256).

The absence of a sense of belonging

It appears that an anonymous crowd does not provide the individual with a sense of identity and it leaves him in chaotic distress. In such an amorphous social reality, people are liable to feel that they have no value or significance, that their very existence might be erased. They encounter unbearable feelings of doubt and confusion, and hasten to defend themselves against this danger.

According to Joanne Field (1981),

> . . . a world that is without form is indeed void. There is nothing in it to get hold of. For any external object to become happily significant for us, it must have some form by which we can recognize it as likely to satisfy our needs and therefore as relevant to our destiny . . . here was the principle of limitation, outline, patterning, the ordering principle which could be hated for its restrictiveness and yet loved because *utterly needed for one's very psychic and physical existence.*" [pp. 99–100, our italics]

Oldenquist (1986), in a socio-philosophical approach, states:

> The evidence is overwhelming that people need social identities— essences as it were—and otherwise they feel isolated, alienated, and without significance. Unless people noninstrumentally value something other than themselves, they will find it next to impossible to value themselves. This is what it means to say we are innately social animals . . . [pp. 472]

Therefore, we regard the primal horde as a basic, universal formation against the possibility of being an insignificant individual, with no identity, within an anonymous crowd. In addition—the multi-faceted distress we describe here is liable to mobilize defensive measures such as splitting, projection, and projective identification (with their double function). We maintain that the primal horde seeks out another, opposing horde, so that the two hordes can behave in the characteristic manner of "us" and "them".

Splitting and projection are well known and widely discussed in the psychoanalytical literature, although mostly in the interpersonal domain, and far less in the inter-group domain (Klein, 1946–1963).

It is also possible that the split into "me/not-me" entities does not suffice as a defence mechanism. A sense of kinship might perhaps constitute a better defence. The group cohesiveness enhances the split, and provides a much-needed sense of belonging as "us". "Us" is likely to be experienced as more reassuring, safer, and stronger than "me". This splitting provides a double measure of protection, since it enables a sense of belonging while projecting unwelcome aspects of "us" on to "them". From a psychological point of view, the process of turning "them" into an enemy can still be considered as having a defensive value, despite the pain and the destructiveness that are inherent in it. A defined, identified enemy that enhances the individual's sense of belonging strengthens boundaries and provides for group and personal identity, can extricate us from feelings of deep anxiety and its link to death, and from depression. Thus, one can say that it is easier to have a defined enemy than to be burdened with the sense of dread that anonymity can arouse.

The idea of the need for enemies is not entirely new. In an article written in 1972, Kohut claims that aggression against the other is an expression of narcissistic rage that stems from an injured self and from a narcissistic deprivation of one's basic developmental needs. He ends this article by stressing that a similar dynamic occurs in group processes, and that its understanding can promote our thinking about social behaviour and hostility between groups.

Kohut says that

> group cohesion is brought about and maintained not only by an ego ideal held in common by the members of the group (Freud, 1921) but also by their shared subject-bound grandiosity, i.e., by a shared grandiose self. Indeed, there are groups, which are characterized by the fact that they are held together by this latter bond—crudely stated, by their shared ambitions rather than by their shared ideals. [pp. 397–398]

In addition, he believes that when group narcissism is interfered with, it causes regression that is transformed into narcissistic rage and aggression against other groups. He says,

> the need for revenge, for righting a wrong, for undoing a hurt by whatever means, and a deeply anchored, unrelenting compulsion in the pursuit of all these aims gives no rest to those who have suffered a narcissistic injury. [ibid., p. 380]

Moses (1982) refers to these ideas of Kohut in an article about the group self. He sees in narcissistic phenomena and their pathological transformations the roots for the polarities between groups and the escalation of conflicts that occurs in them.

As an example, he explores the dynamic process that constitutes the Israeli–Arab conflict. He believes that narcissistic pathology is the cause for signifying the other group as an enemy, and turning it into a sacrificial lamb. In his opinion, seeing the others as aggressive is a collective defence mechanism that promotes the self worth of group members and thus takes care of their vulnerability.

This projection leaves one

> Feeling fairly righteous and pure; even more so when one compares oneself—as indeed one does—with the projectee who is perceived as being bad, cruel, barbaric and inhuman. Such an increase in self-esteem, in what one can call narcissistic affect, is at the root of the mechanism of scapegoating. This indeed is how the original scapegoat was conceived of in religion, and how the chicken on Yom Kippur in Judaism is viewed to this day. The sacrificial animal is discarded with all the badness inside it: the person remains pure and clean.

> The same narcissistic gain from the use of projection occurs when the members of a nation project their hostile and aggressive wishes and tendencies into or onto an enemy-neighbour. The same polarization then takes place: they, the Arabs, are bad and we, the Jews or Israelis, are good. And vice versa, of course. [*ibid.*, p. 56]

Volkan (1988) claims that the need to have an enemy is universal. He traces the origins of social conflict to the crib and argues that fear and hatred of the stranger is deeply rooted in the human psyche. He thinks that the fear of the stranger and projection of hatred upon the other are the psychological foundation of the concept of the enemy. In an article written in 1987, he suggests that the socio-political enemy is an outgrowth of the early need to find objects that will store those aspects one has difficulties in containing by himself. The creation of a mutual enemy provides such a "reservoir", and acts as a collective defence mechanism against drives and wishes that endangered the group identity. He coins the term "suitable targets of externalization" to describe these reservoirs. "The enemy, as an extension of such targets, acts as a reservoir of our externalized bad self and object representations condensed with projected and unwanted impulses, thoughts, and defences against them" (*ibid.*, p. 912).

In our opinion, *the need for an enemy is coupled, consubstantial with the need for a friend*. They constitute two opposite poles of the same continuum and have a contradictory form of coexistence. We believe that creating a place for oneself is enhanced through the creation of an external "enemy". The role of the "friend" is reserved for the group that one initially identifies with and conceives as "us".

The underlying reasons for both these needs are unconscious. The meaningful functions that both these needs have in the process of personal and social development is denied. They undergo a process of rationalization and are transformed into an ideology that is out of touch with the structural roots it is derived from.

We believe that an ideology can serve a double function: it defines and structures identity as well as acting as a defence mechanism. In other words, the dynamic process of forming an identity precedes the creation of a specific ideological content. Thus perceived, an ideology organizes boundaries and provides a sense of kinship under conditions of confusion and doubt. It provides a speedy orientation that apparently has a survival value with regard to critical existential questions that are at stake. In situations such as war or competition, it is especially important to know immediately who is with you and who is against you. Under these conditions, anyone who remains with open alternatives— hesitates, does not define himself, and does not belong—finds that his existence might be in danger. At the same time, the intra-group dialogue about this ideology contains totalitarian characteristics: within the group embrace there is no tolerance for dissidence. It is a form of a "binary" dialogue: it is an "either/or" culture: yes/no, good/bad, with us/against us, belongs/does not belong.

Such an arbitrary division takes on an ideological dimension. The random slip of paper, according to which the groups were divided, turns into a flag that gathers meanings, fashions political and social opinions, and feeds group cohesiveness.

What then, at face value, appears to be a rational choice that expresses a mature, well-considered world outlook, turns out to be, at least partially, an unconscious process over which the individual has a limited amount of choice, freedom, control, and personal ownership.

The splitting into "us" and "them"

The denial of mutual dependence and group development

We believe that isolation and animosity towards others has a price. A flight into group cohesiveness is likely to seal the boundaries around "us" and erects a wall against "them": a wall of projections. To set up such a wall between "us" and "them" denies the space of unconscious as the link with the other. "Them" are thus named to carry, to bear, the projection of *our* refusal to be dependent to the other and to share with it. Both groups will tend to deny the importance of the contribution they make for each other in developing and achieving a sense of kinship and self-definition. Thus, each group is not able to see the other as valuable and meaningful and, at the same time, cannot see itself as having similar value for the others. The possibility of a flexible, open social identity that is continuously updated against a changing internal and external reality, the potential for maintaining real relationships with the changing other, is experienced as confusing and dangerous.

Thus, both groups become enclosed within defensive walls, nurturing a sense of false independence. Because of the refusal to accept the dependence of the other group, their interdependence is denied and forgotten and their deep inter-relationships remain unconscious and unacknowledged.

Basic needs like that can exist in various degrees on a spectrum between recognition and denial. Thus, when the need for the other is denied, the contribution that one group can have for the other is unacknowledged and not recognized because it is deeply repressed

A number of theorists relate to the value of the encounter with the other, and even believe this encounter is vital for individual development. We suggest that the same ideas can be applied to the development of groups, too.

For Lacan, the Other is the place from which a difference is set out for each one. Indeed, the unconscious is *in between* two individuals or two groups.

According to Winnicott, the human world starts with a twosome and not with the individual ("There is no such thing as a infant without a mother", 1965). Winnicott (1975) believes that formulating a subjective identity of value requires the existence of an "other"; an "other" to contend with, destroy in one's imagination, and interact with in order to realize our inborn human potential. Self-definition requires an "other". The other does not just constitute a frustrating and unavoidable reality that must be tolerated, but rather a primary need that is impossible to do without. Such a recognition process first needs our acceptance of the other who is inside of ourselves, that Jacqueline Schaeffer names the *internal other* (*l'étranger interne*).

The other is a subject of fantasy and imagination as well as part of external reality. According to Winnicott (1975) the encounter with externality is crucial for the development of an adequate reality testing, for the realization of one's creative potential and for the ability to enjoy life in itself. He says

> We often hear of the very real frustrations imposed by external real-ity, but less often hear of the relief and satisfaction it affords . . . fantasy is only tolerable at full blast when objective reality is appre-ciated well. . . . the subjective . . . cannot be enjoyed except as a parallel to the objective. [*ibid.*, p. 153]

In Winnicott's view, the other is perceived as a resource, as a poten-tial for diversity and richness. The "not me" has the capacity to save the "me" from a danger of suffocating in paranoid isolation. Hence, we can assume that when there is no Other nearby, we are liable to create one.

Buber and Kaufmann (1970) consider the "I–Thou" dialogue as a worthy existential achievement, while the relation between "I–It" misses the chance for this level of communication. It seems that the division into "us" and "them" contains some aspects of "I–It". We maintain that the splitting into "us" and "them" may represent a move away, and even a fall, from the ability to realize the potential of an "I–Thou" relationship. The hoped for " us–you" state of related-ness is replaced by "us–them", with its accompanying sense of alien-ation and hostility.

Obedience

It is important to mention that there is an alternative hypothesis that might explain the division into groups besides the idea of instinctive splitting we have posited in this paper. The compliance with the simulation's instructions raises the possibility that the participants could have been responding to an overt or latent suggestion by the consultants. If that is the case, the underlying cause for this phenomenon is the need for a leader (Bion, 1961; Freud, 1912–1913) and a deep, primary, dependent obedience to authority.

It was our impression that this dependency on authority was indeed very powerful. In spite of this, however, we feel that obedience alone cannot explain our various findings. It can explain the division into groups based on the instructions, but it cannot, in our opinion, account for the two groups taking opposing stands for the durability of those stands and for the creative investment of each group in establishing a separate and distinct identity. Furthermore, it was our impression that the participants' powerful internal motivation to divide themselves in this way cannot be explained merely by an external factor.

Thus, obedience to authority is possibly a meaningful factor, but not an exclusive one. Moreover, it is possible that this primary tendency for division is the one that seeks a leader—no less than the other way around. It appears that obedience to authority, and dependence on it, joins forces with the primary tendency to divide into "us" and "them" in producing universal patterns of social behaviour.

Cultural influences

In our opinion, the division into "us" and "them" is a universal one. However, culture, religion and historical factors could affect the degree to which this division escalates into extreme poles or is ameliorated and becomes moderate.

We assume that cultures that promote an elitism of the "us" and that devalue the "them," or even recommend in advance that the "them" be regarded as a potential enemy, reinforce a tendency among members of the same society to polarize into two opposing groups.

In other words, the social, cultural, and historical context within which this division occurs can affect the shaping, impact, and content of these processes.

Winnicott (1989) thinks that a catastrophe that has occurred in one's childhood may reappear in later life in a form of a dissociated affective experience, and express itself in overly defensive behaviour. In other words, traumatic events in a person's past that were not worked out might be relived unconsciously and reactivated as an overt preoccupation with bracing oneself against the next attack. ("Fear of break down" pp. 89–90, 91).

By the same token, we believe that a history of group traumas could lead to an emotional climate of collective suspicion and isolation, and could increase polarization between groups.

Winnicott, in his article on democracy (1950), claims that the natural tendency to democracy can be reinforced by first reducing the impingement imposed on the individual by his care-takers, i.e., by having a "good enough mother" in the socio-political sense. Following his ideas we assume that societies that stress openness, acceptance, and democracy help to decrease the polarity that occurs in the division into groups of "us" and "them."

However, in spite of all that has been written before, the division into polarized groups remains, in our opinion, primal and powerful, going beyond societies and cultures, their histories, their cumulative learning, and their collective experiences.

The "third" and the role of the consultants

In addition, the division into "us" and "them" includes, in our opinion, opposition to a third side. For Lacan, the unconscious is the third place (*le tiers-lieu*) that escapes the consciousness. According to Daniel Sibony, in usual relationships, as far as talks are concerned, especially in conversational speech, this third place—the place of the unconscious—is forgotten or implicit: it is taken by a social link, tight or loose though it may be. It is a silent, vigilant link that passes on the voice of the group.

The resistance to the "third" can be explained by Lacan's (1977) concept: the twosome maintains a stable but frozen relationship; the "Other" refers to a third psychological entity generated in the analytic setting that is distinct from the patient and from the analyst: "The Other is therefore the locus in which is constituted the I who speaks with him who hears . . ." (1956, pp. 141). The "third", the other, is the one who prevents repetition and glaciation. We claim that the division into "us" and "them" behaves in the same manner as a twosome (a couple) with its characteristic stability (fixation) and glaciation, in spite of the fact that the relationship between "us" and "them" could be one of rivalry and animosity, and not necessarily of love. The antagonist *di-vision* into "us" and "them"—with the split it underlies—structuring mode

In the simulation, the "Government" group could have constituted a possible "third", but it "disappeared". The government's disappearance, in our opinion, represents the resistance to the other. After the government's disappearance, the whole system, including the two groups, appeared to have "frozen". The relationship between "us" and "them" remained stable (or rather "stuck") until the intervention by the consultants through their statements. The consultants, too, were influenced by this emotional process, and felt the pull to shift roles and join the two existing groups. Nevertheless, they stayed close to their assigned territory and were able to persist in their role. In the end, the consultants appeared to have taken upon themselves the role of the "third", the other. Their ability to maintain their position and their unique function—despite the pressure to be pulled into the two groups—enabled them to be the "third" within the polarized situation. As a result of the consultants' intervention as the "third", the system emerged from its frozen state, and inter-group interactions that had the potential for creating and promoting inter-group dialogue could take place.

We would like to stress that the "other" is a different concept from the "third".

We feel that, in inter-group relationships, the sub-groups are diametrically juxtaposed and they form two entities that constitute the opposite sides of the same coin. The "third" we refer to is outside the polarization of the "us" and "them" and represents additional options. It was our experience that the entry of the " third" into the picture is unwelcome, and is met with resistance by the groups.

The consultants' reflections and interpretations about the participants' compliance with an arbitrary division—based on random slips of paper and their interpretations, suggesting that an ideology might be based on irrational factors—as put forth by the ideas in this thesis, raise fear and anger in the participants. The possibility that a random slip of paper can acquire the status of a well-reasoned political stand is apparently a serious narcissistic blow to the group self. As we have already mentioned, what appears to the participants, at face value, as a rational choice that expresses a mature, well-considered world outlook, is—at least partially—an unconscious process over which there is limited control and personal ownership; the level of choice and the freedom to change it are small. Most often, the boundless strength of the fear of the other—voiced and shown through anger—prevents the encounter.

The ability of the consultants to contain the anger that the participants direct at their interventions, to contain the feeling that they are ignored or devalued by them, makes it possible for the group members to acknowledge their neediness. They become able to use the interpretations of the consultants to decrease the behaviour of closing off and hostility and to increase the dialogue between the groups. They understand the dependency groups have over individuals, and perhaps they will start assuming their own authority, as demonstrated in the work done by David Gutmann and others (1997).

Concerning the unconscious, when we succeed in revealing part of it, we pull down some walls, but the collective unconscious, as a meta-system, gets the upper hand, and this requires more work on traditional resistances in order to fight against them.

Note

1. A version of this chapter was published as "Trauma and identity" (2000), in *Mind & Human Interaction*, *11*(1), pp. 53–72, and in S. Ostroff (Ed.), *Dialogue and Leadership across the Faultiness of Israeli Society: Developing Theory and Practice* (pp. 305–328). Jerusalem: The Joint-Brookdale Institute (Hebrew).

CHAPTER FIVE

The decline of traditional defences against anxiety[1]

David Gutmann, with Catherine Sandler

"Post equitem sedet atra cura" (At the rider's back sits dark anxiety)

(Horace, 65–68 BC, quoted in Raffel, 1983)

In considering the role of anxiety in individual and institutional life, it is clear that we are dealing with a double-edged weapon. Anxiety—in its purest form, an unnamed, diffuse fear of disintegration and death—is one of the primary and most basic emotions we experience. Throughout our lives, we are both defending ourselves against it and struggling to find positive ways of adapting in response to it. By "positive ways" I mean responses that facilitate growth and creativity rather than lead to blockage and regression. In this context, it is important to emphasize the role of anxiety as a vital source of productive tension: it is only through remaining partially vulnerable to our anxiety and responding to it that we can achieve our potential for creativity and innovation. It is equally important, though, to remember that excessive anxiety can inhibit, erode, and even paralyse our capacity to function effectively.

Thus *an adequate level of defence against anxiety is both healthy and necessary*. We can speak here in terms of the need to manage first our own anxiety and, second, that of others. In fact, we are engaged in a continuing process of regulation. However, the amount of anxiety that we take in across our personal and collective boundaries is only one element in determining whether anxiety will contribute to greater creativity or lead to sterility and self-destructiveness. More important still is the *nature of the defences* developed by the individual, group, or society to deal with the anxiety that they experience.

The type of defence used by the individual or group is the outcome of the dialectical struggle that takes place between our urge to keep the unbearable effects of anxiety at bay and our capacity to *contain and harness our anxiety as a force for growth and change*. Our responses range, therefore, from the relatively primitive to the more mature. It is evident that we all make use, at different times, of defence mechanisms such as denial, regression, idealization, projection, and splitting. But the degree and way in which we use these defences is crucial.

If we think in terms of the effectiveness or "success" of the individual or group's adaptation to anxiety, we can summarize three main sorts of response.

1. An extreme and unsuccessful response in which all adequate defences against anxiety are unavailable or break down altogether. In this situation, anxiety becomes an overwhelming and unmanageable force leading to chaos, impotence, despair, and ultimately to madness and even death.
2. A response in which the defences mobilized against anxiety enable the individual or group to survive intact, and to continue functioning, but at a very high cost to their capacity for creativity. This applies to defences of a primitive and limiting kind, the result of which is at best a sterile repetition of past patterns of behaviour and, thus, past mistakes.
3. A response in which anxiety can not only be held in check, but also used as the source of positive creative energy. When this is the case, anxiety and the defences developed against it can be said to play a crucial role in enabling human beings to master and change their environment and to develop. Indeed, anxiety can be seen as a major and essential factor in human creativity.

What characterizes, then, this third and most successful type of response to the threat posed by anxiety—the response that goes beyond defensiveness and becomes a positive force for change? What are its necessary pre-conditions? And what can we do as practitioners in the field of human relations to facilitate its development in the individuals, groups, and institutions with which we work, above all in an era in which many traditional defences against anxiety are in decline?

To begin with, we must acknowledge the necessity of defence mechanisms against anxiety that enable the person or group to generate sufficient feelings of safety or security in order to take the risks involved in any evolution. Thus, defences involving repetitive and regressive behaviour, for example, play an important part not only in the process of controlling anxiety, but also in the process of channelling it into constructive energy. This can perhaps be seen most clearly with children, for whom established routines and repetitive play are necessary prerequisites for emotional development. If these sources of security are not sufficiently present, the child's growth is likely to be arrested and distorted, leading to behaviour in adulthood in which anxiety results not in risk-taking and innovation but in a maladaptive and immature holding on to the familiar and known.

The workings of the financial system in modern capitalistic society provides an illustration at the social level of this link between defences against anxiety aimed at providing a sense of security and the potentially creative outcome of such defences in terms of human development. A large part of the money invested in our society consists of short-term savings, made by individual investors concerned to insure themselves against the uncertainties of economic life. However, financial intermediaries like the savings bank or building society provide more than a defence against anxiety. They enable savings *to be transformed* into productive investment necessary for economic growth. Thus, a force for expansion is released, without the individual saver losing immediate access to his savings.

It is also important to note, however, that the breakdown of this defence mechanism—which happened during the world financial crisis of 1929–1933—has consequences that are as traumatic and overwhelming for society as the breakdown of personal defence mechanisms for the individual. The recent experience of the "great crash" on the Stock Exchange in October 1987 should serve as a reminder of the importance of developing new defences against anxiety if we are not to deal with the challenge and uncertainties of the late twentieth century by simply repeating our earlier mistakes.

Part of the problem in this instance was the blind faith that had developed in the effective working of the stock market and therefore the lack of alternative economic defence systems which might have protected those caught up in its collapse.

Finally, in developing the parallel between the financial defence mechanism described above and individual defences against anxiety, it is worth noting that those investors who take the highest risks are those who expect the highest financial returns. In the same way, at a personal level, the more anxiety one can contain and manage (and therefore the higher the emotional risk one takes), the greater the level of potential creativity.

Returning to our general theme, then, we can add that in both individual and collective terms, the successful use of anxiety by the individual or group must involve the interplay of several different defences. There is no one final solution to the problem of transforming anxiety—indeed the final solution comes only when all defences have either broken down or become supremely self-destructive.

During the life of an individual, group, or institution, anxiety will provoke a response at all three levels of effectiveness. Clearly, it is not always possible to adapt to the pressure of anxiety in a creative fashion. The danger, however, of defences that do not provide the individual or group with opportunities for development and growth is that anxiety that is not dealt with positively is generally *exported* (to remain with economic terminology) *in the form of projections*. The rapid starting up of a system of projections, along with high levels of transference and splitting, is perhaps most clearly seen at group relations' conferences in which very high levels of anxiety are generated and participants' usual defence systems often come under particular pressure.

One example that occurs to me is that of a female health visitor from the North of England who came under enormous pressure to break down while attending a Tavistock-style group relations conference.[1] As someone who had managed to escape her own poor, working-class background and now spent her professional life relating to her original peer group as clients, she became the focus for much of the status anxiety felt by the many other mental health professionals attending the conference—an anxiety that related not just to social status, but also to their status as the sane adult help-ing half of the partnership that they formed in their working with "problem-ridden" patients and clients.

Under the pressure of group projections, the health visitor began to identify with her own clients and became a co-operative vehicle for the role of conference patient or casualty. It was only by leaving the conference and returning two or three days later that she was able to resist losing all defences against anxiety and break-ing down. Her temporary withdrawal from the conference to her home environment enabled her to re-establish her customary defences and thus regain necessary feelings of safety, while simul-taneously obliging the other conference participants—who became very anxious about her—to take back their own anxious feelings and, with the help of the conference staff, defend against them in a less destructive fashion.

The primary task of the staff in this situation was to try to main-tain boundaries within and around the conference institution that were firm enough to create an adequate feeling of safety in the participants, and, second, to use interpretations to assist the members to respond to their anxiety by *learning*, i.e., to produce insights from the raw material of their experiences.

It is clear, then, that anxiety and the defences against it play a vital part in both the constructive and destructive aspects of human behaviour. It is central, therefore, to our work in the field of group relations. It takes on a particular relevance, moreover, at a time that has seen the decline of many of the traditional psychic and social defences against anxiety. These traditional defences played an important role in providing individuals, groups, and institutions with sufficient security to enable them to guard against depression or breakdown, to function effectively, and to develop new and creative patterns of behaviour.

The example of Israel can provide a concrete and topical illus-tration of the decline of traditional, adaptive defences. From its inception, Israeli society has been under constant threat, both physical and psychological, and its members have therefore had to deal with exceptional levels of anxiety. Up until fairly recently, they responded to this anxiety with a variety of defences that, taken together, enabled it not simply to be held at bay, but to be used to fuel an unusual level of creative energy and achievement. The transformation of the desert into cultivated land, the welding of the civilian population into one of the most effective armed forces in the world, the idealism behind the co-operative drive of the kibbutzim, etc., all underline the potentially positive nature of a society's response to constant and acute anxiety.

In the recent period, however, one can develop the hypothesis that this largely positive response to the threats which Israeli society faces has begun to give way to a far more static and regressive set of defences. These are characterized by increased splitting and projections, as seen in the response to the Arab populations in the occupied territories, the return to fundamental Judaism by sections of the population, and the social tensions exacerbated by the economic situation and the influx of Sephardi (and now Russian) Jews.

For us, then, as intellectuals and workers in the field of human relations, the late 1980s present a telling challenge. We must try to use our capacity to interpret both conscious and unconscious reality in a way that enables ourselves and others to deal with anxiety as constructively as possible. At the same time, we must reflect on and encourage the application of new or renewed forms of positive defence against anxiety, defences that will facilitate its use as a force for creativity and innovation.

In order to undertake these tasks, however, we must first understand the present state of the most well-established—and until recently most effective—defences against anxiety. In the body of this chapter, therefore, I aim to give some illustrations of my main working hypothesis: *that the 1980s is a decade characterized by the rapid erosion or even collapse of many traditional forms of defence against anxiety.* While some of these defence mechanisms began to crumble well before 1980, the past few years have seen the dramatic acceleration and culmination of this process. The following are examples of the decline of traditional defences against anxiety.

The use of institutions as a defence against anxiety

Even before the "great crash" of October 1987, recent economic and political developments in the West have ensured an increasing instability in institutional life. In industry and commerce, business after business has faced bankruptcy and collapse. Not only the smaller enterprises, but even apparently indestructible giants such as IBM, Renault, ITT, and ICL have become more fragile, more vulnerable to the pressures of competition and contraction.

The restructuring of industries, the large-scale reduction of labour, and the recent growth in mergers and takeovers have functioned to blur the boundaries between organizations and between the employed and unemployed, adding greatly to the uncertainties and insecurities experienced by employees at every level, managers as well as workers. The acute anxiety of not only the Rowntree workforce, but also the surrounding community in York, provides a current and striking illustration of the psychological consequences of some of these developments.

A similar state of turmoil and uncertainty exists in much of the public sector. The state-run or state-funded institutions that developed in the West after the end of the Second World War have also come under increasing threat for both economic and ideological reasons. This can be seen particularly clearly, not only in Britain, where institutions like the National Health Service and the prison service face chronic underfunding and radical re-organization, and under-invested and poorly-managed nationalized industries have been sold off, at prices often well below their real value, in line with the government's economic and political commitment to the private market, but also in France, the USA, and elsewhere.

The cuts in both the structure and budget of the welfare state, in particular, can be seen as an erosion of one of the major collective defences against anxiety developed since the war. At a time of great economic and social change and uncertainty, we are witnessing the run-down of institutions whose primary task is to contain some of the negative social consequences that are by-products of our industrial societies.

Inevitably, one of the major consequences of these developments has been to undermine the individual's traditional confidence in the continuity of his or her own institution, or at least of institutions in general. In fact, the recent period has seen the undermining of one of the twentieth century's most powerful myths: that of the indestructibility of work institutions. Until recently, this idea of the "immortality" of organizations enabled their members, and especially their leaders, to defend against their own mortality by projecting their wish to be omnipotent, strong, and invincible on to their institution. Today, this no longer applies. (Even in the fantasy world of *Dallas*, Ewing Oil is under threat, while in the real world, this is illustrated by the recent history of companies like Texaco and the *Societé Générale de Belgique*.) As we enter an era marked by the precariousness of institutional life, institutions are becoming an increasingly flawed form of individual and collective defence against anxiety.

The implications of this situation are clear, not only in relation to those institutions hardest hit by changing economic conditions, but also within those that continue to exist and even to expand. Increasingly, the direct and indirect pressures of the developments described above necessitate a redivision of roles, function, and status within work organizations. In order to adapt to the new demands made by the environment, a far greater level of individual and collective initiative is needed in the construction of appropriate task-related roles than was previously the case. As traditional conditions and responses no longer apply, established reference points and guidelines disappear. Organizations which cannot adapt and innovate—and which are unable to facilitate adaptation and innovation by their staff—are faced with the prospect of ossification and, in many cases, destruction.

A further difficulty faced by those with positions of responsibility within institutions at the present time involves the anxiety created by having to carry out negative roles in relation to other members of the organization. Therefore, those in charge of closing down plants, implementing redundancies, or enforcing redeployment may experience very high levels of anxiety indeed, exacerbated in some cases by the conflict between their personal beliefs and the exigencies of their role as manager. In this situation, there is a serious danger that they will defend against unbearable levels of anxiety through a process of unconscious "dehumanization" of those people affected by their decisions.

In the same way, those at the sharp end of cuts and reductions may deal with their anxiety by falling back on traditional forms of defence. At best, they may return to old-fashioned, confrontational trade union tactics; at worst they may resort to anarchic forms of direct action. Either way, they will probably use management, other trade unions, or other groups of workers to carry all the blame and "badness". Unfortunately, such defences only relieve anxiety at the price of a certain dehumanization of the individuals involved, while leading to an exacerbation of inter-group tension and misunderstanding. None of this, of course, facilitates more adaptive defences that draw positively on the resources of all members of an institution.

Electricité de France (EDF), the major producer and distributor of electricity in the world, provides a striking illustration of the difficult situation facing businesses in both the public and private sectors throughout the West. EDF, like many similar institutions, shared the unshakable post-war belief in indefinite expansion. A seven per cent average annual growth rate was taken for granted, even after the economic crisis of the early 1970s, which was coped with relatively well due to the massive development of its ambitious and pioneering nuclear energy programme.

The shock that EDF has experienced in the last few years—on finding that, after all, nothing is guaranteed—has been of cataclysmic proportions. Growth of 1.5–3% is now an optimistic forecast, while massive debts and at least ten per cent over-manning hang round its neck like so many millstones. In the face of the huge challenge that this situation represents, and the enormous anxiety that it involves, EDF is oscillating between a primitive defence denial and burying its head in the sand and a more mature response involving appropriate adaptation to changed conditions. As yet, it is still unclear if the company will be capable of positive innovation or whether the vicious circle of "anxiety, horrified retreat, and paralysis followed by even higher levels of anxiety" will prove too strong.

One last word on the subject of institutions as a defence against anxiety: the 1980s have also brought unprecedented levels of youth unemployment, thereby creating a new sub-class of young people who never had a real opportunity to develop membership of a work organization. For this group, deep feelings of marginalization and devaluation are added to the uncertainties felt by employed members of industrial societies: they are simultaneously exposed to unusually high levels of anxiety and deprived of one of the major traditional manners of dealing with it.

The use of science as a defence against anxiety

Another feature of the post-war Western world that has functioned as an important defence against anxiety is the unprecedented and astonishing growth of scientific, medical, and technological knowledge. Quite quickly, we came to believe that the extraordinary progress made by man over his environment and over every aspect of the natural world would inevitably continue. The past years, however, have seen the hope that science could solve all the problems of the world come under increasing pressure. Public confidence in scientific advance has been immensely shaken by tragedies such as Chernobyl or the Challenger shuttle disaster (and more recently by such horrors as the German mining accident, the Paris train crash, and the Piper Alpha explosion). Similarly, the almost god-like status given to scientists, technologists, and medical men has given way to much more sceptical and questioning attitudes.

Concern has grown among increasingly wide groups of citizens, not just the "trendy left", about the danger of nuclear radiation, about environmental pollution such as acid rain, about the ruin of natural resources (such as the Amazonian rain forests), about the addictive nature of tranquilizers, about the side-effects of other medical drugs, and so on. Underpinning all this, there is the growing recognition that, with the accelerated development of nuclear weapons, humanity has created the means for its own annihilation. Thus, while science continues to offer an enormously important means of reducing human suffering and improving the quality of life, it is increasingly ineffective as a defence against anxiety. Not only can it no longer function as the reassuring embodiment of human rationality and immortality to the same degree as in earlier times, but it is in itself an increasing source of deep anxiety and concern.

The use of ideology as a defence against anxiety

Religion

With the growing secularization of Western society over the past decades, the role of religious worship and activity in the community as a traditional defence against anxiety has undergone a significant decline. Decreasing numbers of ordinary families find religion a major source of comfort and security in the face of economic and social uncertainties. At the same time, the past years have seen a marked growth in the use of fundamentalist religion of one sort or another, whether in Iran, among Catholics such as Monsignor Lefebvre, in the American youth, or in the form of sects such as the Moonies.

Involvement in such forms of religious fanaticism can be seen to represent a harsher and more limiting defence against anxiety, in which the individual abandons personal authority and identity in exchange for an institutionalized ideology and identity. The loss of self involved in fusion with an ideologized group achieves a sense of security and feeds a collective narcissism. But this form of defence is purchased at a high price: through a response to the fear of death, it leads to death itself. The death of the individual identity of the members of the sect or group is followed by the attempt to kill those not in the sect—whether on a small scale as with the Sharon Tate murders or on a mass scale as with Nazism or the Iran-Iraq war—and finally by the death of the sect members itself, as in the case of the mass suicide of Jim Jones' followers in Guyana.

Revolution and "Reds under the beds"

Another form of ideology as a defence against anxiety that has declined in the recent period is that of the idea of a Marxist–Leninist revolution. For much of the period before and since the war, faith and hope in a new and better society tomorrow—whether or not in the form of the Soviet Union—has functioned as an effective defence, and as one that has often resulted in a positive creative drive. The Russian Revolution, whatever one may think of its subsequent consequences, was, after all, a striking example of innovative action as a response to high levels of anxiety and despair.

The idealism among youth and many intellectuals and workers which fuelled the events of 1968, not only in France, but in Italy, Czechoslovakia, Japan, Germany, and parts of America, are unthinkable today, twenty years later. In many parts of Europe the decline of the mass communist trade unions and parties is reflected by a general disillusion with the political process as indicated by low polls and low levels of party activism.

However, at the same time as this decline in revolution as a feasible defence against anxiety has been taking place, other, more conservative, sections of Western society have been finding it increasingly difficult to use the "Reds under the beds" idea as an effective defence against anxiety. In the face of the softening image of both the Chinese and, above all, the Russians, with Gorbachev's *glasnost*, it has become less possible to use the "Reds" as the bad objects on to whom all evil can be projected.

This, I would suggest, has led in turn to greater internal, domestic conflict, with bad groups having to be found more often at home, as with the Le Pen phenomenon in France, or with new enemies having to be found abroad, as with Britain and the Argentinians, all of which defends against anxiety only at the price of considerable destructiveness and internal social tension.

The return to individualism

A final and related aspect of ideology as a defence against anxiety that has undergone significant change over the recent period is the shift from the collectivist and co-operative philosophy of the post-war consensus years to the emphasis on individual effort and competition of the 1980s, a change seen most starkly, perhaps, in Margaret Thatcher's Britain, with its talk of a return to "Victorian values". (Similarly in France, where the attitudes of the Liberal movement have harked back to those of the nineteenth century's most famous premier, Guizot.)

One noticeable result of the promotion of this ideology of individual effort has been the decline in the formation of working pairs (not necessarily sexual) both within and outside institutions as a defence against anxiety. This is the result not only of the growth of disrupted relationship formation in childhood and of fear of potential sexual contact (both of which are discussed below), but also of the replacement of a spirit of mutual help with one of competitive pseudo-independence. Under this new ethos of the "survival of the fittest", the individual is increasingly lonely and alone in the face of his or her anxiety.

The use of "significant others" as a defence against anxiety

The basic organizations of our society consist of the family unit and the pair—both the adult male–female pair, which makes the creation of the family possible, and the mother–child (and to some extent the father–child) pair that enables the growth of a new generation of adults. The experience of a reasonably healthy and secure family structure and the capacity to pair successfully are two of the most important qualities we need if we are to deal constructively with anxiety throughout our lives.

Yet, in general, the use of the family as a positive way of defending against anxiety has become more difficult in recent years. The breakdown of the extended family in most Western societies has already reduced the support networks surrounding the growing child. Moreover, it has left large numbers of men, women, and especially children (i.e., future adults) relatively unprotected from the economic, social, and emotional effects of divorce, a phenomenon that itself has grown at an explosive rate in the last 10–15 years. In some urban areas, such as Paris, almost as many divorces as marriages take place each year.

The accelerated pace of marital breakdown means a huge increase in anxiety for those involved, and a corresponding decline in the extent to which the family can provide a safe, protective defence against the uncertainties of life and a base from which its members can develop and innovate. In particular, the disruption of paired relationships involved in family breakdown may well damage the ability of the children involved to pair successfully in adulthood, whether with a personal partner, or in their working life. (As mentioned above, the return to individualism at a social level acts to exacerbate this difficulty in pairing.)

To summarize, then, it can be argued that the production of children is not only a defence against anxiety but is one of the most creative methods of responding to it. Yet, as a society, we are exposing our children to increasingly high levels of anxiety, in an increasingly uncertain world.

The use of sexuality as a defence against anxiety

The working hypothesis put forward in this paper in regard to the decline of traditional defences against anxiety is perhaps most dramatically confirmed in relation to one of the most classical defences against anxiety: the use of sexuality. The arrival of AIDS (simply the most recent and deadly of a number of new and so far incurable sexually-transmitted viral diseases) has marked a new era in sexual relations. The "golden age" of free-and-easy sex is over. The age of deadly sex has begun. As an infection that operates by destroying the body's own immune defence system, as a result of which the individual experiences gradual weakening and multiple infections, followed by sudden and final collapse, it provides a particularly striking illustration of the theme of this chapter.

The advent of the pill and the "permissive society" enabled millions of men and women to explore a variety of sexual relationships with relatively little fear of the physical consequences. In these circumstances, sexual activity provided a much-used defence against anxiety—a defence that not only helped to relieve feelings of loneliness, insecurity, and so forth, but also provided the basis for much positive creativity. Its defensive role was particularly prominent at times of stress and high levels of anxiety; its prevalence at group relations' conferences, for example, has been a classical aspect of participants' social behaviour.

Despite the unique nature of that period in the history of our civilization, we assumed it would last forever and came to take for granted the sexual freedom it involved. Looking back, the pre-AIDS era takes on a mirage-like quality: we tasted the forbidden fruit, but the fruit now really is forbidden. We are left with a taste in our mouths that is both delectable and progressively bitter. As a defence against anxiety, sex—or sex outside a faithful monogamous relationship—has in any case become dramatically less effective. In wider social terms, the "aid society" of the post-war consensus years has become the "AIDS society" of the Reagan–Thatcher–Kohl era.

The numbers who have died from AIDS in the West may be relatively small as yet, but the insidious, uncertain nature of AIDS and the Russian roulette quality that it has brought to sexual activity make it particularly traumatic. "Safe sex", while a reassuring idea and undoubtedly a sensible one, does little to change fundamentally the deadly reality of the risk that sex now entails. However small that risk may be, the stakes are so high that its presence will always be felt. The "stranger in the night" has become the "danger in the night," both in reality and in fantasy. Thus, even when non-monogamous sexual activity continues to be used as a flight from anxiety, it is in itself a source of tremendous anxiety—more, indeed, than the anxiety against which it was traditionally used to defend.

The recent decision by the influential American Medical Association to waive the rules of medical confidentiality in the case of AIDS sufferers provides a disturbing footnote to these developments. While valid objective reasons for this unprecedented change in medical ethics may exist, it will undoubtedly result in increased anxiety for actual and potential AIDS patients and for their doctors. The important boundary around the doctor–patient relationship represented by confidentiality has been pierced, and in this way a further defence against anxiety has been removed.

The use of drugs, tobacco, and alcohol as a defence against anxiety

A final illustration of the decline of defences against anxiety over the past decade or so is the changing use of drugs and other addictive substances in Western society .

In the 1960s the use of "soft" or psychedelic drugs by middle-class youth represented both their adolescent rebellion against adult power and their reaction to events like the Vietnam War. Smoking pot could be seen as a somewhat immature defence against anxiety, but also as a potentially creative defence which had a certain "liberating" effect and led to innovations in thought and life-style. Similarly, alcohol, when not systematically used to excess, can be said to have traditionally provided a socially acceptable and relatively safe method of dealing with anxiety through temporary and controlled regression.

Drug-taking, and to some extent drinking, among youth in the 1980s, however, plays a very different role: a role traditionally associated with those on the very margins of society, such as the elderly destitute. The use of heroin, cocaine, and now "crack" has spread with frightening rapidity among those at the sharp end both of capitalism's success and of its failure. On the one hand pop stars and city whizz-kids, and on the other hand unemployed and dispossessed youth in the inner cities have turned to drug (and in the latter case solvent) abuse as an anaesthetic—a purely regressive defence against intolerable pressure or intolerable despair. The price paid by those for whom it can offer only the temporary illusion of safety and relief is horrifyingly high.

Finally, even the nature of the role played by tobacco as a defence against anxiety has changed over the past years. As a result of the growth in concern about the health risks involved in smoking, it has become far less effective as a defence. Not only do smokers now worry more about the risk to their health, but smoking also creates greater anxiety for other people in the smokers' environment, who experience a growing sense of pollution or contamination. This in turn leads to more conflict between smokers and non-smokers, as can clearly be seen at group relations' conferences. Thus, there is a general increase in levels of anxiety.

Having said that, it is nevertheless important to recognize that smoking continues, to some extent, to provide a buffer zone for social conflict. In other words, the smoking issue provides a fruitful vehicle for projections which, if absent, might be reflected in more violent and destructive social conflicts. So, where the anti-smoking lobby succeeds in banning smoking from conferences or public places, it may well be found that the unconscious battle for and against a pure, sterile, rarefied atmosphere will simply be displaced to another plane.

The use of interpretation as a defence against anxiety

The final example I wish to give in this list of declining defences against anxiety is a little different from the others, as it particularly concerns our own field of work. As human beings, the capacity to interpret the complex reality in which we live and work is one of our most valuable and potentially creative ways of dealing with anxiety. For those of us working as consultants, whether with institutions, individuals, or at group relations' conferences, the use of interpretation and of working hypotheses is central to our role and, indeed, can be said to be its *raison d'être*.

At this stage I would like to add a point about terminology. Although I use the terms "interpretation" and "working hypothesis" interchangeably in this chapter, it is the second concept, "working hypothesis", that I prefer in practice. "Giving interpretations" can sound a little too much like "delivering the truth". The "presentation of a working hypothesis", however (as well as drawing on the best traditions of applied scientific practice), emphasizes the provisional nature of the consultant's understanding and the existence of other possible ways of viewing a situation. It is more likely, therefore, to encourage those on the receiving end of the consultant's intervention to "become their own consultants" and develop their own hypotheses.

Ideally, we strive in our work not only to understand a situation and to communicate our understanding of it, but also to foster the capacity of all those involved to develop their own insights and make their own interpretations. Ideally, the clients or participants relate to the consultant as a resource rather than an oracle. Ideally, by identifying with and internalizing the consultant's *function and method*, rather than by swallowing whole his *message*, they become less, not more, dependent, better able to manage their anxiety and thus better able to use their own authority to develop and act on working hypotheses of their own.

However, as we know, these ideals are not always achieved. Consultants, like their clients, are not immune to the increased pressures—and therefore the increased anxieties—which characterize the 1980s. The developments described in the earlier sections of this paper place extra stress on those working in the emotional "front line" of human relations.

One result of this, I believe, has been a growing tendency over the last few years for consultants to use interpretation as a means of defending against their own anxiety and confirming their own power rather than as a means of enabling others to learn and grow. Increasingly often, interpretations are given in a punitive or arrogant tone, which makes it hard for those on the receiving end to feel respected as mature adults. A judgemental approach by the consultant makes it more difficult for the clients or participants to mobilize their *own* judgement. It makes it more difficult for them to discriminate between those parts of an interpretation that they wish to accept and those they wish to reject. Above all, it makes it more difficult for them to *work with* the interpretation in order to develop further insights.

In this situation, there is a real danger that the consultant can be experienced as saying "take all or nothing", a totalitarian message that forces the recipient into one of two destructive positions. Either the recipients become passive victims by submitting to the superior wisdom of the professional, or they reject the consultant's view and become rebels or outlaws, and, once again, victims. In both cases, their anxiety, and possibly his sense of guilt, will increase.

In these circumstances, an anxious consultant is using interpretation to defend himself or herself: by subjugating the members or clients, he or she attempts to reduce their capacity to test his or her authority in his or her role. Interpretations no longer function to encourage the recipients to develop their own working hypotheses but rather to block creativity and learning. It is when this situation is taken to an extreme, and the role of the consultant becomes actively oppressive, that we can speak of *consultation camps*,[2] with the consultant becoming the persecutor in the persecutor–victim–saviour triangle.

The dangers of being drawn into such a triangle are multiple: if not experienced as "persecutor", the consultant may become the "saviour", there to solve all problems, or even the "victim"—the scapegoat sacrificed in order to bring about an apparent (and inevitably temporary) reconciliation between opposing groups within an institution. Whichever role the consultant takes within this triangle, he or she is colluding with the clients' attempt to manage their anxiety by avoiding the task, rather than by addressing it.

If I am right in perceiving an increase in such inappropriate collusion on the part of consultants (for example, at our group relations' conferences), how can we account for this? I believe that a number of reasons lies behind this development. In the first place, as I have attempted to show in this chapter, we live in a world that has become increasingly characterized by sources of new, higher levels of anxiety on the one hand, and the decline of traditional methods of managing this anxiety constructively on the other.

In this situation, there is the danger that consultants deal with their own increased anxiety by colluding with their clients, as described above, or by *intellectualizing and/or denying problems*. Intellectualization or simple denial is used when the consultant, and very possibly the clients or members, become too anxious to tolerate the ambiguity and complexity of the situation in which they find themselves. Therefore, the situation will either be understood and explained away at an intellectual or rational level rather than at an emotional one, or else will be over-simplified and the complexity of the problems denied.

Isabel Menzies Lyth, in a recent paper (1987), speaks of the difficulty, for the consultant, of tolerating uncertainty and of suspending preconceived judgements and knowledge in order to listen in the most open way possible to all that is said. She describes how

> One exists most of the time in a state of partially self-imposed ignorance which may feel profound, frightening and painful. One needs faith that there is light at the end of the tunnel even when one does not have much hope . . .

> What compounds this experience is its repetitiveness. If we can hold on to our ignorance with evenly suspended attention, meaning will probably emerge, and we will experience the reward of at least one mystery or part of a mystery solved, uncertainty and doubt dispersed. But it will not last, especially if one communicates one's understanding to the client who accepts one's interpretation and is prepared and able to proceed again into the unknown. One is thrown back again on ignorance, uncertainty and doubt and must experience the process all over again. [Menzies Lyth, 1987, pp. 5–6]

When a diagnosis seems to arrive too quickly, or when working hypotheses are a bit too "pat", it is likely that the consultants concerned have not succeeded in tolerating this difficult state. They are probably drawing more on situations and insights that they have come across in the past, and less on their capacity to experience the present situation in the "here and now". On these occasions, one may have the feeling that "the interpretation is perfect, but where is the evidence?" To work effectively, we must remain capable of being surprised, and of surprising ourselves. But in order to remain in the "here and now", and to encourage this approach in the members or clients, we must successfully manage our own anxiety.

The fact that the products of our efforts are largely intangible, and that much of our work consists of "two steps forward, one, two or even three steps back", makes it particularly difficult to do so. We have to accept, like historians and psychoanalysts, that we can never find "the truth" about any aspect of a situation. Rather, there are always many truths and realities, and we can only attempt to construct that which we feel to be the best fit within our own frame of reference.

Moreover, we have the frequent experience of seeing our small, hard-won advances followed by setbacks and retreats. Recognizing and coming to terms with the *relative nature of our work*, its partial efficacy and its very real limitations, is a painful process. At times, it is far easier to look for the easy solution or the panacea than to tolerate and contain the anxiety and distress that this recognition causes.

If we do not succeed in containing our own anxiety, however, it will be inevitably exported. In collusion with the members of a conference or institution, we shall embark upon the process of seeking a scapegoat or casualty whose primary task becomes that of carrying the anxiety (and perhaps madness) of all of us. Whether this casualty takes the form of a psychotic breakdown or the collapse of a business, it is a reflection, at least in part, of the uncontained anxiety of the consultants and the members of institutions, including both managers and workers.

In addition to the extra difficulties imposed on those in the consultant role, the uncertainties and difficulties with which we live today frequently make the members of institutions or conferences more difficult to work with than in the past. In many cases, their increased anxiety has led them to become more resistant to anything—even, or especially, the best interpretations—that challenges their own defensive mechanisms, however dysfunctional these mechanisms may be.

Furthermore, not only are clients becoming more resistant to interpretation, but it can be hypothesized that they are becoming *better able to resist*, as a result of the growing popularization of ideas about human psychological behaviour and indeed about psychoanalysis. The fact that much of the information that is now widely disseminated through the press, television, paperbacks, and so on, gives a distorted and often hostile image of these areas only reinforces the way in which an intellectual, and often superficial, knowledge of such ideas can be used to resist a real process of learning through experience.

In addition, as more and more institutions seek outside assistance to help resolve their difficulties, increasing numbers of managers (and other workers) come into contact with consultants of various sorts. In many cases this growing familiarity with consultants does not lead to a greater receptivity on the part of the managers. On the contrary, as they become more accustomed to consultants, they also become better able to resist their impact. In other words, managers are less likely nowadays to be taken by surprise by the consultants' interventions. They are more likely, consciously or unconsciously, to erect their defences in advance, in an attempt to protect themselves against the anxiety and pain that the consultants' interpretations may provoke.

We must ask ourselves whether we in this room, individually and collectively, have taken sufficient account of these developments and of their practical implications in terms of the selection and training of consultants, the design of our conferences, and the type of intervention we offer to other institutions. Unless we can manage our own anxiety in such a way as to break the vicious circle of increased anxiety, increased defensiveness, increased anxiety, we shall lose our capacity for creativity and, therefore, our capacity to help others to be creative. *We shall find ourselves defending our status as consultants rather than our role.* The actual primary task of our work can only too easily become to learn, in collusion with the members/clients, how better to defend ourselves against learning through experience—a far cry from the primary task in which we consciously strive to engage.

Historically, those individuals and institutions working in the Tavistock tradition have represented an important source of originality, creativity, and integrity in the field of human relations. The challenge we now face revolves around how effectively we can ourselves respond to an environment marked by heightened anxiety and increasingly ineffective defences. This challenge is itself simply a reflection of that which faces every individual and every institution at the present time.

As I have tried to demonstrate, we are living in an era that has seen the decline of many traditional defences against anxiety. In my view, it is essential that, in the years to come, we as a society can reactivate old forms of defence or build new forms of defence that enable us to deal as constructively and creatively as possible with the fears and uncertainties which beset us. However, a full diagnosis of the present situation and its implications is a first vital step in this process, a process to which this chapter is designed to contribute.

It is not my intention here to discuss solutions to the problems outlined, but I shall indicate briefly some of the possible courses of action that might be explored.

In our work with the members of institutions, and in particular with commercial and industrial enterprises, we can try to facilitate the development of new and innovative approaches to the problems they face. It is only by relying less on a traditional, hierarchical approach to management and more on the development of the authority and creativity of every worker in his or her role that companies such as EDF will find the flexibility and the energy necessary to adapt positively to changing conditions. For its members, a greater sense of autonomy and responsibility and a deeper understanding of the process of change would provide a more effective and constructive means of managing anxiety than the current reliance on a mixture of denial, dependency, and projection.

With regard to science and technology, and the need to come to terms with its limitations and risks, here, too, we may find that the evolution of a new, more realistic attitude may prove very positive. The recognition that science is not omnipotent and that scientists cannot "save the world" can help us to face and come to terms with our mortality. That this process has already started is illustrated by developments such as the hospice movement. If science is no longer used to feed a myth of immortality, we become more able to take responsibility for our own health and well being, and for that of our environment. We can become better able to authorize ourselves to use science as a *resource* rather than as an ideology. (The growth of alternative and holistic medicine, natural childbirth and the like, on the one hand, and pressure groups concerned with issues such as acid rain and nuclear waste on the other, indicate the ways in which increased anxiety can be managed through positive action.)

In relation to sexuality and the threat of AIDS, we can, first and foremost, look to a new, more stable approach to monogamous relationships. It is not a question of adopting a moral stance, but of exploring how we can invest more deeply in those committed, and therefore safe, relationships we already have. At the same time, we must explore new ways of dealing with the sexual desire we may feel for more casual contacts, without necessarily acting on that desire.

In this context, we might learn from the experience of members of religious orders whose life is a celibate one. Monks or nuns are rarely free from sexual feelings and urges, but, if they are to stay in role, they must find ways of containing or dealing with such impulses. Perhaps sensuality, fantasy, and non-sexual creativity can play a greater part in our lives as we struggle to *work through* rather than *act on* the anxiety that so often leads to non-monogamous sexual activity.

With regard to the use of interpretations and working hypotheses, when used appropriately these provide perhaps the best hope of dealing with the anxiety and problems that we currently face. Interpretation does not need to, and indeed should not, be the exclusive province of the consultant or the psychoanalyst. Our work is to encourage in others the capacity to confront and make sense of their reality without undue recourse to defensive mechanisms. The successful use of interpretation in a wider social context was recently illustrated at the time of the hijacking of the Kuwait airliner. Neither force nor humanitarian appeals were likely to resolve the deadlock without heavy loss of life: it was mainly the Algerian negotiator's patient *interpretation* to the hijackers of the situation in which they found themselves that finally succeeded in unblocking it.

Positive courses of action in relation to the other problems described in this paper could also be outlined if space permitted. I shall confine myself now to some comments that emphasize the vital necessity of confronting the situation discussed above, and of developing new ways of dealing with the extra stresses and pressures that it entails.

At a general level, we should remember the crucial point made by Emmanuel Levinas, one of the most important, if not best known, French modern philosophers. In his view, the twentieth century, notably after the Second World War, has seen a concentration of events that is so excessive, so ruinous, and so contradictory that the accumulated consciousness of several generations has been, and still is, unable to digest it.

Bearing this in mind, we can say that, while all members of society should be deeply concerned with the effects of increasing anxiety and declining defences, it is the *youth* of our different countries, above all, who will bear the main burden of these changes. If we look again at the different aspects of the situation, we see that youth is especially affected in relation to most of them. In respect of work institutions, unemployment excludes increasing numbers of young people from membership; in the field of science, it is the younger generation who worry most about the dangers of nuclear war, environmental pollution, etc., and who have least faith in "medical men"; in respect of the loss of hope in revolutionary ideology, adolescence is traditionally the time in which such ideas play an important role; in connection with family breakdown, it is the current younger generation who have suffered most from the rocketing divorce rate and the associated economic and emotional hardships; with regard to sexuality, it is the adolescent, not yet established in a settled partnership, who may be at most risk from AIDS; and, of course, where drug-taking and alcohol abuse are concerned, it is among the young that these "solutions" are most frequently turned to.

In my view, therefore, there is cause for grave concern about the difficult situation of sections of the youth in our countries today, and the implications that this has for the future. The concern felt for youth by us in the middle (middle-class, middle-aged, middle-of-the-road) should not be the result of charity or social compassion. The damage that many young people are sustaining today affects us *all*. Individually, of course, and also collectively, this damage may well prove irreversible. *The social and political consequences could pose a very real threat to democracy itself.* The urban riots of the early 1980s in Britain and the high youth vote for Le Pen in France are just two manifestations of the frustration and distress experienced by many young people. Unless more positive ways are found of channelling their anxiety, energy, and anger, this type of development will become more and not less common.

I shall conclude by underlining once more what is at stake. When anxiety is not managed on an individual level and becomes overwhelming, it leads to personal disaster. *When anxiety is not managed on both an individual and collective level, it leads to social disaster.*

Above I mentioned the simple but vital word "democracy." This word describes a concept that, despite its imperfections in both theory and practice, enables us to be here now, working both to understand the world we live in and perhaps to help it change. When we speak of our democratic system of government, we are referring to a system of values, rules, and institutions. This system enables us to confront the complexity of social, political, and economic life, individually and collectively, without resort to massive projections on totalitarian leaders. Democracy can exist only when we have a sufficient internal and external sense of security to manage and contain our own anxiety, and to be able to authorize our leaders to represent us and take decisions on our behalf for predetermined periods of time. Democracy is also a psychic and political state in which the citizens, consciously or unconsciously, are able to feel some responsibility not only towards themselves, but also towards future generations. In other words, it enables us to deal constructively with our own mortality by offering opportunities to show "social concern". This concern is not only for the other existing members of our society, but also, and perhaps most significantly, for those who will come after us and live on when we are gone.

In fact, if we return to the semantic roots of the word "concern", we discover its meaning to be "to work against splitting." In a period characterized by crisis (which semantically means "split"), it becomes vital that we learn to manage our anxiety and so avert the possible catastrophic consequences that not doing so may well entail. However, while living through a process of successive crises poses a real threat to democracy itself, a certain level of crisis can nevertheless be perceived as a positive opportunity for change (Lawrence, 1986).

It is, thus, possible to describe a "virtuous circle" whereby effective and productive defences against anxiety are not only the main source of creativity, but also the best base for democracy; at the same time, the state of democracy helps us to manage our own individual and collective anxiety. We have to recognize that democracy collapses when the majority of citizens become psychotically defended. Another way to define democracy is as a state in which it is possible to deliver interpretations.

Whether the challenge we face today as a society becomes an occasion for creative innovation or for increased defensiveness depends on all of us. In a small way, this symposium poses the same challenge. Are we going to defend our old positions and resist change, or are we going to take the risk of learning from each other and perhaps creating something new? I very much hope—and I am confident—that the latter will prove to be the case.

Notes

1. This chapter is based on the opening lecture of the first international symposium on group relations (15–18 July 1988, at Keble College, Oxford. The original version was published in English (Gutmann, 1989), and was subsequently published in French in *Nouvelle Conjonctures Sociales*, 342: June 1990.
2. The term "consultation camp" was coined by W. Gordon Lawrence.

CHAPTER SIX

Between tradition and transformation: existential process and primary task for the life of organizations

David Gutmann

For several decades, leaders in charge of organizations as well as institutions have faced profound changes. They have learned that their individual and collective roles must change and that it is no longer necessary to justify the need for change. Recent experience shows that *the way we think about change must change.*

Organizations and institutions have implemented "actions for change" and have mobilized considerable energy in finding and applying solutions. In retrospect, they can realize that the solutions they have chosen have themselves become problematic.

To take into account the existential dynamics of human systems is characteristic of *institutional transformation* (IT). In order to introduce this programme, we can identify the three main strands of IT.

The psychoanalytical approach

Because it takes the *unconscious* into account—which is individual as well as collective—IT allows the exploration of the political and spiritual products that are generated by the psyche.

Traditionally in organizations and institutions, most of the actions that aim to change the structures, the administrative methods or even behaviours stop where anxiety is lived, where representations are created on which the functioning of an organization is based. And, even if these actions involve the top managers, the *links* between psychic, political, and spiritual forces are denied. The search for *How?* has replaced the search for *Why?*

The psychoanalytical approach offers the opportunity to take into account what was previously denied: members of social systems—including the promoters of change—have, in relation to their roles, both conscious and unconscious representations which have been constructed through feelings, thoughts, beliefs, histories, etc., and which determine attitudes and behaviours. *Every approach to change which does not take this into account will fail.*

The systemic approach

Institutional transformation is concerned with the whole organization being in interaction with its environment, as well as with each of its components, which are also interacting with each other.

The psychoanalytic approach, enriched by an understanding of systems—organizations and institutions being systems—focuses on the various dimensions of reality. It also focuses on the interactions between each component of individual and collective realities.

The processes at work show clearly that the path of transformation is neither predictable nor independent: it must be lived, it is in interaction, it must be "understood" and experienced, reflected through actions, decisions, transactions, and the reactions that they generate in the environment.

To work with the transformation of systems is possible through the people that constitute them. They transform their own roles (role is seen as the place for the encounter between the person and the system).

To work with the transformation of systems is possible through the authority (the capacity of being an author) with which everyone takes up his (or her) role.

Learning from experience

Institutional transformation cannot be taught. It can be learned from experience.

Learning from experience—on which this programme is based—is part of IT: it is closer to "maieutics" (a Socratic mode of enquiry serving to bring out a person's latent ideas into clear consciousness) than to didactic learning.

The work of transformation is built on continuous interaction between, on the one hand, the ways in which everyone lives (or does not live) his or her desire and, on the other hand, the functioning and the *raison d'être* of the institution.

Through experience, the capacities to observe (heurism), to interpret (hermeneutics), and to act (praxis) are developed, the one by the other, and contribute to the renewal of leadership approaches as well as leading in the organization.

From this perspective, "to be in charge" relates to the awareness that each person can have of his or her role, rather than being concerned by the title or the status of his or her position.

More precisely, this programme is built on a basic assumption and its consequences.

Basic assumption, consequences, and wording of the central issue

Basic assumption

Our individual anxiety comes from our condition as mortal—therefore living—beings. I am alive when I know that I am mortal.

The push that comes from our desire for immortality is one of the main reasons why we create institutions. (By *institution*, I refer to any organization built by human beings, whose aim is to gather resources in order to achieve a primary task.) However, we only displace this desire for immortality. Anxiety returns in an institutional form, a result of the need to constantly understand and (re-)define the conditions of durability of institutions.

Anxiety has a twin nature. It is *destructive* when it overwhelms the manager of the institution. It is *constructive* when it can be

contained and when it triggers plural and dynamic development processes.
Thus,

Consequence no. 1
There are three ways of existence in and for institutions:

- survival,
- hyperlife,
- LIFE.

Life is seen as a succession of passages and steps, of phases of growth and decline. To refuse such passages creates crises, which lead to survival and hyperlife.
Therefore,

Consequence no. 2
The containment of anxiety authorizes life.
    Containment allows each system to choose between survival, hyperlife, and life. To contain (*contenir (Fr.), cum tenere (Lat.)*: to hold with) is the shared process that makes it possible to hold anxiety and, thus, to open up the possibility of freedom.

Consequence no. 3
The primary task of any consultation is to work on the containment of institutional anxiety.
    This is the *existential* primary task of each consultation. It must be distinguished from the *apparent* and the *functional* primary tasks.

Consequence no. 4
To work on the containment of anxiety makes possible its transformation into creative capacity.
    Containment is one of the basic processes which transforms anxiety into vital energy. Indeed, such a proposal opens consultation practice beyond the field of professional consultants: everybody linked to the institution, within it or from the outside, is concerned by it.

Consequence no. 5
The development of his (or her) capacity as a consultant is an added value for any manager.

This is true no matter which background, profession (managers, consultants, experts, etc.), or field of application (politics, economics, teaching, associations, etc.) a person is located in.

This programme is for consultants who wish to improve their practice, but also for managers within enterprises, public services managers, experts (e.g., in computers), university managers, politicians, etc., who want to take up their role more effectively.

This programme is not designed to teach a profession, but as *a learning process that gives to each participant opportunities to develop and transform his or her capacities.*

Consequence no. 6

To develop one's capacities as a consultant occurs initially through learning from experience.

Traditional—or didactic—learning must be distinguished from learning from experience. We would like to describe both as methodological archetypes between which the different existing teaching practices are set.

The first difference is about what is brought to learning. On the one hand, knowledge held by a master is transmitted to the pupil; on the other hand, an additional richness is created by the encounter of two people. On the one hand, *to learn* (in French, *apprendre*) is *to take* something that already exists; on the other hand, it is to understand, *to comprehend* (in French, *comprendre*), to take *with* somebody else.

The second difference is the *power* relationship that exists between master and pupil in didactic teaching. The exclusive knowledge of the master—an attribute of his or her power and ability to create omnipotence—brings the pupil into a dependency relationship. This power can be set like a screen by a teacher trying to escape from emerging rivalry with the students, as well as by students being anxious about engaging with what is uncertain.

Learning from experience aims to create interdependent relationships in which the authority of self and other interacts. It is not focused on what one person knows and what the other person does not, but on what both know, or do not know yet, but might discover on the way. It might also be that the focus is on *what they do not know that they know*, on what the learning process is trying to push into consciousness.

This process looks like Monsieur Jourdain (in Molière, *Le bourgeois gentilhomme*) who "was speaking in prose without knowing it". The only difference is that what is known here is not technical but existential, ontological.

Thus, the interaction with the Other does not bring any added value but it creates an *altered value* that feeds the transformation process and that is a crucial advantage for the durability of the institution.

Consequence no. 7
Mutuality and interdependency create the containment for learning from experience.

In French, learning from experience is *APprentissage par l'EXpérience*, the abbreviation of which could be *APEX*. The apex is the top, the peak. Apex comes from the Latin word *apere* (to bind). The main meaning is in astronomy (1894): the apex is *the point in the sky towards which the solar system seems to go*. Thus, this path—arising out of a basic assumption and its consequences—invites us to propose *the wording of the central issue*.

Consultation

Consultation is a matter of *mystery* for some people, of *evidence* for others. For us, *consultation is neither mystery nor evidence*. However, it exists and travels between these two poles.

If consultation is only mystery, the task of such a programme would be to *unveil and reveal* the mystery; concretely, to create and increase the number of *initiates* (consultants as well as consulted people).

If consultation is only a matter of evidence, it will accompany the reality that each one of us knows simply because we are alive. Concretely, this process leads to the creation and an increase in the number of *citizens* (citizen is taken here to include democracy, involvement in society) included in a generative process.

Thus, to work on consultation joyfully mixes initiation and democratization.

Life, death, anxiety, containment, learning from experience . . . consultation is a transformation by itself. But what about *passion*? What can it bring to management and consultation? What *impulses* can passion generate?

So, what?

CHAPTER SEVEN

Transformation of language and social transformation

David Gutmann, with Laurence Ponthieu and Christophe Verrier

"We identify metals from the sounds, and persons from the words"

(Baltasar Gracian, *Maxime CCXCI, Oraculo manual y arte de prudencia*, or The Court Gentleman, 1684)

"The ego is not the master in its own house"

(Freud, 1923b)

E ach word that is used or pronounced carries a part of the unconscious with it. Lacan teaches us that *unconscious is structured as a language* and that words are the privileged way of expressing, or revealing, our own unconscious. We propose a hypothesis that is both opposite and complementary: words are not only one of the doors open to our unconscious; words have their own unconscious. Each one carries its own piece of unconscious that testifies its trajectory of its history, of our personal and familial history, but mainly collective, through centuries. Thus, language is also structured as unconscious. How then to better understand what words mean?

Jacques Lacan insisted on the difference between container and contained. As signs, words have two faces, the signifying and the signifier. Through both, words express a hidden content coming from their own singular trajectory. Each word has a history, both conscious and unconscious. But words create history, too. To use a specific word has never been neutral; to confuse two words—for instance *power* and *authority*—has significant practical consequences. This hypothesis is, of course, very fruitful for the work of a consultant because it suggests that to understand words is a primary resource to understand the life of people and institutions. This is why transformation of language and social transformation seem to be closely linked. We will try to present some examples here.

In the work of consultant, and more generally in life, words such as *leadership, authority,* and *power* are *leitmotivs*. Sometimes, they are confused, used one in place of another. Each one carries a heavy affective load that can sometimes resonate. But what do they give us to hear really? How do they resist a demanding analysis?

Authority

The word "authority" carries the idea of being the author of one's own life and to help others to grow up. (The historical dictionary of the French language, *Le Robert*, has been very useful for its etymological data. See the lexis at the end of the chapter.)

Auctoritas → *Auctor* (author): *to the author* (of a piece)

It is the capacity to give birth, to let grow, to increase for oneself and the others, with oneself and the others. It refers to the author of the series of steps that make life in transformation.

Power

Power carries the idea of *possession* (see the Indo-European root *opoti- head of a social group, family, clan, tribe*). Exercising power is to possess, to take the largest part of a cake, while exercising authority means to increase, to enlarge the cake to let each one have a larger part of it.

Thus, for the consultant, the confusion between power and authority is a fine sign of the institutional nature of the consulted organization. A system that is based on power-possession—in which power is exercised as possessive or implies a trend to possess not only goods and resources, but sometimes also the persons, giving them the rank of slaves or serfs—is exactly the contrary of a system based on authority, in which learning and the accomplishment of each is the *raison d'être*.

Leadership

Another example is *leadership*. The Germanic verb *leiten* (to help others to move forward) gives *leader*. The Germanic root *cap* gives *shape* and *-ship* "to create, to shape". Leadership is the capacity to show the way by shaping it, step by step. The group and the way are created at the same time. But the Germanic root that generates *leiten* gives *leiden*, too, meaning "to suffer", as if reminding us of the fact that any experience of leadership involves, among other things, suffering.

Leader (= in German, *leiten*, Swedish, *leda*, Danish, *lede*) all come from a Germanic verb derived from a word meaning *the convoy, the way*.

The leader is the one who leads the convoy and shows the way.

Ship: suffix linked to the Germanic root *oskap* "to create, to shape"

Leadership, then, is the capacity to create, to shape the convoy and the way at the same time.

Management

Another example, not chosen by chance, is *management*.

Management comes from the Italian *maneggio, maneggiare*, which means:

- to handle (*mano*: the hand).
- to direct a horse, to break it in (in French, *un manège* means a horse ring, a riding school).
- the action of driving, directing, *training*.

In Catalan, this is signified by *domar*; in Italian, *domare*: to domesticate a horse.

In other words, a crucial issue emerges: what is management? If one manages persons, does he not take the risk of being unconsciously manipulated by the archetype of the master? Or that of the servant, the domestic? Or by the metaphor of the breaking in of horses?

Consequently, is it not more appropriate to manage resources rather than individuals?

Administrator

An administrator is the one who helps the minister. He is positioned alongside (ad-). The *minister* himself or herself is servant to the *magister* (the master). The minister is *mini*, while the master is *maxi*. The administrator is the one who helps the (small) servant.

This etymologic analysis helps us to understand the unfavourable prejudice that often affects the persons who carry the role of administrators, mainly when compared to operational and management roles. What does the administrator carry? An unconscious load that gives the impression that his role is dedicated to servant tasks of minor importance. To help him or her to understand this burden is an opportunity to help him or her to work on it.

Consultant

There are two issues in connection with this word.

1. The etymological history of the word *consultant* accompanies the history of democracy from the Roman consul to the elected magistrate, through the King's counsellor, the Earl, then the elected head. The act of consulting seems always to present the idea of the power of a chief, totalitarian and concentrated in the hands of a single person. In consulting, the head brings his or her points of view before another (the Other) and sharpens his or her reflection.
2. "To consult" is close to the French verb *apprendre* (to learn). Both integrate two complementary values: to give and to

request, which offer a basis for a learning process as opposed to the principle of the master's power and of the knowledge transmitted in only one direction. Here, the learning is discovered by both during the consultation process, given as well as received (see "Leading consultation and its learning process").

Thus, we try to discover the affective burden that loads any of these words. Our hypothesis is that there is no true language, no original language that would state a truth and guarantee the meaning. Words transform as soon as the affective load that puts each of them in a specific meaning moves them like a new, or innovating, driving force.

As a system, institutions are structures like a language. The meaning comes from the system. An institution is a system that feeds and transforms the meaning of words such as leadership, management, authority, and power.

Each word has a vertical dimension, its meaning, and a horizontal one, its affective part centred in its verbal expression. The oblique dimension might be poetry. The Greeks used to oppose the human language and the noise of an animal, which expresses only sensations, such as pleasure and pain. Sometimes, we forget the nature of the speech in being touched only by the sounds, the voice, with its seductive processes. One risk, therefore, is that the ones who speak well take power. Through the thaumaturgical—and magical—function of language, the word carries within it the capacity to bewitch. However, the bewitchment of poetic language is of another nature, that of authority, because the one who receives it remains free.

This poetic function is the counterbalance to the transformation of language, the primary role of which is to facilitate enslavement, to reinforce domination through distantiation and de-authorization. Indeed, the relationship between words and things gives power over things.

Each of us has to bring his or her own stone to the wall of interpretation, knowing that no interpretation has an absolute meaning. No single interpretation can deliver truth; only its link with its context makes sense in the here and now.

It seems that transformation of language will always try to embrace the human experience encapsulated in the constantly developing meanings of words.

Lexis

Administrator

From the Latin *administrare*, "to help"; "to help with a religious sacrifice", an uncommon meaning in classical Latin, but usual in Christian Latin. The Old French uses *menistrer* (beginning of the twelfth century) in this way. Since Varron, *administrare* qualifies private affairs in medieval Latin and then in French. The Latin verb comes from *ministrare* or *minister*.

Minister derives (around 1120) from the Latin *minister*, formed from *magister*, to which it is opposed as servant is opposed to master. This word is linked to several Latin words (such as "to diminish", "menu", "minor", "minimum", "minute") created by contamination with the Romanic language of two Indo-European roots expressing smallness and lessening. *Minister* means, in Latin, the servant, the domestic, the priest of a god, the instrument, the agent, the intermediary.

Authority

Authority is an old derivation (1119, *auctorité*) from the Latin word *auctoritas*, coming from *auctor*, meaning *being an auctor*, which is a founder, an instigator, a counsellor, guarantor, and author, responsible for a work, and, thus, for its *authenticity*.

Among the various meaning of *auctoritas*, we find the "credit of a writer, of a text", and, particularly notably, in church Latin, "of a revealed text". Applied to the Sacred Texts, these values are found in the first uses of *authority*: "text of Scripture"; "power to impose obedience" (1174); "force of what is judged or decided", in the thirteenth century, when the word is also applied to the force of a reference. This value still exists in Spanish: *autoridad* means also a "quotation used as a model, an example". In the sixteenth century, it means the consideration given to a person for his or her moral superiority. The French expression *d'autorité*, (middle of the seventeenth century) gave rise, in the nineteenth century, to the slang expression *d'autor*, meaning "compulsory".

The main meaning of *authority* "the right to command, to impose obedience", is exploited in the derived word *authoritarian*.

To authorize (*autoriser*) comes from another part of Latin semantics. It derives first through the Latin-like form *actorizer* (end of the twelfth century), from the Medieval Latin *auctorizare* "to confirm", which comes from *auctor* in the juridical meaning of "guarantor". In Old French, *actorisier, auctorizer* also mean "to approve officially", "to give authority to", and "to certify, to prove" (thirteenth century). The main modern meaning, "to allow", appears in Middle French (1439), first regarding things (to allow something), then persons (to allow somebody to do something), where the pronominal *s'autoriser à, s'autoriser quelque chose* (to authorize oneself to do something) comes from.

Thus, to authorize oneself is to take the authority to be guarantor of one's own authenticity, the capacity to be an author.

The derived word *authorization* (*auctorization*, 1419; *authorization*, 1593) qualifies by metonymy *the act which authorizes (itself)*. This word seems to embody much more freedom than the very fashionable Anglo-Saxon word "empowerment".

Coming back to the historical trajectory of the word *authority*, it points out *the legitimate power given by others*, in other words, *the delegated power*. But, if we come back to the root of the word, it means *to be an author*. We cannot be an author by delegation. Here is an interstice that changes the affective meaning of the language.

Consultant

To consult comes from the Latin *consultare*, "to deliberate" and "to question, to request counsel" (1410), frequent form of *consulere* (*consul*: Roman magistrate, then, in the Middle Ages, counsellor of the King [ninth century], an Earl [tenth century], the elected head of a trade colony [1182], the elected magistrate of a city, particularly in Italy [1088]).

Until the sixteenth century, *to consult* is used to mean "to deliberate about something" (*to consult on something*) and as "to confer about a subject" (1468, *to consult with someone else about something*). Its modern meanings appeared during the sixteenth century: "to take somebody else's counsel" (1549), "to give consultations" speaking about a man of law, a physician (1549), and "to look up a text in order to find information" (1585). The verb is archaic when intransitive, meaning "to consider a case in talking about it" and "to question oneself, to hesitate", both being very common in the seventeenth century. Only the meaning that refers to medical specialization still exists in modern use.

A *consultant* (1636) is a "person requesting a consultation", then a "person who consults a physician". The verb *to consult* has, as the French *apprendre* (to learn), complementary values of both giving and requesting (information). *Consultant* is mainly taken as "counsellor" with recent significant manifestations in many professions: *editorial consultant, financial consultant*.

We emphasize the word *consulte* (1708), "collective counsel of the Pope", derived from the Italian word (*sacra*) *consulta* (1588), derivative of *consultare* "to consult". After citing a judiciary assembly in Switzerland and in Italy, the etymology mentions a large assembly gathered to debate an important issue in Corsica.

Leadership

Leader is derived from 1822, from the English *leader*, "the one who leads the fight". Since the Middle Ages, it refers to the heads of the troops, the "born leaders". Leader comes from *to lead*, a verb linked to the Dutch *leiden*, the German *leiten*, the Swedish *leda*, and the Danish *lede*. All these words come from a Germanic word meaning "pointing out the path" and "the convoy". Thus, the leader is the one who creates the convoy and shows the way.

The multiple meanings in English led to the word being adopted in French, first in politics from 1829, then in social life: horse riding, fashion, journalism, sport.

Leadership appeared in France first as a feminine word in 1864, then masculine in 1875, coming from the English *leadership* with *-ship*, a suffix, pointing out "the state, the condition", linked to the Germanic root *oskap-* "to create, to shape". The word was introduced in French about the role of leader in the British House of Commons, and remained for a long time linked to an Anglo-American entity.

While leadership means to shape the passageway, it also means to point out the path that should be travelled together, step by step. Thus, it means to accompany the Other and oneself (as a system) on the path to transformation.

Management

This word is derived from *man*, then *main* (hand), itself coming from the Latin word *manus*, a Romanic word linked to an Indo-European root. Defining a primary organ in the functional as well as the symbolic dimension, *manus* is also the means of prehension that symbolizes strength, authority, command, and the tool we use to fight or to work.

By extension, in the fourteenth century, *main* gave *mainmise* or *main-mise* (takeover), a feudal word derived from the old verb *main-mettre*, which encompassed the ideas of takeover, taking possession, implying that the takeover would lead to shaping or limiting through manipulation.

Management, meaning "action to lead, direct, involve", is used, particularly from the end of the eighteenth century, about the group of persons in charge of the running and the direction of an institution. The English word has been accepted by the French Academy, which, however, recommends a Frenchified pronunciation, *ménagement*.

Power

Podeir (842), then *poeir, pooir*, from which *povoir* and then finally *pouvoir* (power) (1440) comes from a popular Latin word ∞*potere*. This is the refection of the classical verb *posse* "to be able to", "to get importance, influence, efficiency", from the present *poteo* "I can". *Poteo* gave *potis* "master of, possessor of", a meaning which has been retained in *to possess* where "*puissant* (powerful)" comes from.

Potis itself—only its derivations came into French—comes from an Indo-European word *opoti*, which referred to *the head of a social group, a family, a clan, a tribe*. Its roots lie in the Greek *posis*, "spouses", the Sanskrit *patih*, "family head", and the Gothic.

As a substantiation of the infinitive, *pouvoir* (power) is very old in the forms of *podir* (842), then *poeir* (1140), *pooir* (1180), *pouvoir* appearing in Middle French in the fifteenth century. From the thirteenth century, this word is applied in law to the right one has to do something, especially to the capacity to act on behalf of somebody else or to the act through which one gives to somebody else the right to act (1468). It is also applied to the "inherent to a thing" (around 1320) meaning, which would develop later on in the specific languages of physics (1803), chemistry, medicine, and industry.

The expression *plein pouvoir* (full power) (1212) has been transformed (seventeenth century) into the plural *pleins pouvoirs*, as if the temptation of the fantasy of omnipotence, in which "to have all" leads to the *tout-pouvoir*, could not resist the quest of a hold on reality.

By metonymic extension, the word refers to the organs and the persons in whom the power is embodied. It is as if the power penetrated the flesh of the persons in trapping them into the fantasy of omnipotence.

The antonym *impouvoir* (1801) "lack of power" is almost out of use, mainly replaced by *impuissance* (powerlessness). This is an expression of the will to deny the meaning of the word *authority* as a negation of power, hold, process of trapping into possession. On the contrary, *authority* leads to the authorization to grow up in one's own trajectory of an author, in fruitful autonomy and the surprise of vitality.

Note

1. This chapter comes from the Proceedings of the International Conference entitled "At the threshold of the millennium" organized by SIDEA & PromPeru in Lima, Peru, 15–23 April 1998.

CHAPTER EIGHT

Power and authority[1]

David Gutmann

T he first human paintings, dating from before humanity began to use writing, show that power and authority, even at that time, are among its fundamental concerns. The scenes of Lascaux present an example that is both a devolution of power and a distribution of authority established on survival. It is, then, possible for the human being attached to an organized community to play a part not just in the life of people around him, but also in the natural (or supernatural) phenomena that take place.

Today, each thought on power and authority echoes in a particular manner, for we find ourselves confronting two processes that periodically meet to make us ask questions and to challenge us. On the one hand, it is the growing of complexity, or, more specifically, the feeling that this growing is accelerating, and, on the other hand, it is a mutation that reaches not just the economical sector, but also the political, the social, and the cultural sectors. We can pertinently quote Jacob Burkhardt, a Swiss social historian, who said that "The essence of tyranny is the denial of complexity" (1929, p. 89).

The risk is that transformation, if disorganized, leads a human being to a dead end. Disruptions or regressions necessitate reconsidering the whole question of power and authority. Is it possible to transform constraints into assets in this field, and to use complexity in order to control the mutation? The question is worth asking.

Let us remember first that power and authority are really different things, and that they are present in the same person much more rarely than we think. Power and authority take on political and psychological dimensions that we have to precisely delineate in order to understand the real role of the person that embodies power and uses authority.

The vitality of all institutions requires the coexistence (peaceful or not) of power and authority. If we think in a simple way that they have to be homogenized, there is then the risk of dictatorship; if we believe that they have to be opposed to each other in a permanent power struggle, the result then is a blocked or fragmented society.

It seems clear, therefore, that only innovation, followed by a real practice leads to this essential cohabitation of power and authority.

Some practical definitions

In the 1950s, Jean-Paul Sartre told his students to imagine that a rhinoceros had entered the room right now. There is no doubt that such a creature would have great power over us. We might think that he would not have authority.

This example shows how often we tend to make an over-simplified difference between power and authority: power would be bad (or good), authority would be good (or bad). This temptation could create a common belief that associates power and authority with the phenomena of oppression, if not destruction. Rather than take this approach, which is widely used but, in our opinion, wrong and arbitrary, it is better to explore in depth the practical articulation of the two separate concepts. Here, it is useful to give some definitions that will allow us to gain a better understanding of these realities. Let us note now that power and authority do not concern only relations between individuals, or between individuals and groups, but also the relations between institutions.

Power is essentially a matter of organization; it is linked to statute and to the hierarchy. Its legitimacy comes from material sources (the force [Sartre's rhino], the economic competition, etc.) or from spiritual sources (God, the government, the Law, etc.). Most of the time, the legitimacy of power is based on a combination of these two sources.

Power can be given, taken, conquered, and taken back. Those who have it are identified. Their function is known, often acknowledged, recognized, admitted, but not usually accepted. They have status: titles, uniforms, symbols, ceremonials, and privileges.

Power is one of the permanent aspects of all societies and of each individual. Each takes a position with regard to personal power, institutional power, and others' power in a different sector of society.

Authority is linked to roles. The roles are automatically used by each of us in all groups: the family, the company, the school, the army, the trade ... whatever, the group is either closed or open to the outside. These roles are characterized by variety and diversity: a leader or a follower, a person who guarantees to keep existent things or an innovator, an observer or a referee; the list is far from complete. Authority is then attached to each individual, *intuitu personae*. Authority is, above all, the result of the role that "I" want to play and of the role that the "others" want me to play. It depends then on many meetings (many in the institution, but also in time) that lead each other to play the determined role, which varies according to the moment and the place. The limits of this authority are, then, neither defined by an agreed charter nor revealed by symbolic behaviours and attributes attributable to power.

Authority depends little on the title, the rank, or the statute, since it is primarily linked to the person who is acting in a given environment. So, on some occasions, the one who exercises most power is the one who analyses a given situation more clearly, and on others it might be the one who makes the most efficient decisions, or the one who has the most developed judgement skills. Authority, then, is unstable and varied, for it depends on various elements that constitute a particular situation. Clearly, if it is attached to a person through his or her role, authority is not something that can be attained merely by wishing for it. For each of us, and in the most basic sense of the word, authority is not a matter of the possibility of being author.

Power and authority: their development through history

Studies of so-called primitive people living in tribal societies take us beyond the difference between the leader and the wizard or shaman, showing that there are more cunning distinctions between the chief on the one hand, and the hunter or the warrior on the other hand. This is demonstrated in Pierre Clastre's studies of Native American societies.

In these communities was a permanent and irremovable chief and also a contingent of warriors for when they were needed. During periods of war the chief retained his overall authority, but the preparation for, and conducting of, the war was the responsibility of the warriors. One warrior, acknowledged to have the necessary skills, became the leader of the other warriors. He had a role, and not a title; he could be changed if necessary or desirable. Limits were imposed on the chief and on the "first of the warriors" in the practice of their respective roles, and of their authority. Thus, the chief was the only one in the tribe to have several wives, which was a clear sign of power, but he also had to take responsibility for food, accommodation, the education of children, and the settlement of interpersonal conflicts. For his part, the leader of the warriors might well be tempted to continue the war in order to keep his authority and, if possible, to transform it into power. The majority of the fighters followed him because the survival of the group was in question, the chief and the wizard also having a considerable stake in that survival. The role of the leader of the warriors depended on his skills being acknowledged to be the best suited to whatever exceptional circumstances were being faced at a particular time.

In our fast-moving and complex world, such an approach can still be useful. Thus, one of the best examples of the legitimacy of authority can be found in the Temporary Rules of the Army, which state that every soldier has to be ready to exercise authority even if he is the lone representative of the whole army and the nation. The importance of this can be seen clearly when considering the case of nuclear or guerrilla warfare.

Power and authority are not necessarily juxtaposed. Their respective distributions in an institution do not necessarily overlap. Furthermore, the cases in which power and authority are invested in one and the same person are rarer than we might at first think.

We can find in Japan the clearest expression of this separation between power and authority. Structures and values that have gradually evolved have shaped most of Japanese society since the problematic of power and authority became the expression of the cultural identity of the nation. In the political domain—in simple terms—the one who had the power that came with the highest title always ended up having no authority at all as time elapsed. Quite rapidly, in Japanese history, the emperor in power had to abdicate in order to really lead the country instead of his successor! Then, emperors gave their place to regents, who gave their place to Shoguns, who did the same in respect of their own regents . . . Many Japanese think that little has changed in the operating principles of their commercial and industrial companies. This example of Japan invites us to think about the necessity and the possibility of separating power and authority according to the idea that power is unique, but can be bestowed, whereas authority is varied, but cannot be delegated.

Why should we need both a chief and a leader?

Power and authority, as devolved on people, are matters of both political and psychological dimensions. First, there is a political dimension, because all of this takes place in a power struggle: there are rules, procedures, and courses of action to take. Second, there is a psychological dimension, because institutions are also imaginative creations. They are built, develop, and die through phenomena arising from rationality, consciousness, and logic. Every institution (such as a company, a family, a school) is, of course, built with material factors (buildings and equipment, goods and services), and embodies the characteristics of the population in which it exists. However, each institution also exists through the image that it projects. For instance, every company has a different existence in the mind of each of its employees, clients, and partners. In the mutation that our societies are experiencing, this element is all the more important, since the weakest points lie in the relational field. Let us remember the full price we had to pay for our access to civilization. The slow building of a peaceful Europe, or the establishment of the limited and fragile Human Rights in the world, serve to remind us of the difficulty in getting people to agree on a common minimal image of the institution. Such institutions are built on the premise of a certain number of rights and obligations of its members, who repress or transcend the instincts or impulses of aggressiveness and egoism that each of us possess.

When sharing power and authority, those who have the difficult and burdensome task of being chiefs, leaders, managers, officials, or people in charge have to be careful in such situations.

We can examine the role of the leader, who is not necessarily the chief embodying power through rank, through four successive and complementary approaches.

First, the leader is the person most skilled at managing the relations between the group and the environment, or, in other words, the person who specifies and respects the limits and boundaries of the group. He is the link between his group and the system that includes it. Thus, we can take the examples of the chief in a workshop, who gathers power and authority, or an opinion leader, not necessarily from a trade union, working in a factory. It is clear that this role of the leader is all the more difficult to play since the boundaries are blurred and tend to change, which is currently the case most of the time.

If we take this further, we find that the leader is also the one who, in the name of the group members, succeeds in clarifying and taking into account, in his thoughts and actions, the forces and the political and psychological stakes that underpin the group and its environment. This is analogous to a soldier who is a subordinate in his unit, but who appears to be skilled enough to be promoted to head of the unit by rescuing most of his companions and, thus, fulfilling his mission during a fight.

Indeed, whatever the occasion, the leader is almost always the one who is skilled enough to see clearly the fundamental target (mission, main purpose, reason to exist) of the institution. He works on the fact that he and his partners have to focus upon this fundamental target. We can extend the previous analogy by saying that the leader leads his unit according to the target he has to reach, risking his life and the lives of his companions. The target to reach, then, takes into account the nature of the current problem and ways to overcome it, and also the need to use the unit in future fights.

In the end, the leader is the one who (and this is no less diffi-cult) is going to receive a certain number of impacts, feelings, ideas, sensations, and projections, both from people within his group and from those in the external environment. In fact, the more he receives them, the more the rest of the group will be saved and will be able to work in a certain amount of security. The leader plays the role of protector, like an umbrella or a lightning conductor. Thus, he allows the group to carry on the fundamental aim in a calm atmosphere, free from a certain number of harmful restraints.

However, this can lead to a scapegoat phenomenon (cf. René Girard, 1982) when the leader receives nothing other than negative input, such as craving, questioning, destruction, heightened compe-tition, or suspicion. In contrast, the "super-leader" (more charis-matic, perhaps) is the one who receives nothing other than positive returns, such as confidence, congratulations, regard, success, and respect; we can fear then that he no longer plays the role of protec-tor, of boundary guard for his group, which then finds itself, wholly or in part, much more exposed.

The leader experiences a hard reality that we undoubtedly have to accept in respect of the fundamental target of the institution. A saying reminds us of this reality: "When all is going well, every-body is involved. When everything is going wrong, the leader is the only one responsible."

Power and authority: duality and complementarity

Power is as necessary as authority for the good working of our societies. They can be exercised at different times, or with varying strength according to the occasion. Power and authority can often be opposed, and not necessarily to the detriment of the institution in which they are acting. They can be mixed up, opposed; they can coexist and take strength from each other, with variable results. As different as they may be, power and authority can be found in the same person. If not, it is necessary to organize their relationship in a positive way.

Let us take this next example, which is the creation and the life of an institution, whether it is political or economical, cultural or artis-tic. At the beginning, there is a person who is progressively going to impose himself by his authority (invested in him through his role in a certain environment), and by acquiring the material and spiritual tools—and also the symbolics—of power. Afterwards, his successors have the power and its tools, but not necessarily the authority. If a process of regulation does not exist both internally and externally, the damaging of the institution cannot be avoided in the long run. The still existing Japanese imperial dynasty is a good example of the best organization in terms of power and authority (speaking of role distribution) in Japan. It can also be an explanation of the current economical performance of this country. The variety of the roles and varied use of authority accepted by most people appear to be the main reasons for the development of Japanese companies. Those in power seem to have taken into account that they would put in danger not only their own existence, but also the existence of the whole company if such processes were neglected.

In other words, whatever the country and the institution, there is no more important task for those who have the power than steadily renewing the use of their authority, but also contributing to the renewing of the authority by others. The life of the institution depends on it.

But power seems to be much more weighty than authority, particularly in terms of evolution and change. In *War and Peace*, Tolstoï wrote, "The strongest, the most unbreakable, the heaviest and the most permanent link that binds us to our fellow creatures is what we call power". The constitution of a state, of a company, of any institution does not change easily. At any rate, it evolves with more difficulty than does the use of authority. In the same way, a super-tanker cannot change its direction as easily as a tug (yet they are both necessary and complementary).

Indeed, authority is more effective through alternation: one person can exercise authority, and then another after him, or at the same time. Power performs in terms of possibility: if one person has the power, the other is rejected. This leads to radicalism, or at least the exclusion of one or another solution.

Authority is more flexible: over time, each human group needs a variety of roles and leaders. Thus, the leading of a company in a time of growth is different from its leading in times of stagnation or recession. To use a nautical comparison, we can take the example of an advertisement by the insurance profession which tries to demonstrate the relevance, for any ship, of a captain on the open sea and a pilot to manoeuvre the ship in or out of the harbour.

The authority for a person inside a group can then vary according to places and occasions, despite that person's power. The King of the Belgians, a sovereign without power, symbolizes and maintains a feeling of national unity by representing the country in public functions, international meetings, and at times of danger or tragedy. The Italian President of the Republic is in the same position during tragic times experienced by the country.

These examples show, then, that power exists to fix a frame, rules, and procedures. It ensures the permanence and stability of the group. It allows the use of tools founded on a system of values that, at a given time and place, seems to have the agreement of the majority of the members of the institution. It makes control easier, not of people, but of actions initiated by them, in particular the actions of people in authority. For its part, authority represents the bonus of adaptation and innovation. Authority brings flexibility, fluidity, and, finally, ensures the regulation of a system within the rules established by power. Power and authority, then, are necessary parts of all institutions, whether they clash or not, such as when the one tries to get rid of the other, something that usually occurs during a time of crisis. The balance between power and authority is weak. Is that a bad thing?

A dangerous solution: power and authority.

As we have already shown, authority is often a springboard for power. The leader who has exercised authority for a certain time ends up feeling the need for outward signs of recognition, and particularly for signs that confer power. The existing power often refuses then to let itself be led in this way. To have more or less power can also have consequences for the authority that we exercise through our role. In fact, when power is not regulated, it too often leads to becoming attached to outward tributes of power, whereas everyone should exercise authority based on the role that he or she is able to play and his or her skill in exercising it. When power takes exclusive refuge in apparent signs of strength, it is ready to take over, and authority is felt as a real potential power.

Pierre Massé wrote,

> Every power which is not controlled by moral code, one day creates an opposite force . . . the realisation of this consequence should lead not to the suppression of the conflicts, which cannot be avoided and which can be fruitful but to the acceptance of some rules before too heavy consequences appear. [1965, p. 127]

The risk embodied in power is excess, leading to dictatorship, absolutism, totalitarianism, and no doubt, to entropy. In order to prevent misplaced power, safeguards are needed. These are both institutional, as in democracies (the separation of power between the executive, the legislative, and the judiciary, and taking into account the influence of the media), and personal (the exercise of authority through the role). In the ancient monarchies, the court jester, the king's fool, and the troubadour provide good examples of the essential counterbalance that each society creates to curb power through the use of satire or irony.

Thus, power can become too insistent and even too demanding, preventing authority from being brought into play. We can see it when crises occur, particularly during a transformation. The usual reaction is to concentrate power and authority (economic, cultural, and social) in the same hands, although what is needed when there are increased feelings of complexity is an assertion of one and the other, with a complete separation, or, failing that, a clear difference, asserted and experienced.

From that viewpoint, we seem to witness contradictory evolutions in France. The last movement of political and administrative decentralization could be the origin of a new way of doing things, encouraging the strengthening of democracy as well as the development of the local techno-structure. Moreover, the trade unions and the traders having real authority, some people suggest that they should be given power, too, whereas other people realize that their authority could then be in danger.

At a given level, power appears to be a game that leads to nothing. At each hierarchical level and at each group's head, we find only one chief. The struggle for power can even become a play with a negative result. In fighting too much and too long, we can avoid negative effects, but it is beyond the scope of this chapter to describe further the political battle in France or elsewhere.

In contrast, authority is able to transform itself into a game with a positive result: the recognition of oneself as the author and of the positive role of the group is more open and much wider than recognition obtained through the attribution of power.

In times of crisis, most of the members of an institution should exercise authority alternately, without necessarily seeking dedication to power. This would provide the opportunity for the institution to use its resources as best it can, and to increase the value of its potentiality.

Innovation and anxiety

Our working hypothesis is the following: during difficult times, if the research into adaptations and solutions leads to a concentration and conflation of power and authority, is this not caused by a growth in anxiety? If it is true that anxiety pre-exists under a more or less latent state, voiced and perceptible, the working of our institutions must automatically create more of it. Moreover, anxiety is used by these same institutions to further their own development, but, in times of crisis, the institutions have more difficulty in channelling this growing anxiety. It becomes more and more difficult to control, because its expression becomes less and less covered by media.

Whatever it is, the crisis disturbs the status quo, and the complexity, as it is experienced, makes the development of the events less understandable. Anxiety and lack of understanding create worry, and, consequently, the need for urgent research into regaining safety.

The most dangerous, but unfortunately the most frequent, answer is to invest authority and power together in the same person. But, if we do not misunderstand, this grouping does not come only from the desire of some individuals who are particularly devoted, corrupt, ambitious, or Machiavellian. It is also desired by the larger part of the group, who, reacting to fear, use the existing, noticeable, and reassuring power as a reason to excuse themselves from taking any active part. We see then a phenomenon of withdrawal and resignation, and, as a consequence, the inability of the institution to use its own resources.

Faced with this evolution, how can we ensure the existence of power and authority, the standing of power, and the (de)multipli-cation of authority? The answer is not simple: it relies both on belief and history, and innovation that is personal and social, rather than technological, is the only one to correspond to this expectation. Innovation allows a renewing of the institutional working rules, the questioning of personal behaviour, and the use of new techniques in order to ensure this useful, if struggling, complementarity between power and authority.

On this last point, one cannot be certain of the consequences that the appearance of new technologies will have on power and authority, and even less can one set general and universal rules. It took about thirteen years for the effects of the previous generation of technologies to appear. We are experiencing them now. Tele-vision and its role in the appearance of the "state-show" is one of them. In fact, nothing is fixed by advance. We need to separate ourselves from those who, at first sight, describe the new technolo-gies as tools for oppression and from those who, at first sight, too, consider new technologies as "instruments of emancipation".

Either the new technologies will continue to concentrate power and authority, or else they will reinforce the autonomy and the complementary nature of each. Thus, computing and all its deriva-tives can lead to the establishment of an over-concentrated society as well as, for each of us, the possibility of playing our different roles in a better way and then to exercise our authority. Only the political wish, in its first meaning, be it personal or collective, can shift the emphasis of the process in the expected way.

This process can be effective, but we need to view it and to decide upon it; and this during a period in which the development of techniques leads to the growth of uncertainty and anxiety felt by people in terms of their personal future and of the control these new technologies seem to exercise over everyday life. This is why the leaders have a difficult and even dangerous role in the current situ-ation, whether they have any power or not. Michel Crozier speaks of "the one who will be able to face the zone of uncertainty in front of which the group is" (1977 p. 97). He agrees then with a company leader, who was recently elected by his members as the best mana-ger of the year, and who said, "It is in the nature of the manager to cohabit with worry and doubt, fear and good or bad luck".

When crisis and complexity meet, and when fear, insecurity, vagueness, ambivalence, ambiguity, and distress develop, is it not the fundamental role of the leader to bear a bigger part of the anxiety created by the institutions and by life in our society?

Innovation imposes, then, that power should no longer be wrongly preserved. The recognition of anxiety, and the necessity for it to be really taken into account at each level of the institution, not just at the lower or medium levels, are both essential, like a safety valve, and useful for the motivation of people.

Innovation also exists in the creation of institutions in which power calls for the appearance of leaders whose authority is not only used to contest this power, but also to help it to evolve to the benefit of the institution and its development.

Innovation facilitates the appearance of leaders (even temporary ones) who will improve turnover, ensure a certain level of protection against the risks to be taken, and also establish the conditions of the training of staff. Finally, innovation needs special attention in respect of positions or advantages acquired in terms of power in and over society, because if we do not care about it, these advantages and positions will soon be established on a void and will cause much distress.

Mutating society, complex organizations, various crises, sudden emergence of uncertainty and distress, development of expectations and fear . . . how can we fail to notice that the working of our institutions is nothing other than ambiguous because of the flexibility, precariousness, and unsettling nature that results from the mixing of power and authority? And yet, this strange mixing, delicate and subtle, is one of the opportunities of our society's continuity. This supposes that we accept everlasting conflict between power and authority, hoping that those who have power will assemble and, more importantly, bring over to the institution those who are likely to exercise authority.

Note

1.   A version of this chapter was previously published by the *Lettre de la Société Internationale des Conseillers de Synthèse*, in December 1983.

CHAPTER NINE

The paths of authority. From the unconscious to the transcendental: intervention at the Arab University of Jerusalem, December 1996

David Gutmann, with Ronan Pierre,
Jacqueline Ternier-David, and Christophe Verrier

> "Nothing can be taught to others. They can only be helped
> in their discovery"
>
> (Galileo, in Clavelin, 1970)

Since the School of Human Relations, numerous studies have referred to organizational development as an approach in the understanding of men and the systems to which they belong. However, as consultants at Praxis International, and at the International Forum of Social Innovation, our activity is closer to an approach of organizations in terms of institutional transformation (IT) than organizational development (OD).

Institutional transformation differs from organizational development in the sense that its goal is to take into account the unconscious and its expression, whenever possible. As consultants, we try to detect or interpret the unconscious processes in institutions. From this perspective, consultants focus their attention on the exercise of authority, leadership, and transformation within the institutions.

Our practice as consultants in Praxis International (through our activity as Advisers in Leadership) and in the International Forum for Social Innovation (through the organization of "learning from experience" conferences) is centred on a principle: the revealed unconscious, when worked out, can be a resource that opens and transforms blocked situations. To illustrate this, we shall recall our last conference in East Jerusalem.

The International Forum for Social Innovation (Paris), together with Al-Quds University (the Arab University of East Jerusalem), devised, prepared, and organized, under the authority of David Gutmann, the first international Palestinian conference, entitled "Leadership, innovation and transformation". This conference took place in one of the schools of Al-Quds University, 14–19 July 1996.

In the complex and moving context of the Middle East, questions concerning boundaries, identities and relationship are at the core of the life of each individual and each social group's life. Surely, the conference would "resonate" with its environment . . .

*   *   *

The methodology

We will briefly describe the content of conferences such as "Leadership, innovation and transformation".

In the first place, the conference is an *institution*, just like a firm, an association, or a football team, with the difference that it is clearly defined within time limits; that is, it is temporary. In the second place, it is a *learning from experience* institution; the learning method is centred on exploration and interpretation of experience while it is happening, in the *here and now*, by the participants of the conference.

On the experiential field of the conference, participants go through situations they have met within the organizations they usually belong to, in which they must exercise their authority and leadership as well as their capacities of innovation and transformation.

Thus, they can work out the political, unconscious, and spiritual material that constitutes the essence of institutions, and better understand what is at stake in an intellectual or even affective way.

Reveal the unconscious in order to transform the conscious

During these conferences, the consultants are particularly aware of the *political dimension* (what is at stake in terms of balance of power, rules, behaviours, etc.), the *unconscious dimension* (each person's mental image of the institution, marked by his or her fantasy about others, power, institutions, etc.), and the *spiritual dimension* (the belief or faith in the institution, which has something to do with the transcendental) of the temporary institution. The issue is to reveal some of the individual or collective barriers that limit social innovation.

In addition to management (which includes conference administration), the conference's staff members intervene as consultants during the sessions. While it is taking place, the consultants set up working hypotheses concerning the political, the unconscious, or the spiritual material which is at work. Often, such working hypotheses are focused on psychological blocks, resistances, and fears they have observed in the group.

One of the basic assumptions in these conferences is that the collective revelation and expression of resistances is a way of transforming the institution. Therefore, to discuss and debate these resistances is a way to work them out, to go beyond them, and to transform them.

*Respect the boundaries in order
to transform them into resources*

A strict principle on which these conferences are based is the respect for space, time, and task boundaries. That involves a strict schedule: each conference offers a frame where boundaries are continuously clarified and serve as a support for the interpretation of actual experiences. During the conference, several types of sessions are set up (e.g., large study groups, small study groups) according to a strictly defined schedule.

These groups can deal either with the limits worked out during the conference, or the limits separating individuals and systems, social groups and territorial entities. The two may be similar. In terms of transformation, it is necessary that *barricades*, which are impermeable, become *barriers, borders, boundaries,* which can be progressively more permeable. *Institutional transformation* might be: moving from a closed conception of the limit (the barricade) to a more open conception (the boundary). It carries the idea that a boundary marks both a rupture *and* a passage; without boundary, there is no differentiation, but also no transaction.

The words "boundaries" (which contains a form of "bind", the link), "borders", "barriers", and "barricades" form a progression expressing from one word to another a growing demarcation. In terms of transformation, it is necessary that "barricades" become "barriers, borders, boundaries".

* * *

A conference in East Jerusalem

The conference at Al-Quds University in July 1996 took place in East Jerusalem—a city which stands for a symbol of all religious conflicts in the Middle East–during a time when relations between Israelis and Palestinians had suddenly worsened (Rabin's assassination in 1995, the election of a pro-Likud government in Spring 1996).

The main issue for the participants was to understand their place in the transition process from an Israeli authority to a Palestinian authority.

The conference was meant to help members understand the transformations that should accompany the recent political evolutions in the Middle East.

Tasks such as instituting borders, creating territories, building up a democracy, building roads, cities, and moving populations are important, but the transformation raises fears, anxiety, and obvious resistances. Such transformations require an evolution in habits and mentality, which was the main issue of the conference.

Of the thirty-six participants (the maximum allowed), twenty-eight were Palestinians (one of them originally European), six were Israelis (three Jews and three Arabs—two Muslims and one Christian), and two other Europeans (one French and one Belgian). The staff was composed of eight members of different nationalities, religions, and culture. Members came from the Palestinian Authority, from the USA, from France, from India, and from Israel. Along with Islam, almost all Judeo-Christian religions were represented. The director was a Jewish European (French).

It is difficult to recount the actual rich content of the conference. However, some situations deserve description, as well as the main working hypotheses presented by the consultants.

During one of the first events of the conference, for example (the small study group), the group elected a chairman, someone who would moderate the discussion. The consultant noticed that the person chosen was the only Jewish Israeli in the group (which was composed of Palestinians, except for the consultant). The consultant was surprised. Was this situation a sign that, for Palestinians, imagining themselves in a role other than one dominated by Israelis was difficult? Recounted here, this interpretation seems excessive. But, in the here and now, to formulate publicly the working hypothesis is a way to give birth to a debate, sometimes rough, or, on the contrary, to generate encounters. In the best cases, such a pratice can reveal habits, prejudices, defensive attitudes, fears, anguish, and so on, all elements that can inhibit the individual in his relationship with others, and that are resistances in the social innovation process.

The impossible transaction

Another situation met during the conference enabled the consultants to put forward an important working hypothesis and therefore begin to understand what was at stake in the here and now. The interpretation was based on the following observation: the staff had great difficulty in persuading the participants to respect the conference's time, space, and task boundaries.

The external borders were acutely present in this conference, since numerous Palestinians (in addition to the actual thirty-six participants) had been forbidden to enter Jerusalem and could not participate in the conference; others were stopped at the border (the "green line") and could not meet in Jerusalem.

During the conference, the members of staff were confronted with a high number of people being absent or late. Some participants left the conference at the very beginning, never coming back, or returning a few days later. Other participants attended only a few sessions, or came late to the events.

Another type of border was defined in relation to the primary task of the institution. For example, a woman came one day with her child: it was difficult for the staff to make clear to the members, individually or collectively, that she had forced a border.

Thus, the staff noticed on several occasions that it was difficult for the members to respect the limits of space, time, and task of the conference. The consultants presented a working hypothesis: the resistance to the respect of limits (borders) is the expression of a larger resistance to the respect of borders in the Middle East.

The consultants used the following observation: the border as a limit or a separation has been contested since the creation of Israel. An agreement on this matter between Israelis and Palestinians seems impossible, both from a political point of view and an unconscious point of view. The refusal, or repression, of the border as a limit was perceptible at numerous moments during the conference.

Can this type of hypothesis be accurate? One can obviously suggest the cultural background of the Middle East as an explanation of absenteeism or lateness. However, one must keep in mind that such working hypotheses are put forward in the here and now (when situations are occurring), when a public discussion about them can begin, bringing up other elements to work on, and so on. Progressively, by means of successive interpretations, we can hope that some "hidden elements" of the institution will be revealed. (René Girard, 1982, p. 208) wrote *Des choses cachées depuis la fondation du monde* [literally, "About things hidden since the origins of the world"], in which he defends the idea that the "scapegoat" phenomenon is constant and universal in human groups. In our sense, the "hidden elements" are the constant [anthropological] elements of all institutions. They are hidden to those who do not want to see them.) Afterwards, the work of the staff could be analysed in this way: it was interesting to work on the notion of "borders" since it is a conflictual issue in the Middle East.

The most striking revelation was the difficulty for the participants to acknowledge the border as a *place of transaction*, of exchange, of commerce. One situation enabled this point to be revealed: the two Palestinians of the staff (the administrators) were questioned by the members. This questioning was very intense, since members came to the two administrators and asked them why they accepted to "serve" such a staff, composed of individuals coming from primitive people. For a better understanding of this example, let us recall that one of the consultants of the staff was an Afro-American, and another an Indian. Also, in all our conferences, just as in all institutions (firms, for example), the administrator's role is quite unrewarding: he or she is often regarded as a servant. Thus, the two Palestinian administrators were seen as servants of the other staff members, who were largely Western.

The participants' projections on the staff gave rise to the following working hypothesis: the staff was perceived as a strongly hierarchical group (director, consultants, administrators), as if a common project were unthinkable, whereas the *work* of the staff, composed of different nationalities, cultures, and religions, was to be understood as the result of co-operation. We (the International Forum for Social Innovation) believe that the primary task of an institution can only be fulfilled if each person carries out his or her role. Ideally, "managers–managed" relations have to be structured with a view to the institution's primary task, and cannot be reduced to hierarchical links.

In the temporary learning institution of the conference, one of the working hypotheses put forward by the consultants was that the Palestinian members were reluctant to accept any co-operation other than between themselves, as if Palestinians could only rely on themselves. To take on the idea of boundary, it appeared to the staff that differences of nationality or religion were uncrossable borders ("barricades" or "barriers") for the Palestinians. But a boundary is also a place of transaction, and possibly co-operation (between countries, for example). This transaction is both a link (since a transaction links two systems together) and a form of communication by exchange. It is probably the reason why it is so difficult to accept.

A "prison in the mind"

The observation of the identity games in the conference (and in its environment) revealed an image of two societies coming face to face in a mirror-like situation. Let us develop this working hypothesis.

On both sides, everything was happening in a mental state that fuelled a mutual exclusion. This mental state was structured by a closed representation of oneself and of the society one belonged to. The image that came to us was confinement. Each person, whether Israeli or Palestinian, confronted the other with a confined mood. On the Palestinian side, it was a "prison in the mind"; on the Israeli side, it was a "ghetto in the mind".

The working hypothesis, called "prison in the mind", was formulated by the staff during the conference while trying to understand the behaviour of participants who had been in Israeli prisons for a long time. These participants lived as if they were constantly constrained by hostile authorities (embodied by the staff or other participants). Were they not acting as if prison remained within them?

It appeared to us that the "prison in the mind" could be a good metaphor for the unconscious representation of life for the Palestinians: in general, prison is a closed place, where existence is organized around one sex, as if only part of life were possible. In Palestine, the "prison" exists because of the curfew, the temporary closing of territories, the walls, and the barbed wire, all elements that achieve the confinement of a people in the Palestinians' daily life. Observing what was happening during the conference, the staff thought that Palestinians had a "prison in the mind".

Afterwards, it appeared to us that, confronted with this representation, the Israelis presented maybe another type of confinement: we called it the "ghetto in the Mind", as if images from the Jewish people's history confronted that of the Palestinians. The ghetto stands in a surviving dimension, as people desperately try to stay alive.

Thus, each Middle Eastern participant opposed the other, and him/herself, with a confined state of mind. These strongly internalized representations had to be worked out during the conference.

Let us note that these two types of confinement are not complementary. Somehow, they reproduce the political and human situation in the Middle East, which was blocked until the Oslo agreements. These agreements initiated an actual transformation (a concrete, noticeable one). But transformation "in the mind" has been more uncertain, as shown by Rabin's assassination: some are firmly opposed to the peace process, on the Jewish side as well as on the Arab side.

Once these representations were revealed, how could the staff work them out? How does one engage a transformation process? How does one leave confinement?

During the conference, the image of a tunnel appeared as a way out of a confinement. The participants worked on this image. How does one escape from a prison? From the ghetto? Can a tunnel be the answer? The tunnel, just like the one in Jerusalem, was another cause of conflict between Jews and Arabs in September 1996.

But the tunnel does not allow two parties to meet; it is not a Forum, a place of discussion, of exchange; it is a "closed exit". The tunnel places someone directly on the other side, on the adverse side. The tunnel is also a good metaphor for the inevitability of fate. The invocation of fate enables us to act without any responsibility, without any authority.

The task of the staff was to detect these resistances (the "images in the mind") and to reveal them in order to help the participants to take on their own authority, so as to become co-authors of one transformation.

*   *   *

The advent of a secular society

It was not easy to organize this conference in East Jerusalem. The major difficulties were financial. A European sponsor (Electricité de France) agreed to fund Al-Quds University. Without Electricité de France's help, it is likely that the conference would never have taken place. It did eventually . . . and under tough external conditions. Just after the May 1996 elections in Israel, which brought to power a government hostile to the Oslo agreements, tension suddenly rose in the territories as the Israelis closed the borders. Some Palestinian members of the staff, from Bethlehem to Ramalha, from Gaza to Jericho, were forced to give up their project of attending the conference due to the sealing of the territories. However, the maximum number of participants was eventually reached. This allowed us to overcome the most important obstacles.

During the conference, the staff's role was challenged several times by the participants. It is true that this type of contestation is very common in the conferences organized by the International Forum of Social Innovation, and is an expression of the anxiety felt by the members. Anxiety is caused by the perspective of having to deal with the unknown, such as confronting other people first, and, later, learning authority. This sort of challenge is used as a medium through which working hypotheses are expressed by the consultants.

During the Al-Quds University conference, the staff was once severely challenged by the participants. Two Palestinians, who had attended the first session on the first day, came back on the fourth day during the "Institutional Event" and violently expressed their opposition to the staff. (The Institutional System Event sessions are designed to study the relations between members and staff who, in part, constitute the management of the Institutional System Event.) In doing so, they took the lead in an internal challenging movement. Their intervention shook up the other members, who had been attending all the sessions on a daily basis. They had worked together and created solidarity. What surprised the staff was the way the challenge was personified by two Palestinians (who were employees of the university) who had not participated in all the events. The two men joined two other male participants. These four men were sitting together as if they formed a physical "front", thus breaking the initial circle of the room (an obvious association was made by the staff, recalling the "Islamic Front"). Going beyond this first observation, and remembering that the two men were actually chemists, the staff formulated the following working hypothesis: the two men came back in order to set a "bomb" in the temporary institution of the conference, in order to sabotage the current transformation process. This hypothesis was put forward and explored by the participants. Here again, the strong resonance between the conference's incidents and what was happening (the attacks that preceded the Israeli elections of May 1996) was a great discovery. *Thus, in formulating some working hypotheses (sometimes in a metaphoric way), we can help people to be conscious of what is really at stake in some situations.*

Women also played a great role in the conference's evolution. Let us take the case of one young student wearing a veil. On the first day, she hesitated before sitting down and asked a porter to indicate where she could sit. At the very end of the conference, she sat directly in front of the staff. Moreover, right after the conference, she gave the director a set of drawings she had made, which were representing her different mental states throughout the past six days. In several of them, she had portrayed herself without a veil.

One could say that part of the resistances expressed during the conference were worked out and possibly transformed. The conference eventually ended, and a party followed. The event was described in several articles (with photographs) in the Palestinian press. Moreover, a meeting between the International Forum for Social Innovation and some officials of the university was organized during subsequent days. These talks led to a future conference each year, for a period of five years.

In October 1996, this decision was reconsidered by the authorities of the university, who decided not to organize the conference in 1997. We were surprised and concerned. By December 1996, this refusal appeared to be less certain. Today, the situation seems to be not so hopeless. At the same moment, in Hebron, Israeli and Palestinian authorities made new (fragile) contacts. While surveying the political, unconscious, and spiritual dimensions, this conference echoes its environment.

The toughening of the political situation in the Middle East was an important element in the decision not to organize the conference in 1997. But we feel that what was at stake was much stronger and deeper, and not easy to name. When we examine all the valid reasons for this refusal, are they not secondary? When we attempted to work on the reality of the Palestinian society, its highly hierarchical clan structures appeared. This type of relationship was probably strengthened by the Israeli–Palestinian conflict. However, we pointed out the Palestinians' difficulties in locating and respecting borders, as well as dealing with authority. The conference enabled the participants to explore the possibility of a "secular" society (in its etymological sense: "common"), the society of persons, men and women in equality. Such a society contrasts with the actual "theocratic" society that seems to be the reality of Palestinian society, and is growing in Israel.

A quest of the West?

This working hypothesis—the emergence of a secular society—was formulated six months after the conference, when some French members of the staff met (including the director). It enabled us to think about the meaning of our coming to Jerusalem. It is obvious that the idea of an emerging secular society appeals to us, for, as Europeans, we inherited the ideals of the Age of Enlightenment.

What was the staff searching for by coming to East Jerusalem? This coming is probably an expression of our fascination with Jerusalem, as Europeans. Jerusalem is a sacred land we would like to see become secular. We would like to see a land where religious passions are pacified and transformed. This place is a symbol of universal identity conflicts. It appeared to us as a privileged location for such a conference. In a way, we were there legitimizing our experience of conferences. So, when this experience is evoked, our excitement is still vivid and easy to understand.

Somehow, this conference symbolizes a meeting between the West and the East. With the heritage of the Age of Enlightenment and methods born with the psychoanalytic movement (whose inventor was an Viennese Jew), have we not planned to reconquer a sacred land, just as we did with the Crusades, several hundred years ago? Western naïvety? If so, we accept the judgement. We also want to recall that, in these conferences, the staff comes also with its own preconceptions. The staff's main task is to help the "pre-conceptions" become "pro-creation" within the temporary institution of the conference.

These questions show that one can make associations out of mere facts, images, and fantasies. This progressively gives a meaning to some actions. This meaning is in no way the truth, but the sense elaborated, either in the here and now or afterwards, can be a momentary prerequisite for the understanding of behaviours; especially when there are hidden elements.

*   *   *

We feel that this conference enables us to say that working out the revealed part of the unconscious is the only way to fight against the traditional resistances—"images in the mind".

We think that during the conference in East Jerusalem, each participant was able to understand the dependency hold institutions have over individuals. Thus, perhaps they will start assuming their own authority.

Concerning the unconscious, when we succeed in revealing part of it, we break down some walls, but the collective unconscious, as a meta-system, gets the upper hand, and this requires more work on resistances, which will result in another phase of progression and regression and so on (see "The transformation and its zig-zags", in D. Gutmann, J. Ternier-David, and C. Verrier, *Groups and Transformation*, Ubevidste Processer, Copenhagen, February 1995). Acknowledging this perpetual cycle, we can use unconscious elements as resources in order to assist institutional transformation in organizations.

CHAPTER TEN

Transformation and collusion: from conforming to forming an alliance[1]

David Gutmann, with Jacqueline Ternier-David and Christophe Verrier

L ife, in human or animal—i.e., biological—terms, as much as the life of institutions (by which we mean human organiza- tions built to work collectively towards a common goal), includes mechanisms of repetition, reproduction, creation, and innovation. In the case of institutions, our own representation of these evolutions highlights the role of the resistances that they generate and experience.

From that a dialectic tension is born, between the desire for *transformation* and the need for permanence. This tension is mani- fested by dynamics of actions and reactions, progressions and regressions, co-operation and resistances.

Through this approach, *collusion* can be understood as one of the most habitual modes of resistance to transformation. Collusion is a process that individuals adopt, sometimes unknowingly, to oppose it and attempt to set it up to fail. Consequently, having become less clear, more difficult to understand for managers, consultants, or any of their own members, institutions lose some of their legibility and, more than that, some of their vitality.

One cannot explore the concept of collusion without, at the same time, referring to that of *alliance*, which, for us, constitutes its opposite, at least between and within institutions. On what conditions is it therefore possible to build real work alliances that enable all the stakeholders of these institutions to pursue their own transformation and, more generally, to reach their primary objectives?

Collusion is at the heart of a system's transformation: it makes up one of its most efficient modes of resistance. While very often inevitable in any transformation, collusion is designed to make it fail.

For example, one often observes certain people in an institution forming groups, colluding in order to resist—generally in a covert manner—the unfolding of the institution, its primary objective, its management, and the transformation it is engaged in.

More generally, colluding with another person means accepting to share, to put into a common pot, and through this to increase one's own resistances.

Let us take the example of an observer external to a system: he is supposed to be capable of bringing to the latter a representation or a working hypothesis which, even if this upsets the system, can encourage its transformation. However, if this observer starts colluding with this system (albeit collusion may be one of the main levers of its functioning), the observer then tacitly commits not to disturb it. He puts himself in a situation where, like other members of the system, he can neither formulate, nor even conceptualize, this external representation. The system forbids him to, and renders him blind, deaf, and mute. The observer is phagocyted, neutralized, he is from then on filled up with other people's resistances. He has accepted them and, from then on, they live within him.

For him, the only way of recovering his freedom—if such a thing remains possible—consists in shattering and exposing the collusion. For such is the life of systems, and of the homeostatic principle that is one of its ever-present components. We will develop this point when referring to collusion in the work of consultants.

In some cases, *collusion is a primitive form of alliance.* It precedes it when circumstances demand clandestinity. But, when the situation improves or the political game is turned around, collusion in the shadows becomes, through institutionalization, an alliance made public. This is, for example, the case of the Resistance in occupied France, which gave birth, after the Liberation, to the Fourth and the Fifth Republics.

Conversely, a recognized alliance can, when circumstances turn less favourable, "enter clandestinity" and take the form of collusion.

Collusion, therefore, comes across as a rudimentary type of association, while alliance, through its fairly tacit formalization, takes complexity more into account.

Collusion and alliance

By definition, *collusion* is a *secret association designed to prejudice a third party*. (Collusion comes from the latin *cum-ludere* "to play with", which gives *collusion*, "secret, fraudulent agreement".) Legally, collusion is a secret agreement between people to harm a third party. Thus the first characteristic of collusion is its secret, invisible, occult, happily subversive aspect, which feeds any circumstances and any fantasy.

Processes of collusion traditionally inhabit the political game of a country or of any other institution. Nations' current political affairs, in countries such as Italy or France, show us daily how these processes work by leaning in an often decisive manner on power dynamics and vital relationships.

By its occult aspect, its reliance on things being left unsaid, collusion stands in opposition to *alliance*. ("Alliance" and "to ally" come from the Latin *ad ligare* "to link with", which gives *alligare*, "to bind, put together". *To ally with* consists in uniting through a treaty, through a mutual engagement. "Alliance", in French, is also the word specifically used to name a wedding ring. The result of combining metals is called "alloy". "Alliance", in contrast, relies on a contract (a convenant), a publicly signed treaty, which is then advertised.)

Alliance and collusion also stand in opposition in terms of their objectives. While alliance works for, collusion is a scheme against someone. Whatever the meaning or the value given to the action in place, collusion seeks to prejudice the other and his role. It is mortifying and destructive, while alliance is happily negentropic.

Collusion, by its deliberately informal and clandestine aspect, injects confusion into the system; it attempts to generate amalgam and create fusional links between the different subsystems by voluntarily covering up the differences that the system can contain; indeed, it feeds the black box of transformation!

Alliance, conversely, tends to carefully recognize the differences between partners; it generates, from these differences and their complementarities, a relationship based on interdependence and desire.

Paradoxically, the fusion–confusion that collusion introduces is followed by a fragmentation of the system. Collusion leads certain people or sub-systems to gang up against others. Its occult and subversive aspect is a testimony to its illicit nature: collusion is a form of transgression of that which is forbidden. Alliance, on the other hand, gathers and involves the whole system around a leader and/or a primary objective. In that sense, alliance constitutes *the very essence of the idea of enterprise.*

Two examples

Here are two examples that help us better perceive the notions of alliance and collusion. The first summons up a fertile and creative alliance, while the second shows a case of collusion associated with regression.

Biblical alliance

Reading the Bible through the lens of psychoanalysis, some writers have been able to shine a new light on the concept of alliance. Indeed, alliance—the one, for example, that links YHWH to Abraham or Moses and which, through circumcision, is inscribed in the flesh of those latter—constitutes a brake upon omnipotence, because this process implies reciprocity and exchange. Thus, the power of one part is balanced and completed by one of the other, and *vice versa.*

Alliance, thus, introduces the idea of a necessary interdependence between partners. It is that relationship that lays the foundations for the community, and no longer a relationship based on the domination of some by others, as the Hebrews experienced it in Egypt.

In that sense, the crossing of the Red Sea, which leads to the destruction of the Pharaoh's army, is also the journey–transformation from domination to another kind of political order. This emerging order will be based on valuing the alterities and complementarities that bind and support the community.

The period of France's occupation

In the situation of chaos that is the "debacle", *collaboration* develops as a recognized alliance, one known to the public. (Collaboration comes from the Latin *cum-laborare "travailler avec"*, which gives *collaboration* [medieval Latin], "possession acquired by spouses through working together". In its first meaning, to collaborate is *to work together [to reap the benefits]*. The word *collaboration* earned in France a pejorative meaning with the Vichy government.) It serves what appears to be a transformation, the "National Revolution", imposed by the Vichy government and associated with Hitler's project of rendering France subservient as well as the rest of Europe. In fact, it appears rather more like a phase of regression in the long transformation that is the history of France, taken as a whole process.

From then on, the *Resistance*, an authentic movement formed to counteract this pseudo transformation, takes the form of a collusion (clandestine and often fuzzy gathering, born out of disorder, all this thanks to individuals and groups who slowly get organized) before becoming a true alliance (with the France Libre government and then alongside the Allied Forces). The outcome of this process is the conception of institutions for the Fourth Republic, and, more especially, the Fifth Republic.

The role of consultant

Collusion and the role of consultant are linked over more than one issue. First, because the putting together of both these words brings up the issue of collusion between the consultant and his partner. Let us then first examine collusion within the practice of consulting.

In our experience, this practice leans either towards *reparation*, or towards *revelation*. (By *reparation*, we mean the reparation of the effects of guilt present in any institution and which is, among other things, projected on to its leaders either during a period of degeneration, or during transformations. By *revelation*, we mean the formulation of working hypotheses leading to the broadening and increasing depth of understanding that a manager, consultant, or other stakeholder can have of the institution.) The relationship between a consultant and his partner is built from this fundamental choice.

A relationship based on collusion—on connivance, on listening complacently without discernment or distantiation—induces reparation. Thus, it undermines the institution. Such a relationship is based on the principle that the manager—loaded down and helpless in the face of the guilt-inducing projections with which the institution fills him by rendering him guilty of the injuries that it experiences—calls on the help of a consultant to ask him to repair these injuries on his behalf.

In contrast, alliance between a consultant and his partner is a relationship based on partnership, which gives both of them the opportunity to work on the boundary that separates them or, at least, differentiates their roles. In this case only, the trap of reparation can be avoided. The aim of the consultation—to deepen one's understanding of the conscious and unconscious processes at work in the institution, by which we mean revelation—can then be reached.

A consultant who examines the transformation of an institution is usually confronted by mechanisms of resistance, among which we find collusion. His work on the black box (see 'Transformation', pp. 18–20) consists, among other things, of identifying collusions in order to improve understanding, but also acting on them, either by revealing their presence and their dangers (as inhibitors), or by contributing to transforming them into real, favourable alliances (boosters).

As a way of illustrating this practice, we offer the following example borrowed from our experience as consultants to a lifelong learning department within a big French company.

Convivial collusion: connivance

The organizational diagnosis that we established for this institution highlighted that the *affective links between people came before the institutional relationships between roles.*

Thus, this "convivial collusion" comes in the form of a warm, polite atmosphere, with a constant search for consensus, an absence of visible conflict, the desire to convince rather than to coerce—all of which resonates with the lifelong learning approach—and, generally, priority given to the affective domain, which means that "friendship" takes priority over role relations.

However, we also note a tendency to hide or minimize conflicts between people and different ways of thinking, and an aversion to choosing, to deciding: everyone protects him/herself by avoiding asking questions that might disturb the status quo; everyone spares the other, and at times avoids him. Lack of mutual trust leads to wariness, and to people sticking to their area of competence. These observations enabled the following points to emerge.

This "convivial collusion" reinforces the system's confused state. This confusion, rarely overcome, prevents people within this department from working on their collective anxiety and, thus, from developing their creativity. Consequently, differences between roles are not clearly marked, worked on, and utilized. Is the other accepted through his difference? How can we think about working alliances? Are roles being experienced as complementary? It is indeed the issue of otherness and difference that everyone faces.

This fusional atmosphere can be understood as an overt form of resistance to the implementation of a collective and shared management; collusion leads to stereotypes, such as those, for example, that polarize "Parisian intellectuals" and "operationals".

In fact, this conviviality encourages a collective withdrawal of the department into itself in the context of external dangers. In an uncertain environment, the protective role of the institution seems accentuated.

Thus, this "convivial collusion" is full of ambivalence. On what conditions can it be transformed into a true *affectio societatis* (legally, *affectio societatis* is the associate quality necessary to the validity and the implementation of the contract stating the constitution of a company), bringing together recognition, equity (more than equality), and mutual respect, making it possible to build with the other true relationships based on co-operation, role complementarity, and interdependence? To what extent is this model of traditional teaching—reticent by definition in the face of any superior power and inevitably present in this training department—compatible with the implementation of a true management process?

In this example, attempts to introduce a real management process in this service were met with strong resistance that took the form of "convivial collusion".

This collusion draws on the confusion it creates and opposes role differentiation, without which any management process—including the management of boundaries and differences—is made impossible.

Collusion in institutions: four archetypes

Here we propose to enrich our analysis of collusion in institutions by presenting a framework of interpretation of institutional life through, on the one hand, four role archetypes and, on the other hand, a dynamic—that of transformation—around which these archetypes unfold in ways of collusion and alliance.

Of course, these are archetypes, that is to say, four extreme versions, four cardinal points, or even four deep trends running through the whole institution and sometimes finding themselves simultaneously present within the same persons. We are, therefore, not seeking, through a rigid typology, to accomplish a final classification of individuals who are still capable of evolving, nor to develop a radical black-and-white sorting through of entrepreneurs and bureaucrats.

Below are the four roles that we propose:

● the mad entrepreneurs;
● the reasonable entrepreneurs;
● the reasoning bureaucrats;
● the fanatical bureaucrats.

Let us first examine each of these representations before exploring the relationships that these roles can develop.

Entrepreneurs are those who give impulse and shape to organizational life and its transformations, of which they are the initiators. They anchor the institution in a project, an approach, an ambition, a vision.

Bureaucrats, on the other hand, are settled in an institution that they consider to be immortal—since, in their thought processes, it operates on a mode of endless repetition. This illusion claims to protect them. Consequently, their preoccupations focus on issues of procedures, which take over from the primary objective. However, in terms of regulation, bureaucracy is useful as a component of the system (see Max Weber's ideal-type [1965], since some repetition is needed for the development of processes of reproduction, creation, and innovation.

Bureaucrats are set in *repetition*—or at best in *reproduction*—while entrepreneurs support *creation* and *innovation*.

We need to be more precise, though.

Mad entrepreneurs bring, first and foremost, creativity at the heart of the system. Some call them mavericks (translator's note: in the original text: "canards sauvages", i.e., wild ducks). For them, the reality principle, necessary for the development of any institution, cannot be conceived of without the pleasure principle (Eros), which gives to their creative range an authentic, indispensable, and often crucial colour.

(The pleasure principle can be defined as one of the two principles—the other being the death principle—that rule psychic life, whose goal is to avoid unpleasure and to generate pleasure. The reality principle can be defined as the principle that modifies the pleasure principle, in so far as it manages to assert itself as a regulating principle. In the remit of our paper, the reality principle can be understood as the impact "reality" has on the system. This reality matches the environment [the rest of the world] within which the system evolves, but also the system's internal constraints linked to institutional life, its boundaries, its primary objective, etc. This reality principle attempts to transform the pleasure and death principles which inhabit the system, individually and collectively. The death impulses (Thanatos) can be defined as impulses of aggression or destruction that tend to completely reduce any tension, that is to say, to reduce a living being to an inorganic state. They stand in opposition to the life impulses (Eros), which tend to constitute ever bigger units and to maintain them. Based on Laplanche and Pontalis [1992].)

Their natural tendency is to project themselves in all directions within the organization's environment. Their *deviance* is therefore extremely energizing and creative, providing that it does not become too great a centrifugal force, which would result in their running the risk of becoming *marginalized* through disconnection from the rest of the company.

Having said that, their lack of consistency, of control, or their dilettantism render them incapable of taking on, by themselves, the management of any institution.

In order to root their ideas in reality, they need to partner with *reasonable entrepreneurs*. The latter hold on more clearly to the institution's primary objective and its reality principle, which makes them fully aware of its mortality. In a way, reasonable entrepreneurs stand with their backs against the wall and, in order to constantly push back the death of the institution—which they know to be ineluctable—they feed its "life force" with dynamism, through organizing and applying both their own and others' ideas. They select and integrate proposals from mad entrepreneurs.

Reasoning bureaucrats do their job "properly". They usually behave as followers, but at least the few doubts that they harbour regarding their own understanding of the system lead them to keep an open mind. They are particularly sensitive to the notion that a reality principle flows through and influences the institution; in fact, that is their connection with the reasonable entrepreneurs. However, they often use this issue in a rigid and fastidious manner.

As for *fanatical bureaucrats*, they can be considered as bureaucracy's fundamentalists. Their conservative—in fact reactionary—spirit, invariably resistant to any idea of transformation, unleashes a real problem for the institution. Prisoners of their work space, the office, hermetic to their environment, they are tempted to organize the recoiling of the organization on itself. Filled with Thanatos, the death principle, and with the buzz derived from the power that the system gives them, they are capable of taking it on a downward and mortifying spiral.

These four archetypes find several types of associations in a company. But if we observe these in the dynamic processes of transformation, these associations take on a decisive meaning. On the one hand, each of these archetypes, as mentioned, positions itself in relation to the notion of transformation. Some would be boosters, others would be more like inhibitors. Others still would take on a more complex role as supporters of another role.

But, in the movement of a transformation, their associations oscillate between an alliance that sustains transformation *vs.* a collusion that resists it. Let us take an example to illustrate each of these polarities.

First type = (mad entrepreneurs, reasonable entrepreneurs, reasoning bureaucrats)

This type (Figure 3) represents for us the work alliance most favourable to transformation. The crucial presence of mad entrepreneurs is regulated by reasonable entrepreneurs and reasoning bureaucrats. The latter are equally useful, for, without them, an alliance between mad and reasonable entrepreneurs would lead to

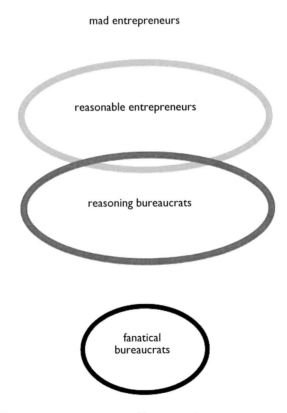

mad entrepreneurs

reasonable entrepreneurs

reasoning bureaucrats

fanatical
bureaucrats

Figure 3. First type entrepreneurs and bureaucrats.

a flight from reality. Reasonable entrepreneurs make up the *epicentre* of this first type: they bring balance and cohesion to the institution between two strong and contradictory tendencies (mad entrepreneurs and reasoning bureaucrats). Here, the alliance between different and complementary components is so fruitful that it can lead to moments, however fleeting, of harmony. It gives real meaning to the word enterprise.

In terms of transformation, the decisive *impulse* given by mad entrepreneurs becomes even more efficient, since it is relayed by the *cascading* process formed by the solid alliance of reasonable entrepreneurs and reasoning bureaucrats.

Conversely, the resistance of the fanatical bureaucrats is isolated and contained, since they have failed to build any kind of collusion with anyone—a collusion that could have helped them to sustain and feed resistances.

Second type = (reasonable entrepreneurs, reasoning bureaucrats, fanatical bureaucrats)

This association, of a collusive type, encourages the development of resistances to transformation and of *regression* (Figure 4). The fact that mad entrepreneurs—if they exist at all—have become marginalized creates such a big gap with the other components of the institution that they cannot succeed in creating a work alliance. Therefore, they run the risk of being expelled. Linked to this excluding process, the other three archetypes regroup in an extremely powerful and dangerous *collusion of resistance*, which threatens not only the transformation process, but also the actual institution in its very existence.

Indeed, collusion between bureaucrats is a constant threat to reasonable entrepreneurs, who could end up being rejected by the system, and can lead the institution into a sometimes violent madness. The epicentre here ends up in the hands of bureaucrats, and can lean towards totalitarianism and degeneration.

Of course, all other types of collusion or alliance between two or three of these categories are possible, and can be observed concretely. They are more or less fertile, or, to the contrary, more or less inhibiting. In the long run, none of them is more helpful to an institution in transformation than the first type.

mad entrepreneurs

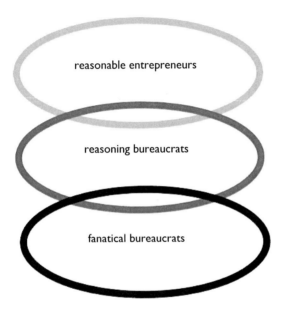

reasonable entrepreneurs

reasoning bureaucrats

fanatical bureaucrats

Figure 4.   Second type entrepreneurs and bureaucrats.

Below is an example in which this framework for analysis is used to better grasp the transformation of one of the main sub-systems of a large French company that we have been able to observe.

The underground company: collusion and clandestinity

In this sub-system, a far-reaching transformation of current management processes was launched. This transformation was aimed at greatly increasing the company's efficacy, in particular in its relationship to clients and to its environment more broadly. In order to do that, it put in place a process aimed at highlighting the differentiation between experts and managers, and at reducing the numbers of layers of management, while at the same time decentralizing decision-making and developing the practice of strategic thinking.

Some way into the implementation of this process, the leader of this institution asked us to help him to better evaluate how much progress was being made. Here are a few points that we highlighted.

Not surprisingly, this transformation generated resistances. Among them, we noticed that a whole group of people had gathered in a seemingly silent collusion: we found those who felt that they were left out by the system and its transformation; the "old ones" for whom adapting is sometimes—but only sometimes—more difficult; trade unions who engaged in conservative behaviours; some grassroots people, too rarely invited to contribute to the transformation process; those who had not yet been affected by the implementation of new modes of functioning; and, finally, many of those who could not locate themselves on the management hierarchy (for example, the experts), now the new organizational trend.

This collusion into an *underground company* manifested itself mostly in central services, i.e., functional departments that work to support central and operational management: administration, HR, technical experts, internal audit . . . indeed, these services represented the old, prestigious mode of organization of this hitherto large, centralized company.

From now on, they would be perceived as the bureaucratic leftovers from a previous age (an age of hegemony); worse still, they had become scapegoats for a type of functioning that people wished to distance themselves from and forget. They also became the point of convergence for people removed from field operations in order to slim down the workforce and increase productivity. Thus, given their difficulty in transforming, central services experienced an avoidance strategy orchestrated by the Board of Directors: they sat and waited.

From then on, the system reacted through making things more complicated: a myriad of costs were inputted, waves of unread memos flowed through the institution, missions increased exponentially, and numerous individuals and flatterers went about with their dismay and their uncertainties.

Then resistances are brought up. They come through as questioning, or even refusal to understand for those held back by doubts, of bitterness for those truly excluded from the process, of difficulty in pulling together for followers, of passive, or even sometimes active, opposition for those supporting transformation, of self-delusion through fantasies, which in turn could generate open attacks or potential conspiracies, i.e., collusions.

In this example, our representation of how role archetypes, in central services, are distributed is as described below.

The hierarchy of managers, which also includes the Director, gives the transformation its impulse. These managers can be considered as mad entrepreneurs.

Middle managers, who manage support services connected to operational management, appeared during the transformation process. They gradually find their place and take up the roles of reasonable entrepreneurs, which include both an aspect of mad entrepreneurs and one of reasoning bureaucrats.

Recognized experts form a group of rather reasoning bureaucrats, while the rest of the central services harbours a large number of fanatical bureaucrats.

The future of transformation, which hesitates between the initial impulse given by the Board and the resistances that it has brought up, depends on the type of association that will ultimately be chosen:

- an unhelpful association of a *second type* (i.e., reasonable entrepreneurs, reasoning bureaucrats, fanatical bureaucrats), in which collusion between reasoning and fanatical bureaucrats can ruin transformation, at least in central services, which will then become a truly underground and resistant network.
- a helpful association of a *first type* (i.e., mad entrepreneurs, reasonable entrepreneurs, reasoning bureaucrats), in which the success of the cascading process—mainly, the initiative of mad entrepreneurs being communicated to reasonable entrepreneurs—is also a guarantee for the success of transformation.

Given this, the task of leaders is to encourage helpful work alliances—including cascading processes among managers—and to

prevent, with much vigilance and firmness, the collusion of bureaucrats. The future of transformation depends on it.

In this example, the collusion between different roles is used to
better resist transformation and, in some cases, block the system.
Given the size of the institution, the collusion also comes across as a
set of intertwined, occult, and far-reaching networks that manipu-
late people in their roles, sometimes without them even knowing it.

As a way of concluding . . .

Colluding, transforming, conforming

Collusion, thus, is one of the main mechanisms of resistance to
transformation. It jeopardizes it, partially or totally, to the point of
shaping the person's or the institution's journey in a process of
conforming rather than transforming. Collusion changes transformation into conformation (Figure 5).

Conformation comes from the Latin *cum-formare*, "to form *with*",
"to give a definite form to", which gives conformation "form,
disposition, arrangement, adaptation", and also to conform,
conformist (1634) "he who conforms to the doctrines and rituals of
the Anglican Church" (from the *Dictionnaire historique de la langue
française* [Robert], 1992).

To conform, to become a conformist (see Bertolucci, 1970), is to
accept entering a mould. It means adopting an evolution towards a
set model that one seeks to attain. This journey is not truly one of

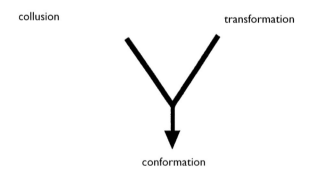

collusion   transformation

conformation

Figure 5. Collusion changes transformation into conformation.

transformation: on the contrary, it is an attempt to do away with it. On the one hand, the objective one is seeking becomes a precise and intangible goal; it is preconceived, conceptualized according to a doctrine, or at least a theory, and not virtual (as in form *B* of transformation [see p. 00]); most of all, the journey of conformation is meant as direct and wilful: it tends to carefully avoid resistances and also anxiety, linked, among other things, to the uncertainty of the result.

Hence, the primary reason that leads some people to conform to a model is probably the wish to forgo transformation.

Is that not therefore simply a way of forgoing life, since it is on this painful and sometimes frightening confrontation of resistances, of our resistances, that the success of our own transformation depends, in other words that which gives meaning and value to any individual and collective existence?

Notes

1. This article was published in French in 1996 in the review *Insight*, 3) and in 1997 in *Management et Conjoncture Sociale*, 507: 9–23). It was originally presented by David Gutmann at the University of Bari (Italy) in July 1994.

2. This chapter was translated by Matthieu Daum, Consultant, Nexus, Paris.

CHAPTER ELEVEN

From envy to desire: witnessing the transformation[1]

David Gutmann, with Jacqueline Ternier-David and Christophe Verrier

T his chapter sets out, on the basis of a case example, to discuss the workings of two major affects—desire and envy—as an integral part of the constructive and destructive processes underlying institutional life.

We begin by proposing a definition of desire and envy as both individual and collective feelings, outlining the nature of their impact in organizations. This is followed by an account of a workshop that revealed envy and desire as key elements of the client organization's dominant dynamic. Finally, we offer some concluding remarks on the significance and impact on organizational processes of the transformation from envy to desire.

Desire and envy: conceptual framework

Desire

Etymologically, the word "desire" can be traced back to the Latin term *desiderare*, composed of *de-* (privative) and of *sideris*, "the stars". Desire, therefore, literally means "to stop gazing at the stars"

(*Webster's Third New International Dictionary*) and, hence, "to feel the loss of", "to long or hope for". Thus, the etymological perspective underlines the close relation between desire and lack. It also suggests that understanding one's own desire consists of having one's feet (back) on the ground, no longer being "star struck", moving on (again), being (once again) in reality.

Desire emerges as one of the fundamental affects of an individual's life. Through it we not only exist, but seek to create: families, works of art, buildings, institutions, businesses, and relationships. Desire, therefore, is not only present in institutions, but is also instrumental in their construction, development, and transformation. This desire is, first and foremost, that of the individuals who make up the institution, starting (but not ending!) with that of its leaders. Desire is ever present. At times it can erupt like a volcano and is too destructive to allow for any creativity. At other times, it is like stagnant water in which the products of our individual and collective histories ferment and are deposited, but have not the effervescence to generate the dynamics of creation or transformation. How, then, can it be stirred? How can the inner source of individual or collective desire be awakened? How can one be brought to acknowledge it, to connect it with one's own desire so as to see it as a resource that can lead to transformation and, in the case of an institution, to share it with others or, more precisely, to have one's own desire resonate with that of others?

Consequently, we have come to believe that the primary role of managers is to reveal and bring into interaction the desire—individual and collective—that exists within an institution.

Envy

Envy is another possible response to lack. Unlike desire, however, which can initiate a constructive process, envy harbours destruction. It involves feelings of anger and indeed hate towards the person having an object or quality that one covets, but cannot acquire. The envious person will therefore seek first to destroy the object of envy and then to destroy the person having the object. Envy is first directed at the object, then the person.

One of the most relevant descriptions of the intimate mechanisms of envy is proposed by Melanie Klein (1946–1963), who describes envy as the most potent manifestation of the destructive impulses that "undermine feelings of love and gratitude at their root, since it affects the earliest relation of all, that to the mother" (p. 36). Klein stresses the projective nature of envy, by recalling that the word envy derives from the Latin verb *invideo*: "to look askance at, to cast an evil eye upon" (*Dictionnaire historique de la langue française* [Robert 1992]). Finally, she proposes a number of interpretations of attitudes observed in adults and in interpersonal relationships, which are of great relevance to the theme of this chapter. Thus, envy drives the very ambitious individual to

> the inability to allow others to come sufficiently to the fore. They may be allowed to play a subsidiary part as long as they do not challenge [his/her] supremacy. Such people are unable and not unwilling to stimulate and encourage younger people, because some of them might become their successors. [p. 152]

On the other hand, "where greed and envy are not excessive, even an ambitious person finds satisfaction in helping others to make their contribution" (p. 53). Here we have one of the attitudes underlying successful leadership.

Living institutions live envy

By nature, institutions that are strong, thriving, and imbued more with the life principle than the death principle, do generate within them affects such as envy. Envy can be necessary—provided it is confined and contained—when it contributes to the definition of roles, their structuring, and the demarcation of the boundaries separating them. It is, nevertheless, often a negative process fostering regression rather than progression, destruction rather than construction, if only by colluding with the envy that any thriving institution arouses. It can sometimes completely overwhelm the institution. How, then, can envy be taken out of the equation when it comes to analysing the processes at work in an institutional context?

Narcissism, envy and guilt

It is our belief that envy and guilt form and fuel a vicious circle. On the one hand, envy arouses guilt in the person who seeks to spoil or destroy the (human) object of envy. On the other hand, however, envy can stem directly from an even deeper guilt. It is the guilt that is experienced by those who know themselves neither to be perfect, nor to conform to the *ego ideal* that their own narcissism continually exalts. (Ego ideal is a term used by Freud in his second theory on the human psyche: a condition of the personality resulting from the convergence of narcissism [idealization of self] and identification with the parents, their substitutes, and collective ideals. As a differentiated condition, the ego ideal constitutes a model to which the subject seeks to conform. See Laplanche and Pontalis, 1992, p. 184.) Envy is anger at falling short of perfection, irrespective of past successes and satisfactions (Figure 6).

In the case of the head of an institution, this guilt, associated with the impossibility of satisfying a narcissistic need, has an impact on the institution as a whole. The inability to attain perfection causes a corporate leader to adopt a posture of omnipotence in which he/she seeks refuge, and which the rest of the institution tends to accept. This is, first, because he/she has a degree of power that can make this attitude prevail and, second, because he/she places this indomitable and insatiable narcissistic need as a vital issue at the very heart of the institution. Thus, envy pervades the

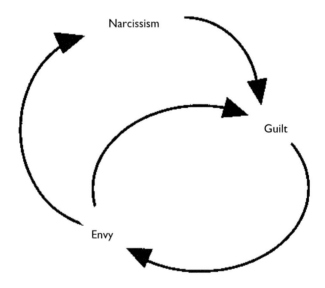

Narcissism

Guilt

Envy

Figure 6.   Process of envy.

institution in so far as each of its members seeks to meet this impossible demand that the leader soon comes to personify. No longer able to "live up to" the demands placed upon them, everyone is dragged into the guilt process. Then all that matters is presumed proximity to the leader's ideal, directly inspired by his/her narcissistic need. Any reference to the profound and individualized desire of the institution's members is then, of course, impossible. And those attempting to progress by standing in the way of this process are destroyed or rejected.

In this way, the leader in an institution overwhelmed by envy is placed in a position of omnipotence, continually imposing on others a guilt-engendering comparison with his/her own ideal: an ego ideal imposed as a permanent point of reference that impacts on all other members of the institution. The hold exercised through this imposition of the leader's ego ideal impedes the working of desire within the institution. The institution as a whole lives under the illusion that it can only be transformed through the action of its leader.

Witnessing the transformation: an account of the workshop

In this section we describe a consultation experience that took place in 1993 in order to offer a number of hypotheses about organizational processes. Our intervention consisted of preparing and running a self-contained workshop, and we shall focus on the workshop itself and on its preparation in so far as it also yielded elements of understanding. However, as is often the case with such organizational interventions, it was the actual fact that such a workshop even took place that proved most revealing of the processes at work within this institution.

For obvious reasons of confidentiality, we do not cite the institution concerned by name, nor do we name the main protagonists. We refer to the corporation in question (an American high technology company), which relocated a part of its facilities to Israel, as HT, and to the Israeli subsidiary as HT Israel.

The genesis of the workshop

HT Israel is the largest of the corporation's facilities located outside the USA. It includes a production unit employing 700 people and a centre for design, research, and development. Much of its success is due to the remarkable and sustained development it has enjoyed over a number of years, and which today places it at the cutting edge of global competitiveness and ensures its short-term survival.

The considerable—and continual—challenge facing HT is reflected in a constant process of ruthless selection and competition among the people working in each of the corporation's sites. This Anglo-Saxon trait runs head-on into Israel's culture and heritage of courage (HT was the only company to remain operational during the Gulf War), to say nothing of its survival-mindedness. It is also to be noted that HT Israel is headed by its founder (whom we refer to here as S), who invented a process that has largely contributed to the company's success, and that consequently confers added potency to his authority within the Israel-based operation.

The Director of the Production Unit (whom we refer to as M), initiated the management's decentralization by reducing the hierarchical ranks from four to three and then two, introduced new work schedules, and appointed a woman (N) as Total Quality Facilitator. However, this transformation was slow in making its way into the day-to-day running of the production unit. At the time of our initial intervention, David Gutmann, one of our team, had been consulting to M as an adviser in leadership since 1991.

One of our initial hypotheses—shared by M—was that nothing seemed to be lacking at the Production Unit. All that was needed for its success was in place. But this "absence of lack" is also an absence of desire. By thwarting transformation of the unit's management, this "completeness" also prevented the institution and the people in it from understanding, expressing, and effecting their individual and collective desire.

In March 1992, M attended the workshop on "Authority, leadership and innovation" organized near Paris by the International Forum for Social Innovation and directed by David. (For some twenty years now, this working conference, renamed in 1993 "Authority, leadership and transformation", has been furthering the tradition of human behaviour training, founded on the ideas of Bion, and first launched in London in the 1950s by Pierre Turquet and Ken Rice.) In July 1992, M suggested that David should organize such a workshop at the Production Unit for the seventy managers working there. Hence, this methodology came to be applied *in vivo*, in a corporate setting, and in Israel, the country of miracles and faith (Gutmann, Ternier-David, & Verrier, 1997).

The preparation

The work done in the run-up to this workshop took much time and effort. It involved our Paris-based team of consultants, as well as our British colleague, Jon Stokes. We finally opted for a two-session programme. The first of these was to be a four-day session with three exercises built up around the central theme of *here and now* (an approach whereby each participant works through certain experiences by exploring the methods proposed during the seminar and learning from these experiences. The discussion sessions then help them to assimilate, transform, and relate these to what they experience day-to-day within their institutions). The first exercise focused on relationships between the roles corresponding to the three hierarchical levels at the Production Unit. The second dealt with individual involvement in the Unit's decision-making process, while the third covered relations with management in a competitive context. *Transformation analysis groups* were set up, and regular meetings were programmed between the two sessions to continue this work. The second session, lasting a day and a half, was designed to give the participants some time out after the first, and to measure the headway that had been made in overcoming resistances (Bion, 1961; Gutmann, Ternier-David, & Verrier 1995).

The project thus presented was approved by M. It was agreed that the consultant staff, headed by David, would be made up mainly of members of Praxis International (a company of Advisers in Leadership, founded in 1989 and based in Paris, whose role is to work with managers from public or private institutions on the transformation of their roles). Then, in March 1993, just one month prior to the workshop, came a dramatic turn of events: S, the Director of HT Israel, decided to call the whole thing off, refusing to "bring in" consultants who were not from HT or Israel.

This about-turn led to a new proposal being put forward: if S opposed the idea of having seven external consultants, then the number would have to be drastically reduced. This meant members of the Production Unit management team—that is to say, the dozen Department Managers—had to take all the staff roles. As a result, the conference staff comprised the Production Unit Director (in the role of Workshop Director) and the Department Managers (who were to act as managers and facilitators), accompanied by the consultants. The staff's role was twofold: to "direct" the seminar and take responsibility for "boundary management" so that all participants were actively involved; to act as facilitators during certain sessions. The "casting" under the original workshop proposal was therefore completely changed: whereas, initially, the Production Unit's managerial team was to take charge of management of the workshop (with M acting as Workshop Director), it suddenly found itself both in a management and in a consultation role, as facilitator.

Provision consequently had to be made for training these Department Managers in readiness for their role as facilitators to the other participants (the seventy Group Leaders). To this end, we set up a pre-workshop, which was to last a day and a half and immediately precede the workshop itself.

After some tough negotiation, this new proposal was accepted. Only two external consultants, David and Jon, would take part in the workshop. H, an internal consultant from the Human Resources Department of HT, was brought in from the USA especially to work with them.

This decision was not, however, taken lightly. In view of the lengthy training needed to prepare members of staff for a workshop of this kind, there was no question of "letting loose" the Production Unit managers as facilitators, although four people—the Director, N, H, and one of the Department Managers—were more prepared for work of this kind than the others, owing to their earlier participation in here and now seminars. Four measures were therefore taken to provide the relevant backup and support:

● Each of the two sessions was preceded by a pre-workshop during which the external consultants "primed" the managers of HT Israel for their role as facilitators. The working groups in which this preparatory work took place were known as *consultation analysis groups.*
● During the workshop, and on the fifth day, the facilitators were supervised by the consultants: the consultation analysis groups met twice daily so as to gain a better understanding of the facilitator role of the Department Managers.

- David, in the meantime, continued to act as leadership adviser to the Director and the staff as a whole.
- Finally, daily staff meetings were held, alongside the consultation analysis groups, to continue the process of clarification and interpretation of the life of the system as a whole, as well as each of its sub-systems. These meetings served to ensure containment of the workshop, that is to say, to guarantee that members of staff did not target other participants with their own projections, and to provide a climate in which individual professionalism could be enhanced by developing mechanisms of co-operation and support between the various sub-systems.

These measures were the final elements in the preparation for the programme, called "Leadership, competition and transformation". As a result of our preparatory work, we had devised an original working approach, whereby professional managers were given a more active part to play in the consultation process. We acted on the belief that achieving success in such a technologically innovative corporation might mean bringing in potential innovation in the area of human development.

The workshop (20–24 April, 1993)

As our description of the run-up period set out to illustrate, this workshop was a learning experience for all concerned: the participants (Group Leaders), the workshop staff (the Director, M, and the Department Managers), and the external consultants (David, Jon and H), but also the members of the workshop preparation team who stayed behind in Paris. It would be difficult to chronicle an event as complex and multi-faceted as a four-day workshop that eventually brought together seventy-four participants. We shall, therefore, confine ourselves to setting out the broad lines of our programme.

We framed this workshop in every way as a "learning institution", if only a temporary one. Viewing an institution as a place of learning for one and all opens up a new understanding—and potentially acceptance—of role differentiation. The institution is no longer perceived as a place where only its leaders hold the truth and are seen as having exclusive access to power and knowledge, but rather as a place where it is possible to imagine decentralized forms of management, and indeed co-management.

During the first part of the workshop, M discovered the role of Workshop Director. Step by step, he found his own mode of operating. During the "competition" sessions, he came up with a very useful working hypothesis when he said "each Department Manager is his or her department's gladiator". In other words, Group Leaders are in the arena of management through a "filtering down" process, through the "sacrificial" mediation of the Department Managers. This does shed light on the imaginary relation between these roles, where the Group Leaders "use" Department Managers while avoiding any direct risk-taking or development of their own authority.

With this image, M expressed not only a working hypothesis interpreting the way Production Unit management take up their roles, but perhaps something much deeper about his own condition as manager of HT Israel. It suggested that he himself is the gladiator for the whole system. S, the director of HT Israel, entrusts to him the responsibility for doing battle (first at the Production Unit, and then from 1994 onwards at the Design Centre), each time "putting himself on the line" professionally, his sole reward being to stay alive, to survive the system, without any special glory or truly recognized merit. Such struggles can be to the death; that is to say, they might even involve expulsion from the system.

We shall return to a discussion of the processes that were brought to light during the workshop. At this juncture, however, we would observe that the workshop as a whole showed just how the members of the Production Unit felt "locked in" to the dominant culture of survival, which seems to foster not only immediate action on long-term strategy, but also a lack of confidence and ill-contained aggressiveness. The feeling of being trapped in the past condemns the future, which is not perceived as an open space where a wealth of possibilities might unfold. The new generation, exposed to the *de facto* cultural domination of the elders, is particularly affected by this (Gutmann, Ternier-David, & Verrier, 1996). A characteristic feature of this sense of being trapped, or locked in, is the blocking of individual and collective desire, which is then not mobilized within the institution. Its members silence their own desire for fear that expressing it might endanger them, have them broach the forbidden, or break a taboo.

This configuration predisposes the institution to accepting and reinforcing the dangerous process whereby one of its leaders is cast in the role of saviour: M, the Production Unit's "voluntary" director, who represents the new generation, or indeed S, the founding father of HT Israel, so deeply enmeshed in this survival culture. One Group Leader's friendly gibe at M during the plenary closing session, "We're all coming with you from the Production Unit to the Design Centre!", was highly revealing. It meant that M was seen as the archetypal leader, much like his predecessor in this region of the world, Moses! The question merits consideration, as there is an association rooted in tradition between S and Moses within this company. If M is seen as the new Moses, this also raises the whole question of leadership succession.

The work between the two sessions

The period between the two sessions was marked by two contradictory tendencies: continuing development *vs.* the (re-)emergence of resistance to change. The work begun in the April workshop was sustained in regular meetings of the transformation analysis groups (twelve Group Leaders, with a Department Manager as facilitator, as at the workshop) and in the working pair built up between M and David.

In July, a half-day meeting was convened, with M, the Department Managers, a few Group Leaders, and David, to assess the progress initiated by the April workshop. As it turned out, some of the groups had made real progress, while others had met only once or twice, and some not at all.

It was as though the element of surprise experienced in the workshop had now worn off. Being caught by surprise or "off guard" can often be a way forward, for it overrides a good many resistances—if only for a moment. Indeed, surprise was one of the processes in April that went some way to making the workshop run smoothly. The seven-month gap between the two sessions seemed to have given everyone space to take time out, to "shut off", and to re-erect their resistance. The work was also made more difficult by the absence of the external consultants.

Second, however, the work between the two sessions was significantly marked by the appointment of M as head of HT Israel's Design Centre. His departure from the Production Unit was scheduled for 1 January 1994, when he was to be replaced by J, his predecessor at the Design Centre. This decision on the part of HT Israel's Director had a number of consequences. There is no denying that it undermined the process set in motion by the experience of the workshop: it was as though this changeover of managers was, consciously or unconsciously, intended to neutralize the results that were starting to come through. The Production Unit therefore found itself preparing for a changeover of leaders just as the transformation of its organization and culture was pursuing its course and it was undergoing an unprecedented learning experience under the "Leadership, competition and transformation" programme.

As a result, it was deemed essential to have the fifth day focus on this central event of the changeover between M and J. The latter was consequently invited to join the workshop staff alongside his predecessor. The objectives being pursued under the programme also had to incorporate this transition in the continuity of action, that is to say, the continuity of the transformation and the learning process.

The period between the two sessions was also a time of preparation for the fifth day. During this stage, N seemed to take it upon herself to speak on behalf of the institution as a whole, expressing focused resistances, which, in this instance, concerned the scheduling and duration of the December session. The tension reached such a point that the second session of the workshop nearly did not take place. An agreement as to the working approach was nevertheless achieved.

A particular manifestation of resistance appeared in the behaviour of many Department Managers. Most of them were clearly determined not to be taken by surprise again, and therefore attempted to prepare for the second session in their own way. Some went to great lengths to try to find out about any unexpected exercises, although they did, of course, know what was on the programme, as they had themselves helped to define it at the July working group. Some entered into a process of collusion, even going as far as rehearsing what they would say and do on the fifth day. This "conspiratorial" behaviour, about which J had serious misgivings, accentuated the diminishing power of M, who was then just one month away from leaving the Production Unit (Gutmann, 1989; Gutmann, Ternier-David, & Verrier, 1996).

The fifth day (over 2 and 3 December, 1993)

It was the recognition of these events and attitudes that led David to realize, on the evening of the fifth day at the staff meeting following the work done with the Group Leaders, that everything had ground to a halt under the effect of these combined resistances. At this point, he took the decision to withdraw from the meeting, taking Jon and H with him. In so doing, he forestalled M, who was on the verge of walking out, but found himself instead left with J and the Department Managers.

This instantly brought down resistances, though not completely and only for a time. Our experience, in fact, shows that resistances rarely give way gradually, but yield all of a sudden, like the onset of a catharsis, or the collapse of the Berlin Wall in 1989. In the dynamics of the workshop, the consultants' departure was also "Un acte de passage prévenant un passage à l'acte" (Balmary, 1986), an action or act of transition preventing an acting out. In other words, by taking this action (act of transition), the consultants were able to get the system past deadlock and got the director off the hook. They avoided his early departure from the scene, if only symbolically (transition in action), seeing as how M was handing over power to J on 1 January 1994, and not 2 December 1993. The consultants were, at the same time, able to pull out of the maelstrom and take time out to distance themselves from the situation.

Upon their return—forty-five minutes later—the mood was one of distress and foreboding. This situation was very telling, and brings us to the core of our working hypothesis, which we will again be discussing later on. What had happened was that the feeling of lack had allowed desire to express itself more fully, and to some extent override the envy that was dominant at that moment. The transformation that had taken place could thus be seen for what it was: it was not about the managers taking over from the consultants, or one manager taking over from another (J from M), but the transformation from envy to desire.

And so, upon their return, M again took charge as Workshop Director, with J at his side, facing the troops—the Department Managers—some of whom were in full regression. The following day, as planned, J took over as Workshop Director during an open work session. The transition phase had well and truly started.

During this second session of the programme, H, who had made a real and enthusiastic contribution in April, seemed to show greater resistance, going as far as to cancel a meeting scheduled with Jon "so I can get some sleep". Confronted with David's desire to continue—with her and his work at HT Corporate, she reinforced her resistance by implying that this kind of process was useful in Israel, but impossible in the USA. She acted as though coming up against this process of discovering a desire, or a host of desires each stronger than the others, should remain a happy experience, but be "done with" at a certain point, as though it had to be "wrapped up" at all costs. It was as if these desires triggered her envy in the face of the success of the process and her fear of having to take authority for spreading word of this transformation in the USA.

This second session was, therefore, an opportunity to mark the changeover from M to J. And yet, judging from the gibe directed at M at the end of the April session ("We're all coming with you from the Production Unit to the Design Centre!"), the personal handover between M and J did not seem to be perceived as conforming to the biblical metaphor referred to above, where Joshua succeeds Moses—who dies—and enters alone into the Promised Land, heading the people of Israel. This is why the work done at the Production Unit on a day-to-day basis, combined with the workshop, no doubt made for a smoother handover, also in terms of technological and industrial efficiency.

In a manner of speaking, reality confirmed this intuition. As soon as he took over, J found an institution that was in "good shape" (shape as in form, as in trans-formation). It was a transformation that, irrespective of this manager's action, was unquestionably not only in progress, but set to last, with a creative momentum that brought excellent tangible results. M, for his part, spent some time at the Design Centre, where he faced a considerable challenge, which he pulled off with success, before leaving HT in 1996.

It was possible to trace impact of the workshop three main areas:

- Day-to-day working relationships within the Production Unit improved, as a result of reducing resistance to the recent de-layering within the senior management team from three to two. The idea or fantasy of a "shadow third rank" in the management hierarchy was removed.
- Most participants were enabled to discover a new understanding of their role and authority within the system. In particular, they were able to increase their capacity to act with authority in relation to the primary task of the factory.
- Although the workshop was not entirely appreciated by either the Director of HT Israel nor by J, many participants were able to gain a sense of distance from the company and to reduce its hold on them. After M left, some other participants also left the Production Unit; indeed, some left HT altogether.

One intended effect that did not occur, because of the interruption to the process, was the transmission of the learning from the Group Leaders to the Production Unit workers.

From envy to desire

This—for us exceptional—experience in Israel led us to wonder about the content the workshop and about the working hypotheses that had emerged from it, to say nothing of the processes involved in its preparation and implementation. What were the determinants and consequences of such a workshop? Could one pinpoint the main conscious and unconscious processes that had weaved their way through the institution during it? It was such *a posteriori* considerations that led us, four years later, to formulate a number of working hypotheses concerning the whole issue of envy and desire in institutions.

As stated earlier, envy and desire, whether at the individual or institutional level, are two possible responses—albeit in fundamental opposition to one another—to lack and, more generally, to a sense of void, imperfection (or the desire for perfection), and to incompleteness. But, while desire may drive one to fill this void through creativity, which is a vital life impulse, envy, by contrast, leads to the destruction of the object of envy and the person possessing that object.

Both these affects play a major role in the life of institutions. After much thought and deliberation following our experience at HT Israel, the main working hypothesis we arrived at was that *the fundamental task of managers consists of moving from envy to desire through the process of transformation.*

An institution dominated by envy

We found HT to be institutionally dominated by envy, as it was long before the actual run-up to the workshop. The resulting dynamics—discreet, veiled, covert, or, indeed, deliberately obscured though they might have been—were nevertheless at work throughout the run-up to the workshop and during the workshop itself.

S appeared not only to be the institution's absolute leader, but was also crowned with a glory born of his past successes in research and development. It was he who founded this corporation and was instrumental in making it the success it came to be. In a manner of speaking, he is, additionally, all this and more *vis-à-vis* the State of Israel, for it was he who "imported" this prestigious American corporation to its territory. S, on the other hand, seemed so possessed by a desire for eternity, so wanting to stay on as head of HT Israel for as long as possible, that he systematically cast aside any potential successors. All the conditions were right for driving S in search of perfection, which he implicitly imposed on his co-workers, and which is reflected in the intense rivalry they were all caught up in.

One possible interpretation of this demand for unbounded narcissism is perhaps to be found in history: some of HT's main leaders (including S and M) lived through the Shoah or its aftermath, such as post-war emigration from Europe. This may have left them permanently scarred and given rise to a narcissism of compensation. This probably accounts for the desire to be entrepreneurial (especially in a field where technology can give the illusion of omnipotence and omniscience), but it also reinforces the posture of omnipotence that can be found, for example, in the discourse of excellence, or Total Quality Management.

Envy appeared to be uppermost in the relationship between M and S, with the added dimension that the succession to the top position at HT Israel was at stake. In a way, the workshop made S face up to this, for he seemed to deny it with all his being. Perhaps this was a reminder for him of his own mortality and the limited nature of life, particularly in relation to the potentially infinite duration of the institution he was instrumental in creating and which, by defi- nition, knows no biological limit. What he envies in M is his—rela- tive—youth and the few years' difference that give him the opportunity of taking over a role that has mattered to him so much personally. Naturally enough, this envy has a rebound effect on the institution as a whole.

What appears to have been at issue at the time of the workshop was, therefore, the future of M, the new candidate to succeed S. Would he be cast aside like all the others? Or would he be able to set in motion what is needed to "release" S from his role as saviour, and the institution from its "locked in" state?

| HOLD | DESPISE (and not SURPRISE) |
| CONTEMPT | |

No more star-gazing

Desire arises when the members of the institution stop looking (up) at their leader as a perfect being, like a star, which is out of reach, and thus refuse to be in collusion with his narcissism. Comparison with an ideal—and idealized—object then clearly appears as a "blind alley". Lack becomes what engenders freedom.

From that moment on, the leader can take a step back, not by relinquishing his role, but by partially effacing himself, leaving a kind of void at the head of the institution. Space is then made for what is possible. Creativity stems from the lack and the desire engendered by this anxiety. From desire arises authority, but an authority expressed by the greater number (critical mass) of the institution's members. With desire "on the up", plural authority enables a new distribution of roles: a stepping-down, an emergence of co-authors of transformations in progress, generativity, and the generation of new leaders.

HT Israel again illustrates this representation of desire: during the run-up to and the actual workshop, there were two stars (S and

M) co-existing within the institution and fuelling processes of iden-tification. And while the one begins to gently wane, the other slowly but surely gains momentum by deploying his authority and talent. At the same time, however, this "changeover" of stars opens up a psychological and temporal space, wherein the rising star has not yet taken over from the waning one: it occurs when there is no one star, and it is laden with all the energy of lack and desire (Figure 7). In superseding S as a star, however, M is also running the risk of having to fill this temporary and fragile void that we identify as the main source of desire at this moment in the life of the institution.

The transformation from envy to desire

And so, on the one hand, a thriving institution knows envy; on the other hand, the life principle of an institution is nourished by the desire of its members, who can only express this when the leader relinquishes a position of omnipotence. Consequently, one of the crucial transformations to be undertaken by managers consists in moving from envy to desire. As we see it, this occurs in stages, three of which we discussing here: *sideration* through envy, consideration, desire. ("Sideration" [from the Latin *sideris*, meaning stars] is a medical term, indicating sudden paralysis. The word's origin reflects the belief that the attack or condition was caused by the malign influence of the stars. Despite its awkwardness in English, the word is maintained here because of its links to the themes under discussion.)

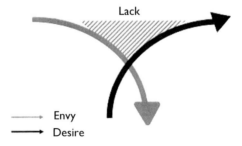

Figure 7, The absence of a star arouses desire.

Sideration through envy

The sideration stage is that of deadlock. Envy has such a strong hold that people are "star struck" to the point of being paralysed by the (idealized) object of their envy. The ideal of the other (that of the leader), becomes the ego ideal, and vice versa. One's own free will vanishes completely, leaving the way open for the processes of mimesis, repetition, uniformity, and, indeed, "cloning". The world seems to be one of absolutes and of completeness: metaphorically, like the world of the exact sciences, repudiating human reality in its complexity, uncertainty, plurality, and diversity.

Consideration

To go beyond the sideration stage, it is essential to move from the singular to the plural. This means going from the contemplation of a single star to that of a constellation of stars. In other words, it is about accepting that processes of identification be directed not towards a single leader, but towards many (Figure 8).

Although this may only be an intermediate stage, the difference is considerable. The plurality introduced opens up a multi-dimensional field making differentiation possible. Identification is no longer about contemplating a single being that transforms you into an object, but attentively observing a diversity of beings so that one is made aware of one's own diversity. This sets in motion interactions between sub-systems (external or internal to oneself): it is the re-emergence of life itself.

This can be likened to the development of a young child, whereby, in order to discover its own singularity and to progress from the relationship of fusion (i.e., to separate from the mother), the infant becomes aware of its father. In so doing, it moves from a situation of identification with a single being—one it has trouble differentiating from itself—to consideration of a two-star constellation. Thus, the infant discovers the plural, the diversity of the sexes, which it then relates to its own inner diversity, its own singularity. Henceforth, it exists as a being in its own right. It is not surprising, then, that the infant's interest at this stage turns to the world at large, starting with its own family.

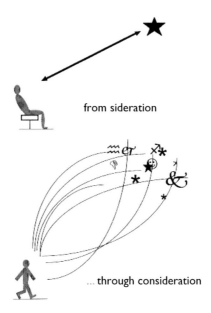

Figure 8.   From sideration through consideration.

Desire

This life "regained" allows each and every one to rediscover his/her own identity, integrity, and singularity as a human and social being and to allow his/her own specific desire to come through as another response to the question of void and lack. The institution can then become an arena for the expression and "working through" of individual and collective desires.

Preparation of the workshop showed how the changeover between the consultants and managers opened the way to a transformation from envy to desire. It is to be remembered that it was S, by refusing to let in foreign consultants, who led to this workshop format being adopted. So it was that the twelve Department Managers, acting as facilitators, took their place alongside M, facing the Group Leaders. By proposing a form of co-management, by showing them that all seventy of them no longer had to converge "towards the one", M was able to release the paralysis of sideration, wherein he was the only focus (thus making him a substitute for S, "the star"?), and so enter consideration, where the seventy could consider the constellation of twelve.

However, everything seemed to indicate that this discovery had begun seriously to jeopardize the sole star and its idealization: the process ground to a halt at this stage, just as the next stage—that of desire—was about to come through. The fact that M left to go to the Design Centre made it impossible to get through the next stages where the collective, plural—but also singular—desire of each organizational member could really emerge.

More specifically, the role of the three consultants was to accompany M in his passage from star to human being. Similarly, for the Department Managers, taking on the role of facilitator meant displaying not their "sidereal archetype" attributes as technicians or managers, but their humanity. They had to do this by starting with their imperfections, just as they were having to take on a role they were unfamiliar with, despite being well-prepared for it. It all seemed as if M had taken the role of Moses, needing an Aaron to take his word to the people, a Joshua to succeed him in the Promised Land, and a Jethro as consultant, for he is not infallible.

The evening of the fifth day of the workshop could be seen as a compressed experience of transformation from envy to desire with its three crucial steps:

- sideration, when there was a strong temptation to idealize M (or J) as a single star chosen from among the many;
- consideration, when this process focused on the twelve Department Managers plus the three consultants, like a constellation;
- desire, when it was finally understood that stars cannot offer more than light.

Epilogue

When an institution expresses more desire than envy, then transformation is under way. In other words, the transformation of envy into desire is a sure sign that the institution itself is undergoing that transformation without which it cannot survive in its struggle against the entropy that threatens its existence.

The workshop gave the protagonists from the Production Unit the opportunity to live a transformation. It took them out of the day-to-day life of the institution where it would have been impossible, or extremely difficult, to undertake this voyage of discovery. It did not, however, take them into a manipulative pseudo-reality that would have made the whole thing nothing more than imaginary role-playing. This workshop, which gave them "time out" (in spite of nearly being stopped in its tracks), also took them from envy to desire as an institutional configuration. This movement allowed organizational members to recognize their diversity, to form alliances, and actually to undertake work together. (The French word *entreprendre*—to undertake—literally means "to take up together", underlining the extent to which human activity calls for alliance and the "crossing over" of differences.)

The passage from envy to desire also casts the role of consultant in a different light, especially when he/she accompanies, or is witness to, a process of transformation and to the work of the leaders spearheading it. During the workshop in question, the consultants were in the here and now, not only observing, but also making the journey of transformation with everybody else.

This experience suggests that transformation requires witness, through a dynamic, cross-referencing presence that encourages it to continue. The consultants of Praxis International provided this witnessing presence, while at the same time being the instruments of the passage from envy to desire. Their role was to recognize this transformation and to have the managers share in the experience. They did this by helping the managers take up the role(s) of director and/or facilitator, simply by being involved in the consultation process. They were there, helping M—and the others—to make the journey of transformation.

Note

1.   This article was published in 1999 in *Group Relations, Management and Organisation*, edited by Robert French and Russ Vince (Oxford University Press).

CHAPTER TWELVE

Paradoxes and transformation in the role of consultant: from reparation to revelation[1,2]

David Gutmann, with Jacqueline Ternier-David and Christophe Verrier

T hose who choose to live and work in an institutional setting have various motivations: they find there an income, relative security (if not effective protection), and they also get a social standing and a way of integrating which is, very often, unique. They also try to enlarge and increase their action, their creativity, and their authority; i.e., their ability to become authors.

The institution enables them to do what they could not achieve alone: in the best circumstances, it is grounded on a shared desire. And eventually, if the main richness for the company is the human one, the company also represents a richness for its members.

Nevertheless, those who choose the institution elect, at the same time, to enter a wider restraining field, born from the tensions between the individual and the collective need to serve a given fundamental target. Life within the institution demands of those who are part of it that they give up the phantasm of total freedom.

Besides, every company or institution is, because of its very nature, a cause of wounds for the people within.

This text aims to explore precisely this very painful side of life within the institution, and to try to understand what the main consequences are.

Every company is bruising; even more, without appropriate regulation, it can become murderous. Then, a strong propensity towards assuaging appears. Yet, revelation can alleviate suffering and heal, or even, to a certain extent, prevent, the wounds.

Thus, revelation and reparation are not only different notions, but both originate from different ethics, aesthetics, and methodology.

This is what we are going to analyse from a general perspective and from a particular example of an intervention we experienced in our consulting practice.

Reparation and revelation

The bruising institution

By its very nature, every institution is constraining, if not traumatizing. Indeed, it applies rules, a setting, and limits in order to achieve the fundamental target it has decided on: that is, generally, to create an added value when working with the environment.

Everyone that lives or works within an institution—not only a private or public organization, or an administration, but also a family, or a school—endlessly has to face the constraints of life in a community as well as the roles differentiation. In fact, each role has its specific prerogatives, different from those of the others. Everyone must face power, and the other's authority, but also his own abilities. Thus, the manager and his/her assistant have different roles, as well as the father and his child, or the teacher and his/her pupil.

If the institution partly meets the desire of the majority of its members, it also regulates the pleasure principle. (The pleasure principle can be explained as one of the two notions which rule the mind's activity in order to avoid displeasure and to give pleasure [Laplanche & Pontalis, 1992].)

Each person learns to recognize what belongs or does not belong to the fundamental target, and to find his/her way within the institution. Eventually, he/she learns to be tested, approved, evaluated, and paid according to these institution criteria and to the reality principle, of which those who are in charge of the institution have always to be reminded. (The reality principle can be seen as the principle that changes the pleasure principle as far as it succeeds in imposing itself as a regulating principle [*ibid*.].)

Within our study, the reality principle can be understood as the effect created by "reality upon the system". This reality is connected to the environment (the world) in which the system integrates, but also to the inside system constraints linked to the institutional life and its limits, to its fundamental target, and so on. This reality principle tries to transform the pleasure principle and the death principle within the system from an individual as well as from a collective point of view.

From what we have noticed, these restraints and limitations may generate wounds that can hurt the individual in his deepest desires and beliefs: they are mainly of a narcissistic kind and are the price—sometimes very high—one has to pay for public acknowledgment.

But the institutions can experience wounds and sufferings from other origins, the first of them being individual and collective anxiety (see also Gutmann, 1989). First of all, it is born from the collective fear that the institution has to vanish (and this is far more obvious in the private firms operating within highly competitive fields), and this fear echoes our own anguish in facing death.

The survival of the enterprise is the price of this individual and collective anxiety. In our own experience, anxiety works as a vital source to create productive tension, if it is properly transformed into creativity. But, conversely, if it goes on growing, it becomes a source of inhibition, not to say of self-destruction.

The *bruising* company is the one that truly recognizes and regulates the anxiety needed for its creativity; but, as far as possible, it must keep from excess. Thus, it recognizes the wounds caused by this anxiety.

These wounds cannot be prevented: they are linked to the very nature of institutional life. Nevertheless, they generate suffering. How can one deal with it?

In some cases—and particularly when every person strongly acknowledges the link between his/her role, the system, and the fundamental target of the institution, suffering is shared as far as responsibility and constraints in the institution are shared too. Thus, "to suffer" is understood in its first meaning, i.e., *to bear and to support*.

Then, suffering is accepted, worked upon, and understood: the meaning it derives alleviates its intensity.

In these conditions, the balance between this suffering on the one hand and everyone's desire on the other, the weight of what is at stake that everyone accepts supporting, and his/her acceptance of the fundamental target, this balance then benefits this person's professional commitment and, thus, the institution itself.

In other conditions, to suffer means to be submitted, or ever to submit. The suffering caused by wounds is neither spoken of nor understood. Then, a feeling of guilt appears.

In fact, in our cultural traditions, the difficulty of understanding the roots of pain very often becomes a tendency to feel guilty, or to make others feel guilty.

When this feeling of guilt is interiorized by the wounded persons, their behaviour moves towards inhibition, withdrawal, or even self-destruction. However, often those who simultaneously suffer and feel guilty are likely to look for an outside culprit in a rush which confuses guilt and responsibility. In the final analysis, this process leads to the making of a scapegoat meant to free them from their suffering, apparently, at least.

But the specific managers' role, answering for the institution, is to remind us of the reality principle and the constraints setting. It is the reason why the hierarchical disposition is such that it focuses this guilt upon the managers, thanks to a projection system, even if the latter are not directly responsible for those wounds that we have found to be inescapable, because of their link with the very logic of the undertaking institution. Thus, the managers are driven into the role of prosecutors and face the harsh guiltiness the whole system is casting upon them. How can one manage such a feeling?

The answer depends upon each manager and upon his/her ability to account for his/her own feelings and to use them. It depends also upon the process established in common to face this situation and to overcome it.

Either the managers develop this ability as well as the possibility of working upon this guilt, to transform it into responsibility, or this work is impossible and, at best, this guilt drives them to wish to heal the wounds caused by the institution.

The wounds we have mentioned earlier cannot be avoided, but they can be understood, accepted, and sublimated. We intend to name them as "first type" wounds.

They are inherent—as we have written before—in the institution which wants to be perennial and which thus also happens to be bruising. But other situations exist, which are even more dangerous.

The murdering institution

Every institution—and especially every company—answers a vital impulse through and for its growth. But it also harbours, at the same time, a Death principle, which some name entropy. (The *death wishes* (Thanatos) can be defined as aggressive or destructive tendencies aimed at the total reduction of tensions, i.e., to bring the human being back to an inorganic status. They are opposed to the *life wishes* [Eros] to create larger and larger units, and to keep them.)

Some institutions are controlled by this death principle: they become deadly, even lethal, and thus generate misfunctions, side-effects, and accidents.

These misfunctions take the form of particular actions we will study later. But, at the moment, we observe that they can result from a want of decisions that can damage the institution as well as its members.

Generally, these actions involve management, but not that alone: misfunctions may also affect the other institutional groups or sub-systems through struggles and destructive quarrels. This morbidity generates new wounds, different from the first-type ones: if they are not deeper, they are more painful, because they could have been avoided, and because they happen in a context submerged in anxiety and entropy. We will name them the "second-type" wounds.

Thus, we think that not only the bruising, but also the murdering institutions are those in which the transformation process from anxiety into creativity has a reduced, rather bad, effect, or even no effectiveness at all.

Then, two phenomena occur: on the one hand, a growing anxiety at every level of the company, in every sub-system and for everyone; on the other hand, and even more obviously, a weakening creativity and a fall in the firm's results, and, more precisely, as far as quality, adaptability, and ability for collective innovation are concerned, in fact, a fall in the profit-earning capacity. A vicious circle mechanism links, in most cases, both phenomena and leads, in the short or longer run, to the inescapable collapse of the institution.

Thus, not only does the murdering institution constrain, of necessity, but it wounds through morbidity.

Its behaviour is pathological, because it cannot constrain itself as well as its anxiety any longer. It generates not only differentiations, but clefts, negative images which are not worked upon any more, or more incomprehension. And here, fusion and confusion are embedded in roles, as well as in activities and feelings, resulting in inescapable sources of suffering.

As in the example of the bruising institution, the wounds caused by the murdering institution generate feelings of guilt and accusation, towards managers particularly.

Since they are overcome by anxiety and confusion, the latter sometimes take on the robes of the prosecutor—which they are offered—and establish a punishing, autocratic, and destructive management. In some other situations, they give up remembering the reality principle, thus putting the institution in an atonic situation, void of any reactivity or creativity.

In both cases, one can understand that the feelings of guilt are focused upon them even more strongly. As far as the want for reparation born from this guiltiness is concerned, they tend to stay in the background, bidden by the managers' manoeuvres.

Of course, the bruising institution and the murdering institution are nothing but standard representations of the reality we have studied. But it would be illusory to believe that the institutions are classified into two distinct and least Manichean bodies.

Actually, both extremes coexist and are linked very closely within the same institutions, although it is possible to detect the chief trend and the main characteristics of such a system or subsystem.

Every institution is always at the mercy of a regression which causes or increases—at least for a limited time—its murdering disposition. Under particular circumstances, an institution might be vulnerable to such an occurrence: particularly during crisis times, when facing its environment, but also during transformation times and when the leaders are replaced.

Then, when anxiety is obvious, when the manager experiences solitude and is unable to answer both this suffering and this trauma (from a double perspective), he can call upon a consultant's services.

This call is generally focused on a precise and factual point: organization, information technology, strategy, prospective evaluation, marketing, or management. But, in most cases, this call deputizes for another one, implicit or ever unconscious: he/she expects the consultant will heal the wounds that have been inflicted by the institutions itself. Then, the consultant has to operate in lieu of the manager, or, at best, beside him/her, sharing with him/her the weight of this task.

But this reparation is a useless behaviour, which understands neither the wounds nor their causes, nor their effects, and even less the means to alleviate or to suppress them.

Thus, a manager, engaged in reforming his/her institution and facing the ensuing suffering, tells the consultant: "Come and help us enforce this reform . . ." But we may also hear: "Help us to heal and bandage the wounds which are, were, and will be perpetrated by this reform."

This understated call for reparation actually imbues the consultant with the position of a bonesetter, a doctor, not to say a redeemer or a wizard!

Why then change and transform the understated contract of reparation?

In our professional practice, the first target is to identify, either alone or with our colleagues, what the wounds are: be they real or imagined, felt or not, one has to heal.

Then, once the understated want is made clear, in the best possible way, our work is to *transform* the initial want for reparation into a stated contract, or, more precisely, *to be explicit* about revelation. To achieve this goal, we must resist, as much as we can this want for reparation (according to a common saying that could be rendered as: *mending is bandaging, thinking is revealing*).

Everything happens as if our contribution consisted in helping the manager to overcome his/her anxiety and to keep at bay the feelings of guilt already mentioned. We have also to take his/her narcissism into account, since it risks being exposed, challenged, and suffering a great deal during the revealing work. Thus, by continually pushing back this guiltiness and this narcissism, we succeed, in the best circumstances, in creating an "empty" space, from a psychological and political point of view, liberated from the demands for reparation and meant to enable the revelation to root itself, to flourish, and to grow.

What do we mean by revelation?

To reveal is to offer a work hypothesis enabling the rise of a further explanation; it is to add a new light to some elements, to pull them out of the darkness in which they are hidden by unconsciousness, habits, dissimulations, be they deliberate or not; it is to give these elements a different perspective to let others see them differently. And, in the end, it is to link again facts and feelings which, when associated, provide an innovating and proactive interpretation for everyday reality.

We are convinced that a manager, whoever he/she is, has but a more or less limited knowledge of what causes or follows his/her action. He/she must overcome the basic knowledge of this action by succeeding in taking account of the feelings, emotions, and affects that encompass it. *Com-prendre* (to under-stand) means, then, to take together, to put together. And we are truly convinced that an institution can live and grow only if its members take part not only in activities, but also in the understanding (comprehension) and thus in the construction, of this institution.

Thus, revealing is not declaring the truth. To claim the opposite, to try to answer the want for a definitive explanation of reality, would be to suppose that the consultant is able to declare *the* truth. Then, the consultant as well as the manager would be led into the temptation and the phantasm of omniscience and omnipotence.

Per se, revelation is bruising.

The revealing company

Revelation can surprise; it often frightens and it sometimes hurts. It awakens emotions and feelings: fear and courage, depression and enthusiasm, pleasure and pain . . .

The way from reparation to revelation, which is a true transformation of the manager's expectation *vis-à-vis* the consultant, is difficult and painful: as for every transformation, it is a zig-zag route, moving forwards and backwards.

But one of the further steps, the one of the revealing shock, itself might be transitively bruising, because it creates added wounds. For us, these wounds are what we call bruisings of the third type.

These wounds have an important narcissisc element; they are sometimes so traumatic that some people or some institutions are not able to bear what is revealed, they prefer to hide it, or refuse to acknowledge it, or even reject it by reinforcing their own resistance.

However, despite these wounds, the target of the revealing process remains to limit suffering, not through giving a meaning to the first-type wounds—particularly thanks to the clear distinction between the first-type and the second-type wounds—but, in the short or longer run, to alleviate or suppress the second-type wounds.

During this period, the consultant is facing the whole of institutional resistances, including those of the manager who asked for his/her help. Then, the consultant might lose the contract because of the obvious challenge his/her professionalism and his /her deontology has met.

To understand and even to thwart those phenomena, it is essential to understand the revelation mechanism and to try it. That is what we intend to do in the third part of this text, devoted to the very process of revelation.

But before we do that, to throw a light upon this matter, we will give an example from one of our interventions.

One example of intervention: the hot potato

Here is, then, one of our experiences as consultant, during which we had to face the antagonistic pair reparation–revelation. We will tell you the story of this example, while adding some comments, as the work proceeds (these comments will be given in italics, within the text).

Our team, which was then made up of two advisers in leadership and one consultant, took action with the management for internal formation in a large French firm (i.e., 2000 people out of 145,000).

The role of the advisers in leadership is to go with the managers, offering them work hypothesis meant to sift and renew their representations of the institution.

Advisers in leadership are distorting mirrors that reflect images for their partners and throw them back interpretations of those images. They urge the leading teams to clarify the transformations they have started in their institutions and to imagine the future without repeating or reproducing the past.

This intervention was meant to achieve a better understanding and evolution of this department two and a half years after they started to change their structures.

We intervened to formulate, share and extend a diagnosis from a real revealing system made of four stages:

- on the one hand, a series of individual interviews with each of the twenty-six members of the board of directors;
- then a synthesis application composed of exchanges between the department manager, Ms A, her assistant Mr B, and two advisers in leadership (a man and a woman).

The synthesis application is the basis of the job of adviser in leadership. It is a long-term working association between the manager and the adviser in leadership working with him/her.

The aim of this partnership is to transform the manager's role and from it, his/her institution, by summoning up unexploited resources such as the clarification of the leader's role, as well as his/her direction team working with the analysis of the institution seen as a system and the examination of the conscious and unconscious elements that compose and build it.

- in the third place, a seminar of the board (*in situ*, for two and a half days), meant to provide the board with the necessary space to appropriate this diagnosis, to develop it, and, most importantly, to share it.

- Finally, a directing committee (the five main managers with the general manager), intending, with the consulting team, to have feedback on the diagnosis and the seminar.

This organization is to be commented on as follows:

- *it is meant to create mirror systems between advisers and managers. Thus, in the synthesis application, advisers and managers work in pair groups. Thanks to the images reflection process, from one pair to the other, what the consulting pair experiences can give clues as to the way the managing pair works;*
- *all the managers of the directing team, who were interviewed individually, were part of this experience during the seminar, the images were sent back in real time. Nobody could escape them, of course; this particular aspect enhances the resistances strength. But, by letting each person face the disclosed hypothesis, it boosts and accelerates the process.*

Progressively, as the seminar was nearing its end, anxiety was growing, including the Leader's words. Once, she wondered whether the seminar had to be held or not, if it was not jeopardizing the department cohesion.

Not only does this anxiety echo a true feeling of fear and of resistance regarding what is going to be discovered, but it also seems to embody a will to protect the institution, therefore keeping the status quo and strengthening its homeostasis, saving it the possibly painful revision related to the revelation process.

The seminar was meant as a temporary revealing institution.

It aimed less to present the diagnosis we had prepared earlier, each member of the directing team having already perceived, with more or less intuition its lines of force, than to extend this diagnosis, to show openly these lines of force so that the managing team could build itself a shared representation of the management of its department.

The seminar organization was managed by a directory in which managers and consultants worked in close relationship. Ms A took the part of the seminar manager, Mr B the role of joint manager. The three advisers' team was also part of this directory, as well as Ms C, who was chief of cabinet of the department manager (a woman) and who played the part of the seminar Administrator.

This kind of directory, reminding the staff on the symposia about authority and leadership, has many targets. On the one hand, it encourages the main managers to get directly involved in the basic target of the seminar, which is the revelation process. On the other hand, it enables the avoidance of two dangers:

- *the danger of the saving adviser who would tell bits of the truth, since the revelation process is common to consultants and managers;*
- *the danger of the scapegoat adviser in the situation where the group of managers, unable to overcome its resistances and its anxiety facing revelation, could do nothing but unload this anxiety upon the consultants.*

Therefore, this organization enables a shared and intensive work to clarify the resistances, between managers and consultants. Thus, at the head of a temporary revealing institution, a true and solid relationship can appear. It is a relationship of synergy, interdependence, and solidarity, which enables the thwarting of the other managers' resistances (those who attended the seminar) and the starting of the revelation process.

At the very beginning of the seminar, the consultants were not *welcome*, symbolically of course. Indeed, every member got a welcome present.

It is possible to interpret this fact as a resistance, expressed by the Adminis-
trator, spokesperson for the group of managers, and which could be linked not
only with the consultant's reputation, but also with the foresight that what
will be allowed to be seen might disturb or be unwelcome.

On the first evening, the seminar dealt only with Dialogues. It is a disposition in which managers meet to dialogue; after they had drawn lots, they were given roles out of everyday life in the institution: members of the directing board, territorial directors for formation and operations, central directors for formation and administration.

This disposition enabled the revealing of some specific facts, among which:

- the weight of administration and book-keeping which cornered the Manageress, whose part was performed by a man; thus, not only the dilemma between management and administration, expressed by incompatibility between global quality and more financial rentability, but also the difficulty of settling this dilemma and going beyond it were introduced.
- the negation of the Assistant Director role, which, spontaneously, everybody refused;
- the way in which, on the contrary, the "Manageress" got many requests putting "her" in the role of the one that knows, which spared the other managers the trouble of finding the answers by themselves.
- the contestation of some roles (some experts, some functional managers) and the evidence that the game of projections daily undermined the department, since everyone was persuaded of the ability to dispense with the others.
- The reaffirmation of some values as references in the department: for example, the efficiency value.

As in the mirror effect, Dialogues are another process leading to revelation.
The interpretation, or Dialogues, is more fecund than each member expressing
himself/herself in relation with the role he/she plays in the seminar, the role
he/she has in the institution; and the combination of both.

These dialogues echoed several work hypotheses, revealing hidden, not to say occulted, aspects of the way the department was working. These hypotheses were elaborated, either before the seminar in the consultants' diagnosis, or during the seminar.

One of these hypotheses was to show the four functional elements of the department, among which formation and administration, which had sought advice from a consultant within the company, and from the management itself. But these elements had no cohesion between them. At worst, they worked one against the other. But never did the last two elements regulate the first two. This hypothesis proved its particular accuracy with the department's board of managers, which fulfilled little or none of its mission.

To compensate for this "un-cohesion", the members of the department pretended a fake conviviality but actually, these affected harmonious relations hid very deep fractures. As a consequence, the management did not - or could not- act as a regulating factor.

The directory had to meet regularly, to study the development of the seminar. Thus, it was agreed that they would breakfast—on the second morning—at a separate table. But the Manageress started a long phone call with the man above her in rank, so that she could not join the others before the end of the breakfast.

One of the advisers in leadership interpreted this behaviour as an obvious resistance to the work of the seminar. He asked to stop the breakfast, to go on with the meeting in another room. Then he worded his disapproval clearly and without any compromise. He denounced with the greatest strictness this manifestation of resistance, which the Manageress's behaviour denoted, whatever the rational explanations for such behaviour might be, and, at the same time, he showed the threat it represented for the very development of the seminar.

For him, this event was the more serious because it had happened in the dining-room, under the other participants' eyes. The latter could not but make—ever unconsciously—a similar interpretation, and implicitly to join this resistance move. The meeting was so intense that it nearly caused a divergence of opinions between the two advisers in leadership. But, nevertheless, the seminar went on.

Here, the Manageress's resistances appear to come from her wish to heal and mend the first-type wounds inflicted by the freeing process she is developing vis-à-vis her hierarchical boss (and his direct assistants).

This struggle, sometimes a harsh one, against these resistances is the price the consultants have to pay if they want to create this empty—or rather, hollow— space that can be the crib for revealing process.

One must notice, too, that here, the consultants are not safe from these regressive games when one of them is tempted to protect the leaders: that is to say, to try to heal the third-type wounds the latter forced upon them. Then, the inner cohesion of the consulting team is threatened, too.

Another work hypothesis appeared during the following meeting of the directory (on the second evening).

The dislocation (i.e., the want for cohesion) was also slicing the department into horizontal strata as long as the strategic information—for example, the tensions within the relation between the department and its hierarchy or, more generally, the influence of its environment— remained in the strict intimacy of the managing binomial (the Manageress and her assistant) without being shared. Thus, the latter (the managing binomial) exempted the rest of the institution from these heavy but essential preoccupations.

Through this behaviour, the Manageress partly gives up one of her prerogatives: the reminding of the reality principle at every level of the institution. Is it due to a reparation reflex, an attempt—in the short run—not to inflict more wounds upon the people around her?

The elaboration of a work hypothesis regarding the absence of sharing of the strategic information was corroborated by the explicitation of another mirror effect between the department and the consulting team. In both cases, intimacy within a binomial— and even within a couple—excludes the rest of the team:

- *in the formation department, a couple of directors excludes the other managers;*
- *in the consulting team, the application of the synthesis was done with the two advisers in leadership, but without the consultant;*
- *but it is at the very moment when the latter enters the core of the intervention—by taking part in the discussions within the seminar—that the hypothesis appears concerning the exclusion of the rest of the service from this specific information.*

This is how this temporary revelating institution works.

Anyhow, the seminar work went on facing resistances. During the plenary meetings, the consultants were either ignored, or confronted about their way of intervening, which was thought too aggressive.

As for the two directors, they were reluctant to express publicly the work hypothesis that had appeared during the directory meetings. Was it then possible for the whole group to progress and transform itself if those who were in charge did not seem to move?

It is obvious, there, how the work hypotheses generate third-type wounds by testing, through their essence and their seriousness, not only the managers' narcissism, but also their ability to see, accept, and express what has been revealed. It is what happens with the department Manageress and her assistant, who, eventually, succeed in facing the work hypothesis with courage, but suffering too.

There again, the directory is a structure that enables a close and intensive work with he head of the institution regarding its own resistances. When the latter rallies the revelation process, it heartens the others to follow it.

The revelation process reached its climax the day after, which was the last day of the seminar, when one of the advisers in leadership explained what the work hypothesis chosen as a basis for the whole revelation work should be.

It intended to show that the culture within this formation department was influenced by traditional teaching, this based itself on the teacher–pupil relationship.

(The teacher–pupil relationship very often wants to exclude any other external intervention, whatever its form may be, seen as alien, disturbing, and inopportune. Experience within our general educative system, from primary school to the Ministry of Education, demonstrates it every day.)

Consequently, the very notion of management was denied as inconsistent with this culture. From that moment, shared management, delegation of authority and demultiplication could not be applied.

The moment when this hypothesis of *here and now* was formulated—some minutes before the end of plenary session—was also significant.

This session had been rather hectic: at some moments the participants had sought refuge in very technocratic declarations, thus rendering their speech rather complicated and obscure for those who, like some consultants, do not know every detail of the department's mechanism; at other moments, they had focused on the consultants' behaviour, taxing them with their intransigency, strictness, and even rigidity.

Everything happens as if the managers, as a whole, managed to neutralize some of the revealing work by succeeding in pushing aside the discovery of the most important hypotheses.

On the other hand, the growing anxiety resulting from the end of the seminar might encourage creativity and thus provoke revelation, even at the very end of the process.

However, people used to this socio-technical approach could have thought a long time before of this very important hypothesis; these people could have been either members of a formation and internal consultation department, or the external team of consultants.

It is also possible that the consultants, confronted with their own resistances, have themselves contributed to temporary occultation of this work hypothesis. Are they afraid to intervene in a service dealing with internal formation and consultation—the activity of which is not very different from theirs—that sends them back, through a mirror effect, to the management of their own institution?

At the end of the session the female Administrator of the seminar, who had to organize the tables to allow work during meal-times, disobeyed the instructions, given that very morning by the Assistant manager, regarding the number of lunch tables. A total mess was avoided thanks to a very authoritarian decision from this assistant, and a re-setting and attribution of these tables at the last minute.

This act of sabotage against the work of the seminar can be interpreted as a sign of the institution's resistance projected upon—and carried by—the embodiment of the administration sub-system: the female Administrator!

The acknowledgement of the central work hypothesis took the form of an utterance repeated many times by the group during the concluding session of the afternoon: *"It's a hot potato"*. This utterance expressed clearly how this hypothesis was disturbing: it was so hot, so "burning", so bruising that everyone tried to get rid of it by throwing it into his/her neighbour's hands.

But, as for every hot potato, its heat progressively lessens. Thus, it corresponds to the exteriorization process of this hypothesis, which, little by little, lets people understand, accept, and transform the revelation of a hidden, but very potent, strength.

(See the input in the third part of the text; the revelation process).

Some time after the end of the seminar, the female Director contacted one of the advisers in leadership to let him know her reactions. She particularly emphasized her fear of seeing the delegates, whose way of working had been deeply criticized, become the system's scapegoats at the end of the process.

(The direction committee was composed of the direction binomial—the female Director and her assistant—and of these three delegates [thus, one woman and four men].)

Some days later, the direction binomial, the three deputies, the chief of cabinet (formerly, the female Administrator of the seminar) and the three consultants met within a direction committee.

The latter, or, more precisely, one of them, suffered harsh criticisms from the deputies regarding the course of the seminar as well as their attitude, which the others found too aggressive and, thus, responsible for the blockage of some participants.

With such a behaviour they try to withdraw from the revelation process that was under way and thus they express the frustrations and the wounds they try to charge the consultant with.

As in every transformation, one can be strongly tempted to go backwards, or to adopt a regressive behaviour when a progression is going on.

Therefore, we could explain the different attempts to sabotage the course of the seminar, as much from the female Director and the female Administrator as from the deputies; indeed, their ambivalence was at its peak just before, for some of them, fully entering the revelation work.

The deputies' ambivalence was at its peak just before the emergence of the most frightening work hypothesis: "*Your department is dead!*". This hypothesis was taking up again some elements of the seminar, more precisely what an important company manager had said, just after he retired. He had shown how the formation department, once one of the company's key departments, had fallen from this position because of its incapacity to react and to anticipate.

Furthermore, this work hypothesis focused on a real distress facing the paucity of the reactions once the seminar was over; indeed, the department was actually dead if its main leaders proved totally unable to overcome their own resistances and shortcomings when confronted with such a merciless hypothesis.

Nevertheless, the emerging image that followed was set by the Assistant Director, paraphrasing Winston Churchill: "Blood, sweat and tears!". And maybe only such a reflex, as strong and vigorous as a declaration of war, could enable this moribund department to rebound.

Maybe one could see here the typical French relation to power and death, which is expressed by the significant adage: "The King is dead, long live the King!"

Finally, the violence expressed by the deputies was found again with two members, but in the direction college. At the end of the seminar, the female Director had instructed each member of the college to write a short memo regarding the management of the department. By refusing this task, the two people expressed a strong and unequivocal disagreement. But their act of insubordination happened also to give strength to the main work hypothesis, which showed that the management was negated within the department.

This one time, the management gave up the process that had led to its negation: since both managers resolutely refused to commit themselves in working on the future of the department (i.e., its rebuilding), the female Director decided, which was surprising and never seen before, to exclude them from the direction college which, this time, took a real part in renewed role and action.

The description of this instance shows how the consultant's work is in keeping with the continual resistance to the reparation desire, to create a space for a real phenomenon of revelation.

In the example we have described, we might think this seminar was an opportunity for the sub-system formed by the direction college to start a transformation both of the manner in which it proceeded and of its production. This transformation is the result of the revelation process we contributed to start with. But this revelation was not initiated without pain, fear, third-type wounds, or even without regressive behaviours from all and sundry.

These regressions may have been essential for the progressions that happened later, even if their consequence was second-type wounds.

Anyway, only the future and the continuation of the efforts that are on their way will enable the achievement of this transformation.

Epilogue: the revelation process

Revelation is a real process, a collective one in most cases: it occurs within a group or a system, when many conditions are fulfilled, among which is the transformation of the want for reparation and the building up of a mutual truth between managers and consultants.

Revelation appears in the *here and now:* the many hypotheses that appear during a process of consulting do not exist before this process. They build themselves during the intervention, thanks to the members of the institution.

Who, within the group, takes the risk of formulating hypotheses? We think that the consultant is often in the best position to open this path, and this for two reasons. On the one hand, he/she uses his/her externality and his/her experience, which give him/her a more critical focus. On the other hand, his/her position as a consultant exposes him/her to the flow of projections transmitted by the system. The latter focuses them upon the consultant because of his/her peculiarity and the proximity relationship he/she has built with his/her client.

Anyway, our basic postulate is as follows: when a tell-tale work hypothesis is expressed, it is in the name of the system and of its members, too.

Conversely, the consultant appears to be in the best position to confront the ambiguity as well as the subversive aspect of the revelation, still in a period of gestation; and yet, at the same time, the rest of the group, which is summoning all its resistance power, is tempted to stifle this revelation in spite of its desire to see it come into full view. These resistances are, in most cases, thrown upon the consultant, too.

Then, our practice consists in refraining from summoning our own resistances to escape these projections (the most traditional, but not the least efficient, way being to express or to understate doubts regarding our own competency). On the contrary, we tend to accept them to expose ourselves, partly at least to their impact, and to progressively absorb them in order to better work upon them. And it is only at this cost that the transformation of the global amount of those projections and information can be settled.

This process is a many-stepped one.

To begin with the *insight*, one could define this as a glow, a flash, or a sparkle that comes suddenly to the mind, illuminating the situation under process. The insight is striking; it is a blow that looms up and reveals one of the explanations for a person's, or a system's behaviour: a *"how?"*, then a *"why?"*

Of course, the insight is communicated to the rest of the system, in the form of a work hypothesis which takes the place of a provocation, taken as its etymological meaning (to provoke from Latin *provocare*, "call outside", "let come", "to give birth" [etymological dictionary of the French language, *Le Robert*, Paris 1992]).

It triggers individual and collective reactions among which are resistances and wounds, but sometimes also pleasure and enthusiasm. These reactions are a sign that the system has started developing.

The insight generates a more particular reaction in the group than in the individual: the input, i.e., the injection of the awareness represented by the insight, into the psychical, political, and technical apparatus of the system. The input is an interiorization, a deep digestion of the insight.

This interiorization validates this insight and can have two consequences: either the input gives birth to new insights, or it creates *outputs*, i.e., a real and visible production, in fact, a transformation of the actions and behaviour, individual or collective.

When we compare the revelation process with what happens in the developing process of a photograph, the insight is the image that appears in the revealing device, after projection of the negative image and its exposure to photosensitive paper. This image is ephemeral, unstable, in constant evolution until its disappearance.

To prevent this entropic process, it is necessary to put the photograph into a fixative liquid, which acts as the input. Then, the image becomes a tangible and non-reversible reality (at least for a certain time): it is the output!

Thus, the output results from the revelation process. It is made not only of the print this process has left in the institution, but also of the awareness that a transformation, within this institution, was achieved to leave this print.

The shock of the output and of the following awareness is as violent as the shock of the insight. The time between both shocks can vary, from a few hours to several years. To conclude, as well as the input, the output may generate new insights or at least, new inputs.

In the example above, and to illustrate our subject, we can identify one of the "insight–input–output" sequences of the revelation process (Figure 9).

The main insight occurs on the last day in the form of the managing work hypothesis, which had been denied by the standards of traditional teaching. Once transformed into an input, it is first interiorized by the consultants, then, on the same afternoon, by the managers: it is the *hot potato*.

As it followed its route, this input generates other insights, among which is the hypothesis of the death of the department, and finally appears in the form of outputs, i.e., behaviour transformations: thus, the two leaders refuse the denial of their management

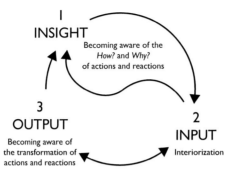

Figure 9. A basic formulation of the process of revelation: insight, input, and output.

by excluding the insubordinate managers from the direction college.

These three stages of the revelation process—-insight, input, output—are not devoid of surprise, unpredictability, or uncertainty either.

The consultant works with his/her client(s) in order to understand, to make clear, and to control this sequence. From the very start of the process to its useful and fruitful results, the stages are many, and far more intricate than a mere intellectual demonstration. They are, at the same time, both fragile and strong.

More particularly, this work goes through some periods of enthusiasm, and some of depression. It can increase the inner resistances as well as those of the environment. This increase, which may be temporary, but which can also last longer, happens in the different stages of the revelation: before and after the insight, during the input, before and after the output. Anyway, these resistances often vanish suddenly. In fact, they are more destroyed than circumvented, by the surprising and irrepressible shocks from the insight and the output (Figure 10).

It is the same with the transformation phenomenon, an often chaotic voyage, made of a series of uncertain, even unknown, halting places, bearing pain but also, before anything else, bearing life.

Is it possible to act differently—we never can tell!—and thus to be spared the pain and the joy of the revelation? Nevertheless, a very well-known quotation by Winston Churchill inspires us to this

OUTPUT

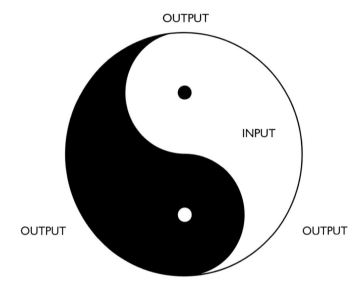

INPUT

OUTPUT   OUTPUT

Figure 10. As in the case with the Ying and Yang, insight and input are inseparable and essential to the production of output.

paraphrase, leading us to suppose that "transformation and revelation are the worst solutions excepting all the other . . ." to assume and secure as best as possible our human condition. (Churchill's quotation is: "Democracy is the worst form of government except for all those others that have been tried".)

Notes

1. This chapter was previously published as a article in Swedish, Den svårfångade organisationen de Siv Boalt Boëthius et Stefan Jern, *Natur och Kultur*, 1996.
2. Translated from the French by Marie-Claude Dufeigneux

Consultation and transformation: between shared management and generative leadership[1]

David Gutmann, with Ronan Pierre

T he cloning process achieved by Scottish scientists with a sheep called Dolly shook the whole world in March 1997. The date is likely to be remembered by future generations: they will definitely have to confront the possibility of human cloning, despite all the reassuring speeches about prudence in experimenting. In this context, it is not difficult to relate to our science fiction literature background. From H. G. Wells to Philip K. Dick, which author has not written a story of human cloning? Traditionally, the human cloning theme is linked with two other themes in science fiction: immortality and/or totalitarianism. For cloning is a way to be immortal by copying oneself, and is also a way to produce masses of identical individuals, a basis for obedient and interchangeable servants.

In these extreme representations of society—what science fiction does best and is meant for—we can recognize two tendencies of *leadership* that unfortunately happen too often: leaders tend to concentrate all powers in their hands and to be exclusive in the exercise of their leadership.

In this chapter, we shall examine the relationship of leadership and transformation, and the importance of consultation. We consider that the first task of the consultant (a role we name

"Adviser in Leadership") is to help the leader to avoid these temptations of becoming all-powerful and all-knowing.

Our assumption is that *leadership* cannot be analysed in itself, but finds meaning in the internal and external environment in which it takes place. The role of the consultant is to help with detecting the conscious and even more the unconscious process(es) in leadership as it manifests itself in the external environment and the psyche of the leader.

Our approach is centred on an institutional transformation (IT) model of organizations, which takes into account the unconscious in its institutional expression. By *institution*, we mean any social organization or structure with a primary task, like a firm, or an association, or a football team. By *trans-formation*, we mean *passage from one form to another*, which we consider to be a condition for innovation. Our experience of transformation is directly related to our work with leaders in helping them to comprehend their moving, complex environment. As consultants, we try to see what resistances are at work in organizations when a leader tries to trans-form and "govern" an institution. We have to remember at this point the very enlightening etymology of "leadership". "Leader" derives from a Germanic word "leiten", which refers both to the path and the convoy: a leader is the one who conducts the convoy and/or shows the path. "-ship" relates also to the Germanic root "skap", which means to create, or to shape. In this perspective, leadership means to shape one's way, to shape the path and the convoy together.

The thesis we are proposing here is: no institution can sustain itself without transforming itself. However, there is no transformation without leadership, as well as no leadership without transformation. This implies that leadership has to be both *generous* and *generative*. Therefore, as Advisers in Leadership, we must focus our intervention on institutional transformation. The consultant's role within the institution then completes a sustaining triangle, composed of the *leader*, the *manager*, and the *consultant*, which is essential to the institution's dynamics. We further describe the thesis in the sections that follow.

No institution can sustain itself without trans-forming

A perennial institution is the dream of any manager. This is especially the case in the economic sector, where firms (small or large) are organizations that, beside their collective primary task (generally profit), give work and a means of living to each of their employees.

However, a perennial institution also takes the risk of being outdone by other organizations in its environment with the same primary task. This principle is at the core of the classical economic theory (Adam Smith, Jean-Baptiste Say) which gave birth to the capitalist system that is today our business environment. Later on, Schumpeter analysed the evolution of firms in a competitive environment as being a "creative destruction" process (Schumpeter, 1939). This process implies that when a firm enters the market with a new product, its success is short-lived, for the innovation is somehow integrated into its environment, and new products appear, cheaper or of better quality. Therefore, the firm is confronted with new tasks in terms of innovation. Often, the firm disappears. This destruction has, however, been a gain for society, since it has given rise to new and cheaper products. Therefore, it is a "creative destruction" process.

This economic scheme has a counterbalance in the psychoanalytical field. We think that an institution, like an individual, is constantly confronted by a question of self-renewal, and can be in a process of *repetition*. With this Freudian concept (Freud, 1920g), we designate the tendency of the subject to reproduce sequences that originally created suffering. The impossibility of obtaining the wanted thing creates suffering (repetition is guided by the pleasure principle in the first place, but its obvious relation to suffering and pain led Freud to the idea of "beyond the pleasure principle"). Following the same idea, we think that repetition can sometimes put the institution in danger. In this case, the danger is either concrete and physical (destruction, as in the Schumpeter theory), or can be more subtle, and diffuse itself within the institution, endangering members (again, either physically or psychically). Also, despite the pain it creates, repetition is a defence from anxiety (Gutmann, 1988), because the fear of the unknown generates high levels of anxiety. We can say that for an individual or an institution, attempting to avoid repetition is often much more difficult than the search for stability, which brings less anxiety within the institution or for the individual.

If stability is threatening, could instability be less endangering? Of course not, but it is a condition for innovation, for avoiding repetition. Any effective innovation demands time, energy, and often entails much more anxiety than letting things remain "untouched", "untransformed". In our experience, innovation can only be achieved if an institutional transformation process is at work. What is transformation? As consultants, how can we detect and help transformation?

Unfortunately, the "modern" conception of management and leadership constitutes a science that promises managers and leaders they will be able to analyse, forecast, and monitor behaviours in the organizations they are responsible for. How can this be so? In the history of sciences, we are only beginning to apprehend the complexity of human behaviour (Foucault, 1966). Freud made his major contribution to the discovery of human nature only a century ago. Discovering the unconscious and the oedipal determinism of human beings, our civilization also became aware of the frailty of the myth of self-possession of the human. With regard to this history of science, one should be careful and modest when claiming that management is a form of knowledge or a science that can be taught or learnt.

The other main reason why forecasting and monitoring human behaviour is a fantasy is that the roles of representations, imagination, affects, and drives are, of course, determinants in the life of an institution. On this particular point, it is interesting to note that a growing number of scientists in domains in which a strong rational and "Cartesian" culture traditionally prevails use some intellectual material or even corroborate some results of the social sciences. For instance, the role of emotions in the decision process of an individual is now a hypothesis in which neurologists take an interest. In order to process all the choices that an individual can make, the frontal cortex of the brain creates images of the different scenarios of actions to be taken. These images create an emotional reaction linked to their content. Emotions are generated by a "change of the corporeal landscape": each emotion connects with a different aspect of the body. This theory of the role of emotions offsets the belief in the rationality of the decision process (Damasio, 1995). Although it is not established, this theory enables an understanding of the complexity of decision taking and, furthermore, allows us to take into account some "unrational" material in management, for example. Thus, consultancy inside organizations has to take note of these aspects. This is why we consider the dynamics of organizations in terms of "institutional transformation".

Our point of view is that the transformation process is not simple. Each institution is a system open to transformation forces that come either from the exterior environment or the interior. The institution integrates these forces but, according to the *homeostasis* principle, it works them out, it resists them, modifies them in order to keep itself stable as long as possible, to keep the system as it is. For this, several modes of resistances are used.

Often, when a director or an executive, a ruler or a manager, formulates consciously the future of his institution from state A, he represents it by an objective; let us call it state B. Despite what most "managerial" experts claim, *there is no evolution of the institution that can be rationalized or forecast*—there is no "from A to B" (a "to be"). *B is a fantasy. The closer you get, the more it transforms itself.*

We can explain this phenomenon with the help of chaos theory (Chabert, Chemla, & Dahan Dalmedico, 1992). Since the institution is a product of human behaviour and imagination, it is chaotic in the sense that no rational prediction can be made about its evolution. According to chaos theory, in terms of evolution, a small disturbance in initial conditions can result in huge disruptions after a period. An obvious example is the weather. A well-known aphorism says that the flap of a butterfly's wings on the banks of the Chiang Jiang River in China can generate a hurricane in the Atlantic Ocean. Chaos, however, is not disorder, for chaotic states are determined, but unpredictable. In a similar way, the future of the institution cannot be predicted, because of all the various disturbances (external and internal) that can affect its evolution, but it is determined, which means that it can only evolve towards determined states.

The passage from one state to another (*trans-formation*) is neither regular nor continuous: it is chaotic, erratic, and discontinuous. Because it comes up against irregular resistances, the movement of transformation adopts a path composed of zig-zags, progressions and regressions, constructions and destructions. Let us recall our personal experience: a sentimental or an academic failure can also provide the impetus to spring back to life again. We even think that the presence of these resistances are so many clues, confirming the authenticity of a process of transformation that distinguishes itself from a simple measure of superficial regulation.

To schematize, this sinuous passage is comprised of blurred phases that are strange, if not incomprehensible, and seems lost in the obscurity of a "black box". By definition, these segments of the passage are never seen, known, or understood. The black box is the uncontrollable, determined but unpredictable part in the evolution of the institution. Inside the black box, one could find all the "non-rational" elements that are at stake in the interactions between members of the institution and between the institution and its environment, in which affects and unconscious drives are determining factors.

Also, other segments, as if they overran the black box, are identified and apprehended by certain members of the group. For example, the raising of the turnover rate inside a firm can be an indicator for future difficulties. These points emerge like the tips of an iceberg above water: they necessarily imply the existence of a hidden mass that is even larger, beyond what is apparent and its appearance. In other words, it is a question of an unknown itinerary that is long and tangled, lost in the darkness of the black box. In addition, these emerged segments do not, alone, allow the reconstituting of the totality of the path, or even formulating a view of the whole.

Other steps along this path are visible but, *a priori*, untouchable: they seem out of reach or outside the capacity for action, influence, and regulation by the members of the group. Often, they seem unreachable because it seems that transforming them would entail consequences too dangerous for the institution. These elements can be found in a transparent "glass box" that itself contains the black box (see Figure 1, p. 10).

We think that if the leader incites people to believe that "B" is an absolute certainty (instead of a fantasy) it will be demobilizing for those concerned with the primary task. This is especially the case in our Western society. In contrast to our civilization, the Chinese culture for example, both in its Taoist and Buddhist aspects, acknowledges that one can never see the whole of a thing (Jullien, 1992), which creates in essence a certain degree of relativism in the way one considers life (Figure 11). In a sense, accepting the unknown is also accepting the Other.

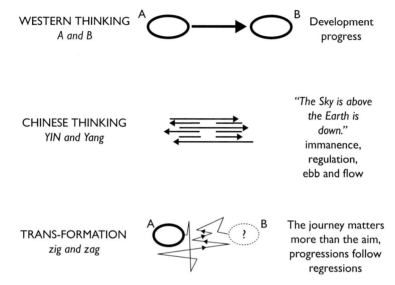

WESTERN THINKING
A and B

A   B   Development
progress

CHINESE THINKING
YIN and Yang

*"The Sky is above
the Earth is
down."*
immanence,
regulation,
ebb and flow

TRANS-FORMATION
zig and zag

A   B   The journey matters
more than the aim,
progressions follow
regressions

Figure 11.   Considering trans-formation.

Each one of us, in our personal and professional life, goes through a transformation process; is in transformation. Thus, he or she lives periods of progression and regression. Is it possible to deal with these moments of regression, to accept them, when one is at the head of a corporate institution? In our work, we often observed that decision makers who have had a model career (top universities, important jobs, successful achievements) were particularly vulnerable to a sudden obstacle or misfortune in their life. In such cases, just as with a revelation process during a psychoanalytical treatment, they went through a depression, but the problem was that such individuals, being in situation of power in an institution, were also harmful for the institution at that moment of their life. They often became omnipotent or, on the contrary, invisible in their exercise of leadership. As Freud observed, the depressive structure (melancholy) is characterized by the impossibility for the subject to be in mourning for the lost object (Freud, 1917e). This particular task is at the core of leadership "ethics": The leader is responsible for taking into account his or her full personality, in the way he or she fulfils his or her role in the institution. *The consultant can help him or her in this work.*

Just like individuals, institutions are confronted to the incapacity or unwillingness of accepting regression, which can either make it vulnerable to brutal inner or exterior evolutions, or make it omnipotent. For example, Microsoft holds 80% of its market, and has been growing since 1983. It seems as if it overcame each difficulty. But what can happen to a firm that is not in the habit of confronting regression when unforeseen trouble occurs—for example, the huge success of the Internet? Will it be able to transform itself? This question can also be raised concerning leaders or managers.

First, in order to help institutional transformation, the consultant in the role of Adviser in Leadership must use the information in the "glass box". Some elements of the institution can be revealed and worked out, which helps innovation in individual and collective behaviour. Working with elements that are observable in the glass box is a *heuristic* process (discovering facts). The consultant's role is also to reduce the unknown, the black box, whenever this is possible. At this step, the consultant can only interpret. The black box is unobservable. For this task the consultant engages in a process of *hermeneutics* (the science of interpreting facts). Thus, being an Adviser encompasses both heurism and hermeneutics. However, the heuristic process must be at the core of a consultant's practice.

Often, this process, either detecting facts or formulating working hypotheses about what is happening inside the black box, is disturbing for the members of the institution. The consultant points out certain elements that were "forgotten", cast aside. We consider that conflictual matters have to be worked out and not systematically avoided. To make them appear is a way of regulating and containing them. Conflicts are therefore reframed constructively.

The consultant's role is to disturb. He or she says things that can hurt. But it is necessary so that it can be discussed and worked out. In the "here and now", to formulate publicly a working hypothesis is a way to give birth to a debate and to generate encounters. In the best cases, such a practice can reveal habits, prejudices, defensive attitudes, fears, fantasies, anxiety, all elements that can inhibit the individual in his or her relationship with others, and that are resistances in the social innovation and transformation processes. Progressively, by a series of working hypotheses, we can hope that some "hidden elements" of the institution will be revealed.

There are some elements that make transformation especially difficult or impossible. They are often related to the notion of "difference" or to the incapacity of members of an institution to accept co-operation. The words "boundaries", "borders", "barriers", "barricades" form a progression, expressing from one word to another a growing demarcation. In terms of transformation, it is necessary that "barricades", which are impermeable, become "barriers", then "borders", then "boundaries", which can be progressively more permeable. Institutional transformation might be moving from a closed conception of the limit ("the barricade") to a more open conception ("the boundary"). It carries the idea that a boundary marks both a rupture *and* a passage; without boundary, there is no differentiation, but also no transaction.

This idea of *passage* is important also in the leadership phenomenon. Because leadership has to be *generous* and *generative*, a leader must generate other leaders and accept that they deviate from the path the leader has chosen: in a succession process, for example, both a rupture and a passage have to be achieved.

No leadership is possible without transformation and no transformation occurs without a leader.

What are the links between leaders and the dynamic structure that supports them? The historical examples of leaders' assassination as an expression of unconscious global resistances are numerous: Abraham Lincoln, John F. Kennedy, Robert Kennedy, Martin Luther King, Gandhi, Anouar Saddate, Yitzhak Rabin. All assassinations were more or less linked to a global, political issue and, ultimately, an expression of the resistances the leader had brought up by undertaking transforming action. It seems as if every time a leader rises, unexplained forces, which express themselves through a defined element (in the examples above, a murderer), tend to break him or her and to bring him or her down. Overall, leadership has to be understood as a complete and global phenomenon. Transformation and leadership are related in a complementary way.

First, our point of view is *that there is no transformation without a leader*. This necessity is so strong that talking about a "transformative leader" is, in our sense, redundant. This statement can be interpreted as a general paradox of democracy: whereas each individual is equal one to another, it seems that no task can be achieved by itself, and desperately needs someone to lead. Thus, each individual might be called upon to take the role of leader at least once in his or her life.

Second, without transformation, the institution is both threatened and threatening in its interactions with the leader. *No leadership can exist without transformation* (of its role and of the institution). For example, two kinds of altered leadership can occur if transformation is lacking. In both cases, the leader is confronted with the risk of "psychic exhaustion".

The first possibility is that a *superleader* can arise. In this case, the leader is flattered by his surrounding entourage. Positive projections are all he receives: trust, congratulations, success . . . the leader cannot play a role of protecting the group, or guarding the institution's boundaries, thus exposing himself and the group to destructive projections. The suicide of Kurt Cobain, lead singer of the rock group Nirvana, is a good example of such a phenomenon. In this case, a sudden and huge (worldwide) success became in fact Nirvana's Hell. Before Cobain, famous rock or movie stars also went through a self-destruction process: Jimi Hendrix, Janis Joplin, Jim Morrison, Brian Jones, and Marilyn Monroe, for example.

Or, the leader can also play the role of a *scapegoat*: this happens when the leader receives negative projections, such as envy, destruction, suspicion, rivalry, and so on. The scapegoat, or, more precisely, the sacrificial process, is not wanted consciously by members of the instutition, but it is functional: it enables the restoration of order in the organization by allowing internal conflicts to focus on a victim (Girard, 1972). Of course, the person at the head of the institution is also a potential victim. These two "distortions" of leadership are typical of "non-transformation" states.

Besides these two kinds of altered leadership, the lack of a transformation process can produce, out of institutional transformation, a leader who becomes an autocrat, if not a dictator. If this happens, the institution engages in a vicious circle, which we call the "saviour, victim, persecutor circle". This happens when the leader emerges in particularly difficult circumstances; for example, a well-known manager hired by shareholders in order to help a firm face its great losses or some threatening competition, or a young and therefore promising politician elected in a crisis situation. He or she first stands for the institution's saviour. A politician or a firm's executive take up their post amid tremendous hope, but actually may lose their popularity soon after the election or the arrival in post. This phenomenon seems inherent to all leadership take-overs in an institution in crisis. Confronted by important resistances, the leader then is an easy prey for critics. The leader becomes rapidly a scapegoat for all the ills of the institution and receives strong negative projections. Thus, he becomes the victim. In reaction, he or she tends to concentrate power in his or her own hands, makes a series of hazardous and arbitrary decisions, and thus becomes the persecutor.

Overall, the emergence of a leader is a complete, global, and systemic phenomenon. The consultant can only help to clarify the emergence of unconscious resistances that alter leadership—but not in the emergence of leaders.

During the period of the twentieth century, we can say that some transformation processes have actually occurred. For example, we see several transformation "peaks" in the USA, which are mainly represented by Roosevelt's Presidency (the "New Deal", the decision to enter the Second World War), or Kennedy's mandate (Medicare and Medicaid), the concrete results of which still prevail today. Since 1973, the end of the "Golden Years", the elite has tried to close its eyes to the depth of the Western countries' crises, and firmly believes in "change". Politicians and experts persist in advocating "change", whereas transformation is what is really needed. Few transformations have taken place, unfortunately. This is probably one of the causes of the rising anxiety in our societies.

As an exception, during the 1980s, a process of transformation did actually take place in the UK, under the leadership of Margaret Thatcher, whereas elsewhere in Europe, and even in the USA and Japan, no real political impulse has succeeded. It is true that this process of establishing systematic economic liberalism in sectors of the British economy generated a large number of poor people, part of a growing "underclass". However, there is no doubt that the UK, founder of the Welfare State in Europe, did go through a transformation process by setting up a new structural capitalistic society. As a sign confirming the existence of this transformation process under Thatcher's leadership (and John Major's, which followed), which was a progression *and* a regression for the UK, let us note that it is Tony Blair's *New* Labour party that was brought to power in 1997, as if a transformation had brought something new and opened another era.

The desire for trans-formation is an expression of the vitality of any institution or system, whatever it may be. It is both the result and a condition for the feasibility of social innovation. On this particular point, *desire* seems to be a prohibited word in our society. It is associated with a form of guilt. Moreover, desire in its expression is linked to an image of death (because of AIDS, of sexual delinquency). *However, desire is also life.* Many institutions, whether firms, political organizations, or social institutions, do not take desire into account. They are more preoccupied with surviving than actually living. Through institutional transformation, we have faith that institutions will not only perpetuate, but also innovate, accepting through their leaders both the fate and the face of transformation, i.e. incompletion. For an individual, living means also accepting death. In the same way, one of the qualities of the leader is to accept the incompletion of transformation.

Generative leadership and shared management: a condition for the transformation of the institution

It has become so difficult to think about leadership today, probably because of what we learnt or experienced with some leaders during the twentieth century. The traditional perspective in which leadership is studied is in relation to the "Theory of the group" elaborated by Freud (Freud, 1921c). This model sees the group, or crowd, as a unique functioning entity, which interacts with one individual (the leader) in a fascination–domination relationship. What holds individuals together in a group is the belief in a supreme leader who loves each of them equally. In the Catholic Church, or the Army, for example, the link between each individual and the supreme figure (Christ, the commander, etc.) creates mutual dependencies. In short, what holds the institution of the group together is a libidinal link between members and with the supreme figure. The leader is in this case the ideal of the ego, the superego (Freud, 1923b). There is no doubt that, in huge corporate organizations, for example, the leader tends to be at the centre of a strong political, unconscious, and spiritual game. What is a leader?

A leader is a visionary. He or she stands out and is followed. In our experience as consultants, more specifically as Advisers in Leadership, we would like the leader to have seven characteristics (Figure 12). Of course, these features can somehow be found in other roles or persons than leaders, but only leaders can mobilize them all and, according to the different circumstances, can use them or not. Our view is that *leadership has to be generative.*

First, *vision* is the most obvious quality that a leader must have. To take an example in the political field, De Gaulle's departure to London in 1940 and his call of 18 June, which gave birth to the French Resistance, was visionary, as was Churchill's absolute refusal to compromise with the German Nazis after 1939. This was visionary in the sense that very few would have thought it was the right attitude at the time. The leader must perceive the primary task of the institution he or she belongs to and conduct the institution according to this objective. With vision, the leader will be able to set up an institution following a more or less unknown path, and to announce the "B" desired and fantasized task, which is the next step of transformation.

For example, the progress of medical and biological technologies is an issue in which vision is vital, since mankind has today the opportunity of interfering with human creation. Any hesitation in our ethics about research or experimenting on human organisms today could generate disasters tomorrow (see the chaos theory).

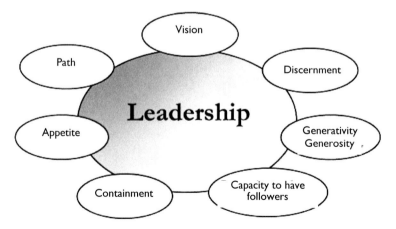

Figure 12. The characteristics of leadership.

Concerning this "bio-ethics" issue, no one is qualified to tell what rules have to be adopted: options and opinions are too divergent, since cultural practices, beliefs, and nationalities can influence the individual's opinion. However, possible scenarios have to be clarified: we have to know what can happen to mankind in relation to these biological and medical revolutions. In a sense, vision is required to make the right choices in terms of regulation. In this instance, vision is a condition for ethics ("ethics" being understood as "the art of directing one's behaviour"), since it helps individually and collectively to follow a clarified or, at least, voluntary path.

The construction of the European Union after the Second World War stands for another example of vision, both in its economic and political aspects. In the early 1950s, French leaders Robert Schuman (Minister of Foreign Affairs) and Jean Monnet (the "Father of Europe"), along with political figures such as Konrad Adenauer (German Chancellor) and Alcide de Gasperi (Italian Prime Minister), set the foundations of the European Union. The movement towards the EU was a succession of progressions and regressions. Still, there are true visionaries behind this movement. The vision was perpetuted by political leaders such as Helmut Kohl, German Chancellor, and François Mitterrand, the French President, who set the basis for the single currency (the Euro).

A second feature of the leader, *discernment*, implies that the leader must be constantly aware of clarifying his internal and external environment by taking into account the economic, political, psychic, and spiritual issues that are at stake within the group. Discernment is *staying with one's desire*. Because leadership has something to do with energy, a leader has to convince people, fight resistances. In a sense, discernment, to the leader, is quite similar to what the "sublimation process" is to the artist, that is, to give way to desire in a more or less socially acceptable form. This definition of discernment, "staying with one's desire", was given to us by a Jesuit priest. Only in desire can one find the energy for innovation and transformation.

Let us think about how today's high-tech economic successes, such as Microsoft and Apple, started in the 1970s. Teenagers fascinated by computer science spent days and days on their machines; at the core of their task was a desire for innovation and transformation. Discernment led to vision. As another example, George Lucas's insistence, in 1977, on creating licences for products derived from his *Star Wars* films not only made him rich, but also generated a model of merchandizing which is now systematically used by the whole film industry in Hollywood. His decision was strongly criticized at the time.

Third, the leader must have *the capacity to be followed*—and this is not so obvious. Followers play an active role in creating leaders, and are part of the institutional transformation. In our sense, they must carry out an "authoritative followership", which means that their support for the primary task of the institution is *deliberate and chosen*. This condition renders followership entirely different to that associated with totalitarian systems or dictatorial regimes, in which people are forced into following. An "authoritative followership" is a relationship with the leader that allows each individual to be an author, more precisely a *co-author*, and also in which the leader seeks systematically to enable acts of authority from his followers. A leader who has lost his passionate love and requirement for his people cannot continue to lead them, for he cannot enable them to become co-authors. Moses, leading his people to the Promised Land, stands for an example of the love and requirement a leader must have for his followers. In contrast to "authoritative followership", an omnipotent leadership is based on a dependency relationship between the followers and the leader. This dependency structure is recognizable in many of the firms whose leader is also the founder. It hinders the capacity for other managers, or even ordinary employees, to take charge of their authority and develop vision in the firm.

One of the great responsibilities of the leader towards followers is his or her constant effort to clarify and abide by the (internal and external) boundaries of the institution. Boundaries between public and private matters are especially important to enforce. A leader has to beware of boundary confusion, since it systematically affects the primary task of the institution. Examples might be a manager who uses the firm's resources for personal purposes, or a sect-member employee who preaches to his colleagues.

Above all, a leader must be able to set up a *working pair. The leader must find a manager*, a person whose mission is to prepare and organize the means and resources that are necessary for the primary task of the institution. Any institution, then, needs two roles, usually taken by two different individuals. In a way, the manager's role is to implement the vision of the leader in the daily life of the organization. *Management has to be shared.* An important role of the manager is to help members of the institution to "manage themselves". This process is what we call the "authoritative followership", which implies that the leader's followers have authority over themselves and their activities within the institution. Such a process allows better efficiency in the achievement of the primary task of the institution.

Unfortunately, working pairs are uncommon in both the economic and political worlds. As an example of a working pair in the mid-1990s, which fills business circles with admiration, let us take the case of Bill Gates, President of Microsoft, and his executive director Steven Ballmer (Executive Vice President of Sales and Support). In this pair, Gates takes the role of the visionary leader, and Ballmer of the tactician manager. Seven key executives back them up: not only is the working pair effective, but the head of Microsoft demonstrates an example of shared management. In the political world, the building of the European Union (towards the single currency) during the last decade was essentially achieved under the impulsion of French and German leaders (Mitterrand and Kohl), but their vision was taken in charge by great civil servants such as Jacques Delors (at the head of the European Commission), who played there a role of manager.

Also, the leader must share and create authority within the institution, and therefore, contribute to the grooming of potential leaders to take his or her place: generativity–generosity (fourth characteristic).

It is imperative that a leader succeed in engineering his *succession*: too many firms have fallen because of a failed succession. This is especially the case with firms whose corporate leader had a strong personality, and is also a crucial economic issue in small and medium enterprises. Often, such institutions depend on the personality and the energy of their founder. When the leader's departure is at stake, the tension and anxiety (no longer contained) about his succession are so strong that they can often destroy the institution.

To go further, several strategies connected with the succession of a leader are usually at work in an institution (a firm, for example). The most obvious strategy is conducted by what we could call the "presumed successors", that is, the individuals who form a "court" surrounding the leader. Always agreeing with the leader's decisions, they form the irreducible and inevitable support of the leader. They personify the legitimate successors. The second strategy at work is employed by the traditional opponents of the leader of the firm. They exist in any institution. They constitute a group that personifies the systematic opposition to the leader's decisions and way of ruling the firm. They are tolerated and often secretly desired, since they represent something that appears to be a counterbalance to the leader's power, and are also perceived as being a medium through which lack of satisfaction of the members of the institution can be expressed. It can be a good guideline for the leader, also. Third, a group of outsiders have their own strategy in the succession process. The "outsiders" play a role that is perceived as very individualistic in the institution; the clown, the genius inventor, the clerk, etc. They are perceived by the others as not having integrated the institutional logic or collective game, and can therefore be cast aside. Each member of these three sub-systems is a potential leader. The model described here is a caricature of what is really in play as strategies for the succession. However, some careful observation of the collective representations and roles in the institution can always reveal such behaviours.

We are very concerned about the question of how the leader can generate other leaders, for we observed that many failed successions implied the failure of the institution, probably caused by the tremendous anxiety that bursts out during the crisis caused by the departure of the leader. In our experience, in order to achieve succession, the leader's successor has to be carefully "chosen". The potential leader must not display a concentration of features that could be noxious for the future institution.

The difficulties of a succession process are much like the difficulties of innovation. In a sense, to innovate implies psychically betraying one's parents (Mendel, 1992). A successful succession is also a form of *betrayal*. To explain this by a metaphor, one has to escape from the prison created by the shadow of his or her predecessor. Each individual is confronted with the necessity to succeed his parents. Within an institution, the potential successor is, in addition, confronted with the image of his parent in the person of his predecessor. He or she has to "betray" him or her psychically, in

212 FROM TRANSFORMATION TO TRANSFORMACTION

order to achieve the succession. As one example among many, let us quote the case of a young and brilliant civil servant, nominated as the head of one of the most prestigious universities in France. He took over from a much older and well-known director—himself nominated for a very important function, equivalent to the Supreme Court. One of his first decisions was to allow first-year students to have a second attempt at their final examination, a measure that had been refused for years by the former director. Considered for a long time as the "pupil" of the former director in the university, the newly nominated leader thus symbolically killed his father. For each such successful beginning to succession, how many failures are there in firms, organizations, political parties, etc., which plunge institutions into disturbance?

The biggest difficulty in succession is to avoid repetition and to achieve innovation for the life of the institution. To show how institutions can be in repetition processes, just like human beings, let us take the case of the Italian car industry, dominated by the Agnelli family. Today, Giovanni Agnelli, the "Avvocato", does not think of his own son Edoardo as his successor, but of his nephew, the executive chairman of Piaggio. This is not surprising, in view of the family's history. Their empire was founded at the end of the nineteenth century by Giovanni Agnelli, "il Senatore", who never thought that his son, also named Edoardo, would succeed him— indeed, the son eventually died in a plane crash. Instead, he named his grandson, Giovanni Agnelli, the "Avvocato", at the head of the Fiat firm. Now that the Avvocato's own succession is at stake, all the signs show that he has chosen his nephew Giovanni to succeed him, which is probably a repetition process. The anecdote would not be complete without adding that, in Italian, the same word is used for grandson and for nephew (*nipote*).

A leader, when the time for his succession approaches, has a tendency to concentrate even more power in his own hands. As a result, he or she can encroach on the role of manager (often) or even consultant. But, by putting himself or herself in another role, he or she cannot be generative. Unfortunately, leaders often raise— consciously or unconsciously—a confusion between the roles, either by increasing their monitoring of the administration of the firm (being a manager), or by leaving the primary task and acting as a fake consultant.

In a context of crisis, whether it is caused by external factors (tough competition, oil crisis, political instability, etc.) or by internal factors (from the coming departure of the boss to an employees' strike), leaders typically start confusing roles. Probably, crisis is an environment in which role boundaries are difficult to distinguish, to establish, or to accept. But it is an occasion where they should obviously be carefully worked through and be respected dynamically.

The fifth characteristic of the leader, *appetite*, is the tendency that pushes the individual to satisfy his or her needs, desire, etc. It exists for every individual, but for the leader it must be particularly acute, as the leader should enable himself (or herself) to let appetite conduct his or her leadership. Unlike a depressed individual, who has difficulty in having desire for himself (or herself) or for others, a leader must have appetite for himself (or herself) and also for others, in order to carry people along with him or her. On the other hand, the leader has to bear the reality that his or her appetite will never be totally satisfied, which has something to do with containment.

The process of taking charge of the group's anxiety, the destructive part of anxiety, can be called *containment*. The leader must have a strong capacity to contain the (dis)satisfaction of the members of the institution, as well as his or her own (dis)satisfaction. As transformation of the institution is always in process, the leader must contain the state of incompletion. Non-containment of anxiety and violence implies that dissatisfaction can burst out at any time. Good examples of this are the Los Angeles riots in 1992, or the Black Riots during the 1960s, where the absence of real and recognized leaders within both the establishment and the rioters pushed the situations to the point of explosion because no one was "in charge", that is to say, in charge of containment. Non-containment of negative feelings and affects can also create overwhelming disorder in an institution.

So, the institution and its members have to rely on the leader and his or her ability to contain. There is a relationship between them that could be identified as "dependability" (not dependency). Also, the "authoritative followership" and shared management allow the leader to rely on his or her followers. It is a two-way dependability.

Finally, the leader is a person of *path-making*. In an uncertain, shaky environment, in which any attempt to achieve a defined project inevitably fails, the leader has to keep his or her path steady.

This *path* is a translation of the leader's vision, whereas the *project* is a reduction of the vision. The leader, the individual who is the path-maker, has the capacity to live, to carry, and to bring *surprise* to the others. For only surprise can enable him or her to escape from the grip of the institution. This "grip" is utilized by the system and its environment in order to put an end to the ongoing transformation and to generate a process of repetition.

The leader of an institution is, in effect, writing the members' biography by giving a meaning to their own path. By doing this, he also writes his own biography, and forges his own path. This may be the reason why it is important to study leadership "inside" the transformation process. It is less important to emphasize the *qualities* of the leader than the *relations* of the leader with the other members of the institution, and its relation to transformation.

Consultation and institutional transformation: the sustaining triangle

The *working pair* that has to be introduced in the practice of leadership is fundamental: it enables each role in the institution to be clearly defined. The *leader* defines his vision, is generous and generative (he or she accepts that other leaders diverge from his path). And *managers* try to create and organize the means in order to fulfil the primary task of the institution, and also to enable each member of the institution to manage himself. However, another role has to be introduced into the dynamics of the institution: the *consultant's* role.

We call the threesome composed by the leader, the manager and the consultant the *sustaining triangle* (Figure 13). It is a conceptual archetype that represents the conscious and unconscious interactions that can take place between the three roles carried by individuals or groups, in order to maintain an equilibrium within the institution and to foster institutional transformation.

We cited Microsoft as an example of working pair, with Bill Gates and Steve Ballmer. The head of the computer giant also offers a good representation of the sustaining triangle, if we consider the role fulfilled by Nathan Myhrvold, Technology Director of the company. His very close relationship with Gates, as well as his

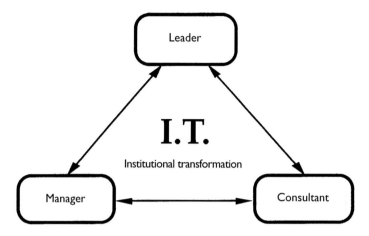

Figure 13. The sustaining triangle.

multi-disciplinary profile (computer expert, doctor of physics and mathematics), his numerous passions (palaeontology, cosmology, fishing, racing, photography), and his reputation of inspired visionary make him an effective consultant. Many of his notes have inspired Gates's strategy in the last years. The sustaining triangle at the top of Microsoft would then be Gates as the leader, Ballmer as the manager, and Myhrvold as the internal consultant.

The consultant's role is necessary for the members of the institution and also its environment, because the consultant represents the Other in bringing diversity and otherness. He or she thus plays a role similar to the "mirror" in the constitution of the ego of each individual, as defined by Lacan (Lacan, 1965). According to the words Michel Tournier, one of the greatest living French novelists, puts in the mouth of Robinson Crusoe after his encounter with Friday:

> The Other is a powerful element of distraction for us, not only because he bothers us continuously and keeps our mind busy, but also because just the possibility of his appearance throws a vague glimmer on objects of our universe which were before located in the margins of our attention, but can become its centre at any moment. [Tournier, 1972]

The consultant's role cannot be better defined.

In reality, the consultant breaks the potential one-to-one totali-tarian relationship between the leader and the manager: He or she completes and enriches it. He or she can therefore be—in the best case—the spokesperson for what is never or rarely expressed within the institution, and for the members who never or rarely speak. The consultant's intervention is naturally conflictual. Thus, the consultant's role or figure enables a permanent fight against the temptation for a leader (or the working pair) to be all-powerful, omnipotent, and all-knowing, omniscient.

An important state-owned French company was the theatre for such a scenario at the end of 1996, when the chairman decided to dismiss the four managing directors and, at the same time, to replace them by an executive council of seven members over which he would preside, the former CEO and vice-CEO becoming vice-presidents and losing their "operational" posts. Changing or reor-ganizing the head of a company is usual. Also, choosing his managers is understandable for a chairman. But this particular decision was particularly amateur and autocratic. First, since the creation of the company, a legal document holds that the company will be ruled by a chairman and a CEO; there is a specific reference to a "dualist" form of government. In regard to this document, the chairman's decision was invalid. This should have been thought about before he took the decision. Most of all, the conditions under which the decision was taken and announced to the CEOs, without ratification by any internal institution such as the board, was quite brutal: no consultation, no negotiation. The way the whole process was engaged had nothing to do with the practices of a modern company, but much more with the tendency to autocracy of an incompetent chairman. As a result, the chairman lost his credibility among his employees, and the French government had to inter-vene, maintaining the post of CEO, which was assigned to the former vice-CEO.

At the head of this important French company, the sustaining triangle is now restored, but with different relationships. The CEO is assisted by two managing directors. This offers the possibility of a threesome in which the CEO is the leader, the two managing directors are the managing entity, and an adviser in leadership completes the triangle. But also, each one of them can evolve through different roles (the leader, the manager, the consultant).

This sustaining triangle is a conceptual archetype: it is necessary that each person's role in the institution evolves. First, each person has the capacity to be, at any one time, a leader, a manager, and a consultant. The different roles are carried out by each person according to circumstances, in interaction with the others. Second, everybody is able, or might be able, to carry each of his or her three roles; moreover, each role can be more or less present at the same time in an individual or a group (Figure 14). Sometimes, one of these roles tends to be prevailing, indeed even exclusive.

The working conferences, "Institutional Transformation", organized by members of Praxis International through and by the International Forum for Social Innovation (IFSI), offer an example of this exchange of roles within the sustaining triangle. In these conferences, the members of staff fulfil two roles. First, they act collectively as management of the conference, thus assuming the

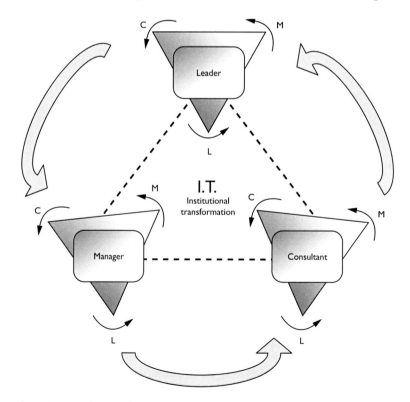

Figure 14.   Evolving roles in the sustaining triangle.

responsibility for managing the boundaries in such a way that members may confront the primary task of the conference. Second, staff members intervene as consultants during events. The staff, in their interaction with the members, must be absorbed by either role. For example, if staff members focus on the role of management, they might not fully offer their own perception and experience of events as they occur during the sessions, which eventually hinders social innovation. As another example, in these working conferences the director does not take the role of a consultant in what we call the large study system any more, whereas he or she did before—he or she does not now attend the large study system sessions. Not being the consultant in a here and now session is not meant in order for the director to take the role of manager in a better way, but to allow him or her to work on his or her role of leader. Not being a consultant, he or she can better carry out the leader's role, for him- or herself and for the others, inside the temporary institution of the conference.

The principle around which we tend to organize our institutional transformation working conferences is that *being eternally enlisted in one role can be a source of suffering, entropy, and impotence.* In different periods of our life, we must carry out different roles. We noticed that a lot of consultants feel the need to become, after several years of practice, a manager, or a leader in an entrepreneur role, and to create their own firm. Also, many counsellors to the President in the USA are former "big bosses" in the economic sector.

Finally, we want to focus on the role of the consultant, i.e., the adviser in leadership, in the institution. Advisers in leadership build a long-term relationship with executives in order to apprehend the evolution of their role. The aim of this partnership is institutional transformation. The efficiency elicited as a result of such a process eventually pervades the entire institution.

Advisers in leadership are not experts, but enlighteners: they bring a different and outline perspective on a decision, a role, a system, or a strategy in an institution. With their partner, they can thus share in an energized and renewed vision of the institution. It enables leaders and managers to get out of collective inference processes and lead action in a different way.

In a sense, advisers in leadership are complementary to the leader or the manager's loneliness and isolation. For there are some decisions that an individual at the head of an institution is forced to take alone, on his or her own responsibility. The consultant is there to offset this particular characteristic of leadership.

To conclude, any *living* institution (as opposed to one that is merely "surviving") should create an internal environment where *management* is *shared* with as many people as possible and where *leadership* is not only creative, but also *generative*. Generative of ideas, goods, and services, of course, generative of followers with authority, and, finally, generative of new leaders, so that one of them will succeed the "old" one, in a risky process. As we explained earlier, a successful succession is necessary for the vitality and the very existence of the institution. The presence of a consultant does not bring about a miracle, but he or she can help to prevent the search for omnipotence and immortality by the bosses. Helping in the path of transformation, he or she will accompany the differentiation of roles by being part of the sustaining triangle of leader, manager, consultant.

We would like to end with another example of a leadership that failed because of an impossible transformation: the worldwide known "Club Méditerranée". A few years ago, Serge Trigano succeeded his father, Gilbert Trigano, the founder of the firm. The group was confronted by several difficulties and, in Spring 1997, the stockholders (which, incidentally, included the Agnelli family) imposed a new chairman on the company: the successful chairman of EuroDisney, Philippe Bourguignon. Our working hypothesis would be that in this case the son (Serge) refused to acknowledge his differences with his father (Gilbert). Gilbert was both a leader (his vision of "a new kind of holiday" led him to create the Club Méditerranée) and a manager. Serge refused to see that he could only succeed his father in the role of manager in the first place, which would have constituted his period of "learning by experience". In the second place, his leadership should have grown in a different way to that of his father, through his developing his own personality. Serge may have been caught in unconscious drives that prevented him from sticking to his desire, from psychically "betraying" his father. In the same spirit, his refusal of a consultant (an adviser in leadership) reflected this state of mind. It seems that in this process of succession, the family and entrepreneurial dimensions were mixed up by Serge Trigano, and this confusion altered his quest for autonomy as a leader. In a sense, the transformation process was refused, and instead a conformation process was achieved . . . until Serge Trigano's dismissal by stockholders.

Coming back to the example with which we began this paper, conformation (or "cloning") cannot be the solution for leadership, whether one is at the head of an organization, or is a simple member of it. Leadership is effective when one is taking his or her full authority and displaying, more or less, the seven attributes we listed here, and cannot be separated from a transformation process in which each individual should be co-author.

Innovation should allow transformation. Each one of us has the capacity to be a co-author of institutional transformation. This entails the capacity to envision other options than repetition and reproduction of past behaviours; it implies the ability to transform roles, relations, systems, and, most of all, projections.

Note

1. This chapter was previously published in F. Gabelnick and A. W. Carr (Eds.), *Dynamic Consultation in a Changing Workplace*, Madison, CT, Psychological Press.

CHAPTER FOURTEEN

The unconscious and politics: how to explore black and white in colour

David Gutmann, with Christophe Verrier

This chapter is based on the workshop "Diversity, racial relations and transformation", organized by Color Cubano (La Havana, Cuba) and The International Forum for Social Innovation (based in Paris, France). This event took place from the 4th to the 7th of November 2006, in The National Council of Houses of Culture in La Havana, Cuba.

This experience is about the difficulty in recognizing and touching processes of discrimination based on racial issues in a political system that promotes equality in a voluntary way. Thus, as anywhere else in the world, the act of uncovering hidden dynamics based on unconscious processes triggers strong resistances, both within the workshop and from its environment, but also some astonishing revelations. However, through the processes of interpretation in such an institutional setting, it was possible to uncover some of the links between politics and the unconscious. In other words, this chapter could also be entitled "The politics of the unconscious" as well as "The unconscious of politics".

Origins of the workshop

From the beginning of our interest in Cuba, we were fascinated, but also very challenged, by working with Cuban colleagues, within Cuba, on the main issues and subjects that are the core of IFSI work over the past thirty years: promotion of leadership and authority in social systems, institutional transformation (including its political dimension), learning from experience on innovation and transformation (here in a country driven by the Revolution).

The co-operation began in 2001 with the CIPS (Centre for Political and Sociological Investigations [Ministry of Labour]).

These three institutions are based in La Havana, Cuba. A working conference, partly international, has been set up and organized almost every year. The most recent one—called Liderazgo, Participassión and TransformaCtión (Liberation, participation and transformaCtion)—was co-organized in April 2007 in Cuba by the University of La Havana (Faculty of Psychology) and IFSI, with the support of GESTA and FORDES.[1]

Some years ago in Cuba, Gisela Arandia founded (and still leads) Color Cubano, an association that aims to work on the problems of racial relations in Cuban society. She took part in this workshop in April 2006 and, as a black woman, she understood how this process of intervention could tackle in a critical way the understanding and the transformation of racial relations in Cuba. Taking into account the conscious as well as the unconscious dimensions of the issue, it could help the members of a workshop to work out their own relation to race issues and transform their practice of racial relations in Cuban society.

This starting point led her to launch a co-operation between Color Cubano and IFSI around the possibility of creating a specific workshop on this theme.

To join in this new venture, Gisela Arandia and her daughter had to extend their training in IFSI approaches after their initial participation in La Havana in April 2006. They took part as members in various working conferences: "The Passion of Entrepreneurship", organized near Bologna by ISMO (with the support of IFSI) in June 2006; "FLAM" ("Femininity, Leadership, Authority and Masculinity"), held by IFSI in Saint-Raphaël, France, and the Praxis International Network meeting in Paris in October 2006.

The organizing institutions

This new workshop, called "Diversity, racial relations and transformation", was organized by Color Cubano and IFSI at The National Council of the Houses of Culture in La Havana, Cuba.

The International Forum for Social Innovation (IFSI) is based in Paris. It has given itself the task of facilitating social innovation and, thus, of contributing to the institutional transformation of organizations: public or private companies, public administration, associations, teaching or educational institutions, whether religious or secular. Indeed, IFSI considers institutions as living systems that, as such, need to transform in order to exist. This transformation is a matter of authority in the role, leadership, and transformation of the system-in-the-mind, many crucial elements that are experienced in various events organized in IFSI. (One possible definition of system-in-the-mind [SIM] is the systemic construction—the system—through which every individual represents, in an unconscious way if it is not worked through, his or her environment. This construction at least influences, but often determines, his or her relationships, behaviour, decisions, vision of himself/herself, and place in the universe. SIM comes directly from the person's history and his or her relationships with his original institutions (family, school, etc.). It structures the individual and conditions his or her relationships with institutions in the here and now.)

Since 1978, IFSI has organized in France an annual international working conference on the theme of Authority, Leadership and Transformation. In 2005, it became the TransformaCtion® conference. Over many years, IFSI has also been developing and conducting conferences in many different countries (Australia, Belgium, the West Indies, Catalonia (Spain), Cuba, Finland, India, Ireland, Israel, Italy, the Palestinian Authority, Peru, UK, Ukraine, USA, among others), in partnership with universities and other organizations, on similar and complementary themes.

Since 2001, it has been running, in partnership with the Business School, University of Glamorgan, and then with the Business School of the University of Hull, a training programme for managers and consultants: Leading Consultation (MPhil, PhD).

In January 2004, IFSI developed a new international annual conference on the theme of Femininity, Leadership, Authority and Masculinity: the FLAM conference.

Let Gisela Arandia herself define her association. She describes Color Cubano as a working group that aims to create the conditions for a cultural, political, and social dialogue able to enhance the national consensus on reflection, analysis, and recommendations regarding the racial problems in Cuba. This project has been working intensively for more than five years. It has instigated debates and actions that approached in a coherent way the theme of racism, racial discrimination, and prejudices.

The proposal was to lead a dialogue able to express the diversity of criteria that transform the colour of the skin into social inequalities that still exist today.

This process of theorization involved well-known academic experts. It quickly identified some of the manifestations that had survived the impact of the revolution and that have, in certain sectors of Cuban society, even extended their influence in either a hidden or an open way. Essentially, this project aims to be an emancipating quest in its most historical and libertarian sense; at the same time, it highlights the reinforcement of a nation united in an inclusive way, facing up to the new challenges imposed by the neo-liberal model.

What is its aim?

The fundamental objectives of this group start from an intellectual and political concept tending to structure the struggle against racism through defining it as a manifestation opposed to the principles of revolution and social justice promoted since 1959.

In this way, the aim is to promote a cultural process that helps to open avenues for a debate reinforcing these ideological and cultural alliances in order to show the urgent necessity of accepting this problem in all its magnitude, and the dangers that neglecting this theme once more would bring.

The group has evaluated, in a responsible manner, the incompatibility between any kind of racism and the socialist ethos that Cuba is building, and how these manifestations damage the political fabric and undermine any possibility of equality. The focal point of this group opens various directions.

First, the objectives were directed to the writers and artists insisting on analysing racism as an ethical process that is in opposition to any process of liberation. From this premise, the group worked on using the opportunities opened by the artistic vanguard to draw the attention of the general public to the need to confront the problem.

Concurrent with this intellectual rapprochement, Color Cubano dedicated special attention to the community project Concha Macoyú La California, created in 1995, which was the initial inspiration for a proposal to explore racism. Since then, we have been able to demonstrate considerable progress in the black community in a practical way.

Considering the three perspectives involved (writers and artists, the academic world, and the community project), the group favoured participative discussions as a way forward, gathering a sample of the state of opinion on the theme through a spectrum in which various voices converged. This ongoing debate allowed the group to access views representing the various opinions that exist today in Cuban society about the need to confront racism, discrimination, and racial prejudices as a way of thinking diametrically opposed to the revolutionary ideology.

From this perspective, and in a modest way, Color Cubano also elaborated critical reflections and recommendations in order to find the appropriate processes for achieving racial equity in the country. As a synthesis of its aims, one can say that its work had a significant impact in Cuba, as well as in various events organized abroad, in which, for a long time, the island did not have significant representation on this theme.

Now, the immediate aim focuses not only on the debate, but also on the creation of proposals for inquiries and recommendations for building, in a participative way, an action plan useful for the Party and the Government seeking to improve Cuban society in the matter of equity.

The words "Color Cubano" were used by the national poet Nicolás Guillén in 1939, in the prologue of his book *Songoro Cosongo*.

The *Consejo Nacional de Casas de Cultura* (The National Council of Houses of Culture) is a part of the network of Cuban institutions registered by the Minister of Culture of the Republic of Cuba. This institution performs a work of academic and methodological consultation in the entire country as part of this network. The system of Houses of Culture is integrated in a National Council, fourteen provincial centres, one municipal body, and 328 houses of culture.

The aim is to promote the access of the people to culture (which includes the social problems between the various regions), to provide all the population with services and cultural opportunities, and to promote a healthy use of free time. It privileges cultural work in schools, urban districts, and communities.

The fundamental condition for the work of this system is to offer workshops of appreciation and creation of the various art manifestations, such as plastic arts (sculpture, ceramics, etc.), dance, music, theatre, and literature. As result of this work, which has been carried out since the triumph of the Revolution in 1959, the country has facilitated considerable development of amateur artists as part of the contribution to the individual and collective human development of all Cubans.

The context in Cuba

A long process of mixing blood

In common with most of the former European colonies in the West Indies, the land of Cuba, "discovered" by Christopher Colombus in 1492, carries the memories of the Indians (Taïnos and Karibs) killed in only few short years by the Conquistadores. Then a triangular trade developed, providing black slaves from Africa owned by white European colonists from Spain. This process lasted from 1513 until 1886, when slavery was abolished. Cuba became independent in 1898, but was under the control of the USA until 1909. In January 1959, the Castrist Revolution took control of the country, launching an egalitarian communist system. Today, half (51%) of the eleven million Cuban people are mixed blood, 37% are white, and 11% black.

The promotion of an egalitarian system

The presentation of Color Cubano is very significant. As anywhere else in the world, Cuban society seems to present an official appearance and a hidden aspect, more difficult to reach. Here, the appearance is very specific, because of the tremendous efforts of the communist system to promote equality. Any discrimination is forbidden. The status of women is promoted. The percentage of children in education is very high. The good reputation of the Cuban health system (particularly in public health) is not contested.

But the reality shows that some manifestations of racism and prejudices have survived the "revolutionary impact". Social groups, apparently based on the colour of the skin, may share some common specificity: access to power, place in society, incidence of imprisonment, for example.

We believe that the historical context of a country drives unconscious forces at work in its society. This seems to be particularly true in the Caribbean islands, where history has been very violent, including slavery, colonization, and domination. Moreover, the traditional difficulty in accepting differences among human beings deeply influences Cuban society. Then, the rest is a matter of having the ability to acknowledge these processes in order to work on them (as in the workshop). Not to do so creates a phenomenon of denial, with all its consequences.

Ostracism applied to foreigners

An interesting aspect of this discussion might be around the concept of the universality of human beings. In Cuba, whatever the reality of daily life is, the political system—in its permanent quest for equity and equality—clearly should be inspired by such concepts to fight against racial discrimination and prejudices. However, the discrimination against foreigners seems to be strong and obvious, based on daily life: difficulties in relating outside institutional settings, no authorization to share the same spaces (hotels, shops, etc.). Despite this, discrimination is not necessarily based on racial criteria: the result might be the same when viewed from the basis of any idea of universalism that affects the whole country systemically.

A difficult working environment

This workshop has also been notable because of the difficulties in setting it up. Its organization had constantly to overcome obstacles at a late stage before it was due to happen. For instance, a middle-aged Cuban man, initially hired for the role of Co-ordinator of Resources of the workshop, suddenly lost his permission to work. He had just been excluded from his institution because it had been discovered that he had applied for emigration to Canada.

Another thing that happened at the last minute was the cancellation of the availability of the spaces planned to be used as the workshop venue. A "plan B" was found, thanks to the help of the National Council of Houses of Culture, which offered most of the rooms in its office in Vedado, La Havana. But the workshop had to be held in parallel with the daily life activity of the Council, creating several problems of boundaries between the two. Even more, the staff was accommodated somewhere else, quite far from the venue, resulting in huge transport problems.

Of course, daily life is not easy in Cuba, but these specific difficulties might be related to unconscious resistances to the workshop: its known capacity for revelation, for identifying and working on issues that are usually denied as taboos, seemed to be anticipated by the system, which developed a hidden but active resistance to it.

The final working conditions remained uncomfortable, particularly because the available spaces were very limited. As a result, the members were crammed into these rooms, calling to mind the barranqueros, the districts in La Havana where black and mixed blood people were living during colonization and that still exist today.

The working approach

A four-day specific programme had been conceived for this workshop. As usual, the members were invited to take part in two kinds of sessions: the here-and-now and the reflection sessions.

The first sessions provide the members with institutional settings that they can use in order to explore and experience the themes of the workshop. This exploration is very practical and vibrant. It is done individually and/or institutionally, with or without the involvement of the staff. It includes action, environments, and roles (taken or projected), but also feelings, emotions, and physical sensations that help to touch and discern individual and collective unconscious processes.

Working through these sessions, members usually enact whatever the situation requires, in interaction with the other participants, but also what comes from themselves, from their inner personal histories (for instance, systems-in-the-mind repeated within the workshop, patterns inherited from childhood, from the family, or other early institutions).

The next sessions, dedicated to reflection, are designed to offer the members opportunities to associate in a creative way about their experiences in order to become able to identify and interpret them through working hypothesis. As soon as a discovery is made, or an example of learning from experience is shared, members are invited to transform their behaviour accordingly, using the workshop as a contained space particularly appropriate for testing responses, or exploring new experiences.

In direct connection to this workshop, we must acknowledge the inspiration of FLAM. Created by Jacqueline Ternier-David and David Gutmann, this international working conference is the most recent of IFSI's projects. (For more information about IFSI, please consult www.ifsi-fiis-conferences.com.) The central theme is about femininity, leadership, authority, and masculinity in institutional life. It is interesting to note that one of the intuitions of its founders was that nowadays social and institutional structures and systems may shift from a model built around a unique centre to one offering a polynuclear configuration. The place and the dynamics that each person negotiates within these centres influence his or her institutional life and behaviour.

This intuition provided the basis of the structure of the first here and now event—called the Systemic diversity—the primary task of which was to study the experience of racial polarity in a large study system, and to understand the dynamic of the relations created consciously and unconsciously among the members within the system. The seating arrangement devised for this session was a line of chairs arranged in a continuing double spiral.

The second here and now event was the Sistema de Relaciones Raciales y Relaciones Raciales Aplicadas (System of Racial Relations and Racial Relations Application). These two related types of sessions were based on the design, methodology, and experience of the Institutional Event in FL.M: FLAM and Flam'n Co. It offered a space for learning by experience, where the participants were invited to liberate themselves from their traditional representations of diversity, racial relations, and transformation.

Members created relationships and sub-systems among themselves. Then they had to build a system of representative government that invited the expression, exploration, and transformation of their representations.

The management invited members to create, by drawing lots, four sub-systems: diversity, race, relation, and transformation. Then it announced that a government would be composed of one representative of each sub-system. At this point, the government would take up the role of management of the session, publicly electing its own President, while the staff would relinquish this role and become the team of Advisers.

To reflect and associate on these experiences, members were offered some reflection sessions such as Plenary Sessions, an Active Meditation Event, a TransformaCtion Analysis Group (or TAG), and a Discernment Session, where they had to study their experiences of the various roles taken within the workshop in order to anticipate transformations in the workshop and in their real-life institutions.

The eight-member staff of the workshop was composed on the basis of diversity: besides David Gutmann, a white French director, the staff included four Cuban women (two mixed blood, one black, and a white), a Peruvian white woman, a Trinidadian black man, and a Spanish Catalan white man. The diversity showed also in terms of age (from twenty-six to sixty-six) and religion (Catholic, Protestant, Jewish, and/or agnostic).

Thirty-five members, from twenty to sixty years old, registered for the workshop, all Cuban except for one black man from the USA. The membership represented very diverse sectors of Cuban society, comprising intellectuals (professors and students), workers, and artists (painters, sculptors, poets, writers, rap singers). The majority of the members were black or mixed blood. There was no white man among the members. There was a majority of women.

The final and central element of the workshop, its primary task, was to explore the relationship between diversity, racial relationships, and transformation through the experience within the workshop, taken as a temporary learning institution.

The course of the workshop: challenges and resistances

What happened within the workshop was obviously very rich, even full of passion and emotion. We have selected some parts of this complex institutional path that appear to us as the most significant.

The leaving of the only foreign member, and other events

This member left the workshop during the first day, just after the Active Meditation Event. He did not say why, and only shared his feeling of "entering into a religious workshop". He was a black man, a professor in the USA staying for a while at the University of La Havana. Beyond the various associations that this situation suggested (such as discrimination against foreigners, the link with racial relationships in the USA, the focus on a black man, etc.), the first systemic hypothesis was to link it to the trajectory of another member who was the only white woman of the government.

The most revealing aspect was that she was sitting in a corner while her three black and mixed blood government colleagues were standing up. The director interpreted her role as a "white Queen with her black slaves". Being unable to differentiate between the systemic projected role and the chosen role, she began a kind of strike, refusing to really participate in the following sessions of the workshop, in which she was merely present. This could indicate an attempt by the membership to explore from experience how a Cuban system deals with differentiation processes and a sense of privilege.

In another dimension of the workshop, the difficult material context of its realization had not improved. One of the three co-ordinators was an older black Cuban woman, head of Color Cubano and co-founder of the workshop. She suddenly appeared as the black "good mother", for two reasons: the constant efforts she had to deploy to maintain, with many contradictions, the boundaries between the workshop and the daily activity of the Council; she tried many times to soften the casual relationship between members and staff.

Maybe a mirror process appeared between staff and members: in the staff, a white foreign director paired with a black Cuban good mother, this couple having created the workshop; in the membership, an inverse couple of a black foreign man and a white Cuban woman, both unable to really deploy their authority within the system, as if this couple was created by the membership as an answer to the huge impact that the staff of the workshop (representing also its primary task) had on them.

A black female President (vs. a black female dictator)

During the System of Racial Relations and Racial Relations Application, the membership chose four women as the government: two were black, one mixed blood, and one white. Then, the government publicly elected its blackest member as President.

Apparently, the system seemed to be very anxious not only to experience such a democratic process, but also to discover its potency. Members had much difficulty in containing emotions, and the process ended in physical attacks on staff members during the last session.

After this trauma, the next morning, a black female "dictator" emerged from the system during the following Diversity System. Then she was excluded from the session by the other members, through a deeply difficult process.

This sequence was seen as strong ambivalence between political models. On the one hand, a democratic process was proposed and applied, despite much resistance and hesitation. On the other hand, the model of a repeated revolution spontaneously emerged, but was unable to create the conditions of the real transformation that was required. In addition, some ambivalence might have been expressed through the repeated emergence of black female leaders as an inverse image of Fidel Castro (a white male).

In other words, the members elaborated first a real progression in electing a fully interracial government. Even more, it was composed only of women! Of course, there was a majority of women, both in the staff and in the membership. But, in a deeper way, this might represent a desire to transform the traditional leadership by trying a totally unusual configuration, mirroring the fact that interbreeding between races can only happen through women.

In this phase, they were certainly influenced by the title and aims of the workshop, as well as the way they could perceive the director and the staff in general. They might have looked for a connection with them in a way that did not exclude seduction and a certain "politically correct" spirit. But such a "zig" (progression) can frighten, even terrify, and created then the conditions of a "zag" (regression), which actually happened and lasted until almost the end of the workshop (except for the very last sessions).

This "zag", and more particularly the physical attacks on the staff, was triggered by a song chosen from a CD by the staff: "My Way", by Frank Sinatra. In selecting this song, the staff aimed to openly draw the members' attention on their own specific way of acting, based on repeating habits. (Actually, "My Way" is Frank Sinatra's English adaptation of a very well-known French song called "Comme d'habitude" ["As Usual"], written and sung by Claude François in 1967. Maybe the members had (unconscious) knowledge of this information, which reinforces the focus here of the staff on repeating habits.)

This process, and the feeling of being unveiled, created a strong irritation, a frenzy, leading the members to perpetrate physical attacks on the staff! Only the director was not touched, not because of any impressive physical aspect, but probably because the members felt that he had to be preserved at all costs.

We believe that this feeling of the members' came from the specific role that the director takes in this kind of conference. In fact, the members had a special awareness that the director is specifically linked to the unconscious (on behalf of the entire workshop) and ultimately represents its primary task, as well as the potentiality and faith inherent in this task.

This experience might reflect the uncertainty and anxiety created by the process of transition that will take place after the Castro brothers are no longer the leaders of Cuba. Moreover, our hypothesis is that the unconscious content that emerges from such a workshop can mirror what will really happen on the Cuban political scene in the future.

In other words, what is the meaning of the fact that a black female dictator appeared the day after? We think that it may announce that a black general will succeed the Castro brothers, reproducing what happened in Haïti during the decolonization. (Toussaint-Louverture [the glorious leader of the Haïtian liberation from the French colonizer], the former slave Christophe, is a general of Jean-Jacques Dessalines at the liberation of Haïti in 1804. After a successful coup against Dessalines [1806], Christophe becomes President and then king of the North part of the country, known as King Henri the First, or Henri-Christophe [cf. Carpentier, 1949; Césaire, 1963.].

Along the same lines, we can now offer a further interpretation of the leaving of the black North American male member. In reality and symbolically, he was the only foreign member. Our hypothesis is that the transformation of Cuba will happen only with and through the Cuban residents: neither the "gringos" (even if black), nor the Cuban emigrants will take part in this process, and any direct intervention from outside which aims to interfere in the future of Cuba after the disappearance of the historical leaders would be doomed to failure. Even the physical and psychic attacks against the staff could be seen in the same way.

We have to remember that Che Guevara, being an Argentinian citizen, was the second-in-command in the Castrist regime. Very quickly, he took charge of exporting the Revolution from Cuba, first to Africa, and later on to South America, especially Bolivia, where he was assassinated.

More broadly, in terms of spiritual dimension, the director could be perceived as a white god coming from abroad, over the sea, with his black and mixed blood believers and two white servants, creating a new religion and mirroring Fidel Castro. Of course, in such a configuration, the staff was also mirroring the white Queen with her black slaves.

Resistance against leadership and authority

The resistance to inventing a new way of government and to using the opportunity to create and take up roles of leaders in the context of the current Cuban system raised a lot of anxiety. Authority and leadership appeared as not necessarily wanted. Roles seemed to be taken with no desire. As a result, the government seemed depressed and inconsistent up to the point where the youngest representative—who happened to be the daughter of the founder of Color Cubano—took up her leadership and decided to mobilize her authority and experience in a challenging and constructive way.

She tried not only to re-mobilize her three female fellows of the government, but she also took a decisive stance and led the last session of Diversidad, opening the way to an impressive discovery and revelation.

In recreating a dictatorial system within the workshop, members seemed to express—at least in a large part of the workshop—a strong tendency to repetition and a huge denial of the opportunity that was offered to them. They even created the most unrealistic system, as if they wanted to demonstrate that no other way of government could exist. This was expressed by the predominance of women in the government as well as among the anti-task leaders who tried to restore the traditional Cuban political system. Male members, in contrast, were much more hidden and silent. However, this is not the reality in Cuba, where the male is predominant, particularly in politics.

Finally, the role of the staff, both in the role of consultants (reflection sessions) and advisers (here and now sessions), together with the impact of the methodology and the role of the pro-task members, had a determining effect on the whole process.

In the last plenary event, the Session of discernment, the members were asked to propose collectively a word that expressed their state of mind at that point of the workshop.

The result was the word *reto*, which means challenge. This word testifies the transformation that happened during the workshop. Helped by the clarification, hypotheses, and interpretations formulated during the various reflection sessions, the members' state of mind moved from resistance, anxiety, uncertainty, and doubt to a clearer space where the issue of racial relations could be—at least partly—uncovered, examined, and worked out. The future is seen as a challenge, but practical working plans emerged: the members created a webpage, called RETOS, where they recorded their experiences and continue to update them; they also organized recurrent events gathering most of the members in order to continue to apply the learning from the workshop. Now, one year after, they still meet.

The pantheon of distinguished women

Five women emerged to carry determining roles for the course of the workshop. Did they represent the five main archetypes of Cuban women in power and/or authority? Or did they express five facets of the same imaginary character?

The first one was the only white person among the four female members of the government. Being associated as a "white Queen with her black slaves", and alternating attitudes of arrogance and sulkiness, she could represent the traditional power of women, and particularly of white women.

The second woman was the very black dictator imposing power, and being finally excluded.

The third was the black President of the government, who was able to express her desire, but who finally entered into a "depression" from which she had much difficulty in escaping.

Gisela Arandia was the fourth. With her unwavering good will, as a black good mother who actually gave birth to the workshop, she assumed the role of go-between in mediating several conflicts, to the point of risking losing her own authority. Only her strong and deep desire to learn and to discover, but also to help the others' learning and discoveries, prevented her from falling. In fact, it enabled her to continue her quest for social transformation.

The fifth woman was Gisela Morales, the daughter of Gisela Arandia. Carrying the mixing of races and colours, she finally proved able to take authority for herself and for the system, through many zig-zags and periods of rejection. Then, too, she was able to lead the system in the direction of discoveries and learning.

How significant is this series of women? It is as if the attempts made by white or black women "failed" one after the other, laying the ground for the success of the last one, who was concretely carrying the métissage.

The director as the gate to the unconscious

During the last Diversity System, the white director felt a very potent push to pair him with the youngest black member of the government. This inspired in him a profound intuition, leading him to ask the members which of them had a partner, husband or wife, of the "opposite" colour. The answer was very significant: only the three remaining members of the government could match the criteria! This opened up a set of interpretations about the unconscious conditions that prompted the taking up of leadership. Out of thirty-five members who knew little or nothing about each other, they unconsciously "chose" for the government that would try to transform racial differences and prejudices the only ones who had an official companion of the other race. The fourth one was therefore impelled to create an institutional couple with the director, "doubling" the initial working relation launched by her black mother.

However, it also raises some new questions about the nature of the role of director in this kind of workshop or working conferences. Indeed, the very difficult conditions in which the workshop was carried out (reproducing here usual daily life in Cuba), as well as the constant presence of Cuban sensuality and creativity, led the staff, and particularly the director, to use resources that are not often used in other circumstances. The rational and the conscious level were constrained and constraining, pushing the director and the staff in another direction.

Maybe the first condition necessary is the capacity to consider the unconscious as the most beautiful and powerful available resource to foresee, understand, and act. This path is a zig-zag, never a straight line. A zig-zag expresses the complexity, the difficulty of the process, the uncertainty that can submerge things, the alternation between progression and regression, the required doubt and faith connected with succeeding.

Thus, the second condition is the capacity for a staff member, and particularly the director, to let himself or herself be invaded by the unconscious. The director offers him- or herself to the unconscious production of the institutional system but he or she can only do it in working on and constantly weakening his or her own resistances.

Through this work, the director obtains an "access" to the unconscious. He or she becomes the gate to the unconscious. Or, possibly, merely the porter at this gate, a kind of liaison officer, or he or she might alternate between both roles.

However, this role is rather passive. Even if he or she has the capacity to take this role, he or she must move aside. If he or she is the gate, this is a very passive role; if he or she is the gate porter or the liaison officer, this is a more active role, but always conscious of his/her limits. The main quality of a director is to be touched by the unconscious, to take the risk of giving it expression.

As the director, it is not a matter of facing the massive irruption of the unconscious, but merely to move aside; to be in and within the unconscious, to have the capacity to think that you can lose control of what is happening, knowing that you can rely on the two basic processes: containment and pulsation. Then you can let go, abandon control, and tell yourself that you can do it . . . and do it really. Indeed, the danger lies in the possibility of being over-whelmed, swallowed, unless you mobilize those two elements, containment and pulsation, with the help of the rest of the staff.

Although this experience obviously has a spiritual dimension, this is not a religious experience. The director is not a go-between for the unconscious, considered as an untouchable and unreachable divinity, on the one hand, and, on the other hand, for the congre-gation of the faithful. He or she is a "passeur", a "ferryman", passive or active. And the other staff members contribute by reliev-ing the director of any other tasks.

Then, the director can help the other staff members, followed by the membership, to enter, to gain direct access, not only to the insti-tutional unconscious of the conference, but also to what it means for each of them as a living part of the system, exercising a role. At the same time, the unconscious "invades" the conference and its partic-ipants. The path of transformation results from the interaction of all these forces, thanks to an authentic process of containment and pulsation.

Indeed the aim is not to create a director who expresses work-ing hypotheses as the Pythia stated oracles in Delphi. But it is to lead a path, followed and relaid by the staff members and the membership, where each one can discover how to learn from expe-rience, including about unconscious processes.

How to explore black and white in colour?

Many questions remain open after this experience. For instance, what is the capacity of any political system to erase such uncon-scious processes as racial discrimination and prejudice through the rational and voluntary promotion of equality?

This kind of question is not limited to the specific case of Cuba. It concerns any political action. What does happen when a political action is limited to rationality, in denying the historical and uncon-scious roots of the issues that it proposes to improve? How can the political action avoid being limited to superficial changes and engage in real transformations/transformActions?

After the past fifty years of the Castrist system, the racial problem remains at the core of Cuban society. Black and mixed blood people seem to be the most eager to explore it—with ambivalence— and to transform it. White people—and above all white men—seem to be the most resistant. The workshop has been a lead cast, even a thunderbolt, which both illuminated and cleaved through the current stratifications. The process of revelation, of revelAction, however painful it is, may be the only way to avoid being an inmate of a present prison that will determine the future.

The sudden appearance of the unconscious may be the most efficient element for shaking and questioning the existing systems in the mind (SIMs) and breaking the cycle of their established immobility. The impact of the unconscious, struggling against the hold of the past on the present, brings surprise, joy, and liberation. This happens in the psychic and spiritual dimensions, but also in the political one.

When one finds the capacity to give space to unconscious forces, to express them without being too afraid, they free the future. To live this process in a managed, contained, and pulsated way is an opportunity to avoid repeating the past—meaning to act out in losing and forgetting our freedom and authority.

The relationship between conscious and unconscious cannot be seen in black and white: it is a permanent back and forth between both, which focuses at certain times on the conscious root, and at other times on the unconscious root. For this reason, it must be seen in colours.

Surprisingly enough, we might now give another meaning to the well-known concept of transference, not only the projections and introjections between staff and members, but also the ability to transfer the unconscious in the conscious world, and vice versa.

In fact, this workshop worked on *democracy*, i.e., the *liberty* to think, to feel, and to act, the *initiative* to innovate and to transform.

Appendix

The programme of the workshop

Nov 2006	Saturday 4	Sunday 5	Monday 6	Tuesday 7
09.00–10.00		Diversity System	Diversity System	Diversity System
		Break	*Break*	*Break*
10.30–11.30		System of Racial Relations Application	Diversity System	Transformation Analysis Group (GAT)
		Break	*Break*	*Break*
12.00–13.00		System of Racial Relations	System of Racial Relations	Sesssion of Discernment
13.45–14.45	Opening Plenary	*Lunch*	*Lunch*	*Lunch*
15.00-16.00	Diversity System	System of Racial Relations		Transformation Analysis Group (GAT)
	Break	*Break*	*Break*	
16.30–17.30	Active meditation event	Active meditation event	Active meditation event	
	Break	*Break*	*Break*	
18.00–19.00	System of Racial Relations	System of Racial Relations Application	System of Racial Relations Application	
	Dinner	*Dinner*	*Dinner*	
20.30–21.30	System of Racial Relations		Transformation Analysis Group (GAT)	

Note

1. GESTA: Centro de Gestión Empresarial, Superación Técnica y Administrativa (Ministry of the Steel and Mechanical Industries). FORDES: Centro Coordinador para la Formación y el Desarrollo del Capital Humano (Ministry of Telecommunications and Information Systems). CIPS, GESTA and FORDES are based in La Havana, Cuba.

CHAPTER FIFTEEN

Anxiety and passion: about the inescapability of depression

David Gutmann, with Pascale Ravot-Loucheux

A t the end of this journey into the core of the consulting profession, and most obviously to reach a better understanding of the transformation process, we come now to the most important part of these considerations: the connection between *anxiety* (the word "anxiety" is deliberately chosen instead of the word "stress", which is more often used in a "politically correct" way (cf. Chapter Five) and *passion*.

These two concepts may seem puzzling, not to say out of place, in a book dealing with management and government. And yet, we cannot be closer to the point. What is at stake here is vital in a firm's life, as well as in our own lives. Far from wandering from our subject, we come back to the very start, where everything begins: it requires every part of us to build our own identity, and this is also what drives us to live and to act. Let us explain the reason why.

Two phenomena are acting in both people's lives and within institutions' lives:

- anxiety, on the one hand, born from the fear of death, which comes from the death instinct (Thanatos);
- passion, on the other hand, born from desire, which comes from the life instinct (Eros) (Figure 15).

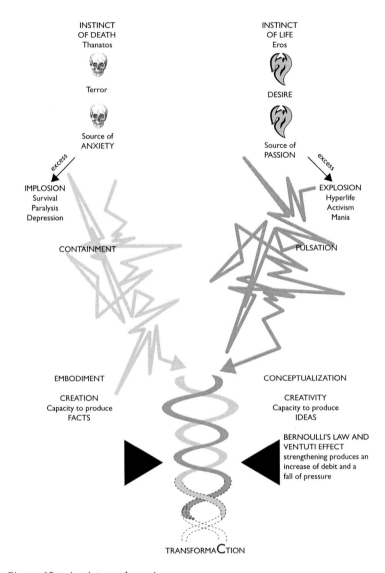

Figure 15. Anxiety and passion.

If both of these forces are not transformed, they will not be able to save the institution from inevitable self-destruction.

Too much *anxiety* leads to survival, paralysis, and depression. When submitted to pressure that is too strong (the fear of death, which it is unable to regulate), a business locks itself into a repetitive behaviour mechanism that it cannot escape. This system gets jammed and eventually shuts down. Although it might believe that it is escaping both troubled times and unavoidable issues by constantly repeating the same schema, it will, on the contrary, accelerate the conditions of its *im*plosion and thus, inevitably, its disappearance. Conversely, too much *passion* leads to *ex*plosion, i.e. hyperlife.

Activism wins, and hyperlife becomes the rule. The firm wears itself out in hysterical, perpetual motion. The danger of "burning out" overtakes its employees and its managers. It is the reverse side of depression and, tightly linked to the latter, it also tries to escape Thanatos.

As in manic-depressive episodes, stages of activism and depression follow in turn, each of them producing the other.

Anxiety and passion must both transform themselves to avoid the institution being steered into the wreckers' yard of survival or hyperlife. It must find the way to effective life once more.

By the process of *containment*, anxiety will change into a state that allows a factual evaluation, which will give birth to actual, material achievements. Thus, the leaders' great works or plans, whatever the state of the times or the political or religious environment, are the embodiment of a self-controlled and transformed institution, facing the death terror, building firm foundations to ensure its durability, and surviving the leaders' disappearance.

Passion is an overflowing phenomenon, but it can be regulated through the *pulsation* process. Therefore, the Japanese ideogram meaning passion is a symbolic drawing of the heart (Figure 16).

Pulsation, as well as being a function of the heart as a muscle, controls and follows the rhythm of passion, and imposes on it diastolic and systolic phases that provide the pauses necessary for normal breathing, without panting, gasping, excessive slowing

Figure 16.   Koï.

down, or even cessation. Through this transformation, passion gives birth to *creativity*, i.e., the ability to produce ideas and concepts. Thus, we see *pulsation as the best possible antidote to pulsion*. Let us present some practical examples at the institutional level.

One of the unconscious strategies, characteristic of institutions that do not want to grow out of ultra-conservatism, is to isolate the "crazy "creative agents by making them unable to establish links with sensible creative agents, or even with zealot bureaucrats. This achieved, they are totally unable to create or to change things. At an extreme degree, their isolation can unleash the dormant "craziness" in them.

In other situations, power is totally entrusted to the zealot bureaucrats who, if they are unable to connect with the creative agents—be they crazy or sensible—will not be able to create anything.

However, if all the conditions allowing the connection between these two energies are achieved—via the containment/pulsation process—a *generative trend* can appear. It will result from the intimate intricacy between these two processes. One cannot exist and succeed without the other. Thus, to mix them, to let them coincide, is to allow them to be complementary, to feed mutually by fully accepting their complementarity.

The subsequent ideas and facts that will appear will testify that transformation is actually under way at the core of the institution. At the same time, an increase in the field of restraints and oppositions will be noticed. A constriction (cf. the Venturi effect) of the transformation area will ensue, creating not only an acceleration, but also a diminution of the pressure, thus a depression. The risk , then, is to fall into the manic–depressive pathology again.

We have just mentioned a physical law, well known to scientists and particularly to engineers. Of course, we did not invoke it randomly. The deep and fractal consistency of life—from cosmos to cell—can and must encourage us to enlarge the field of the understanding of our ways of acting and behaving.

To illustrate what we have just said, there is a clear example in the application of Bernoulli's law—and more precisely the Venturi effect—on the flowing of air (Figure 17). The wing of a plane, with its characteristic profile of a flat surface beneath and a convex one above, forces air to flow more across the top of the wing than under

Figure 17.   The Venturi effect.

it; this then causes an acceleration of air above the wing, and a depression that draws the wing upwards ("the lift"), enabling the plane to fly. But, this very phenomenon that makes a plane fly can, if deceleration is too strong, lead to stalling and eventual crashing. What is needed, then, is to keep an optimum "pressure" in the key step of constriction, and to accept the concomitant depression phenomenon.

Analogy with the energies present in the transformation process is obvious: in the vital moment of transformation, the concepts of dynamics, speed, and acceleration are paramount. Thus, as in the example of the plane, if one cannot control a slower speed, the whole process is bound to collapse.

Another example can be found in climatology: it demonstrates a similar process in the forming of depressions that can lead to tropical storms, typhoons, cyclones, or hurricanes.

Therefore, we must admit that along the whole transformation journey there is an element of depression; what is at stake, then becomes of vital importance. Our options are

- to transform transformation by interaction with the containment process;
- to let go and be sucked down in an endless fall; we fall then into a melancholic depression (individual or collective);
- to compensate, as well as we can, using the manic–depressive process, although this cannot last long because, again, we will be at risk of implosion in the depressed state, or of explosion in the manic state.

The example of "B", a large South American bank that is a leader of its traditional market, is telling. In this bank, the operating chart allowed some crazy agents to be linked to a larger number of sensible agents and to a few zealot bureaucrats. Then, the zealot bureaucrats' leader, X, attempted to become the overall leader. By clarifying and slightly accelerating these processes, our interference enabled the zealot bureaucrats to be ousted and power to be given to Y, the leader of the sensible agents. Similarly, the crazy agents' leader, Z, was ousted too. Eventually, the one that seemed to be a crazy creative agent, as well as those who were thought to be his allies, the consultants, were also evicted.

On a practical level, this is what happened. On the verge of retirement, Z, who had initiated the project, finds a new incentive in Eros and creativity and wants to achieve a dream that so far had escaped him. He had a very strong *passion* to make the bank more useful, more efficient at serving his country, by evading the dominating–dominated hierarchy that was fundamental in the bank's practice, as well as being rooted in his country's deepest traditions. According to this wish, our intervention started immediately. Very quickly we started working at full speed (indeed, in overdrive); the rhythm of the sessions, particularly the ones dealing with the formation of a group of internal consultants, became very intensive: five or six workshops a year. Real dynamics aimed at transforming the institutions began. The work achieved together took the form of a stage play, meant as a mirror for the way the bank and, thus, its main managers, was acting. It was, immediately, a great success, and generated excessive joy and euphoria.

But very soon, fear succeeded happiness. After "everything" had been given, a feeling of emptiness took place. Similarity with post-partum or post-coitus depression is obvious. And it proved impossible to start the machine efficiently again. Workshops were systematically postponed, then suppressed. The plane of transformation started gliding, eventually stopped, and fell.

This fall was accelerated by a terrific earthquake during the summer of 2007, which necessitated the whole country, as well as institutions and individuals, to concentrate on survival, thus killing any form of desire. A few days after the earthquake, we arranged a workshop to keep up people's spirits. But it was already too late; the flame of passion had been quenched. Within the bank, roles had been reversed. The Board had been changed. Z, who had initiated the project, was out of the game. Then, as he was of an appropriate age, he retired.

One must be conscious that when the journey to transformation is actually approaching the required achievement, the very proximity of this achievement generates a strong desire to draw backwards.

It is a very fragile instant when, in the face of the violence of this sudden awareness, the resisting forces are such that either the achievement is "forced", when resistance suddenly collapses and TransformaCtion is possible (perhaps because "everybody is tired out" and there is a momentary freezing), or "there is a tough clash" and regression eventually takes over.

The transformation phenomenon is, *per se*, a continuous, self-generating process. It does not mean, of course, that the consultant must always stand by the institution, but he has to help it in the key moments of the journey by assisting the manager and/or the leader to be aware of the mechanisms operating within the institution but to remain confident, and must then keep the pressure going, even in the worst moments of uncertainty. It is the reason why the consultant's role is always immanent and temporary.

The adviser in leadership can enable the transformation of a lot of "things" in the institution, by the actors or co-authors who are part of it, by the people surrounding it. *But nothing is ever absolute or final. A final victory cannot exist.* Things happen as if one could only temporarily defeat Thanatos. This acknowledgement is neither pessimistic nor defeatist; it is part of the human order. It is an aspect of the adviser in leadership's activity. One has just to accept it, to remember it, and to take it into account in our intervention.

The consultant's mission is to escort the institution as far as possible in its transformation work. When one knows that, anyway, the process will stop—and one does not know when—one has to be even more efficient, by enhancing the "zigs", and opposing the" zags" (by way of the" blockers").

What is at stake is to help the journey to go its way, even in the teeth of the wind, and even if pauses or stopovers (shorter or longer) are necessary. But one must keep in one's mind and one's heart and one's guts that, despite storms and withdrawals, one can and must be on course.

At some stages, it is as if the institution is worn out, is not able to stand the journey of transformation any longer. Resisting forces overwhelm what has already been achieved, and the process is bound to be halted. In these circumstances, consultants, as well as people within the institution, face frustration and dissatisfaction, dejection, and even breakdown.

But the seeds of transformation are already in the ground, and the time will come when they will be able to bear fruit.

Processes go on, according to their own rhythm, and people go on—intentionally or not—carrying out, in their professional or personal lives, what they have discovered . . . for their own good, but for ours too.

An (un)expected postscript

A t the end of this book, my first intention was to avoid concluding, whatever the conclusion might be, since the purpose of such a reflexion is to stay unended and open.

Nevertheless, I found it indispensable to remember the key element that marks the end of the first years of our century: the world crisis which affects us and which will go on affecting us for a very long time. Twenty years after the fall of the Berlin Wall, which opened the way to every exchange, we are experiencing—paradoxically—the excesses of the absence of boundaries. Do we have, thus, to rebuild new walls to install order again? Actually, the only wall we can go on building today is the wall of interpretation, not to say the wall of interpretaction. It is a long-term process, element after element, stone by stone, without destroying the former interpretations but adding new prospects.

For example, the main (or the only) credit of George Bush Junior's two terms of presidency of the USA was, without doubt, to enable Obama's election! Because we know that, in the zig-zag path of Transformaction, the zigs cannot happen without the zags, if, of course, the blockers stop the zags before one cannot put the clock back.

Furthermore, we can ask ourselves if this major crisis, by far the most important one in every field since the Second World War, is not, in fact, an auto-immune disease of postmodern capitalism, where the body destroys its own protections; even a sort of organizational AIDS from a triumpher acting out without any real regulation on fallow lands, where pulsions have overcome pulsations (cf. Chapter Fifteen, "Anxiety and passion"), thus enabling the negative affects which were allowed unlimited development. We can also understand that the absence, or the loss of, an external regulation leads inevitably, in the short or longer term, to the sudden production of internal antibodies fighting a non-vital external aggression and, thus, poisoning the body they were expected to defend.

It is amazing, then, to notice that the Seven Deadly Sins and their corollaries became almighty sovereigns: gluttony and greed, sloth and blindness, jealousy and envy, stinginess and covetousness, lechery and ostentation, and, most of all, pride and omnipotence.

A new pact with Mephistopheles was concluded at the dawn of the twenty-first century, trying to deny, in the most absurd and destructive way, our existential anguish and anxiety, which, conversely, help us to accept with courage and lucidity the fact that we are, at the same time, mortal and able to desire, which is the definition of the human being.

REFERENCES

Balmary, M. (1986). *Le Sacrifice interdit: Freud et la Bible*. Paris. B. Grasset.

Bertolucci, B. (1970). *Il conformista*. Film.

Bion, W. (1961). *Experiences in Groups, and Other Papers*. London: Tavistock.

Bion, W. (1962). *Learning from Experience*. London: Heinemann [reprinted London: Karnac], reprinted in *Seven Servants*, 1977e.

Bion, W. (1977). *Seven Servants: Four Works*. New York: Aronson.

Bion, W. R. (1961). *Experiences in Groups*. London: Tavistock.

Bollas, C. (1995). *Cracking Up: The Work of Unconscious Experience*. London: Routledge.

Buber, M., & Kaufmann, W. A. (1970). *I and Thou*. New York: Scribner.

Carpentier, A. (1975). *The Kingdom of this World*. Harmondsworth: Penguin.

Chabert, J.-L, Chemla, K., & Dahan Dalmedico, A. (dir.) (1992). Chaos et déterminisme. In: *Points Sciences*. Paris: Le Seuil.

Crozier, M. (1977). *L'Acteur et le système* (in collaboration with Erhard Friedberg). Paris: Le Seuil.

Damasio, A. (1995). *L'erreur de Descartes ou la Raison des Emotions*. Paris: Odile Jacob.

di Lampedusa, T. (1958). *Il Gattopardo* (*The Leopard*). Milan: Feltrinelli.

Dumézil, G. (1959). *Les Dieux des Germains: essai sur la formation de la religion scandinave*. Paris: PUF.

Encyclopaedia universalis (1990). Paris: Encyclopaedia Universalis France.

Field, J. (1981). *A Life of One's Own* (2nd edn). New York: Putnam.

Foucault, M. (1966). *Les mots et les choses*. Paris: Gallimard.

Freud, S. (1912–1913). *Totem and Taboo. S.E., 13*: 1–161. London: Hogarth.

Freud, S. (1917e). Mourning and melancholia. *S.E., 14*: 239–258. London: Hogarth.

Freud, S. (1920g). *Beyond the Pleasure Principle. S.E., 18*: 7–64. London: Hogarth.

Freud, S. (1921c). *Group Psychology and the Analysis of the Ego. S.E., 18*: 67–143. London: Hogarth.

Freud, S. (1923b). *The Ego and the Id. S.E., 19*: 3–66. London: Hogarth.

Freud, S. (1925d). An autobiographical study. *S.E.. 20*: 3–70. London: Hogarth.

Girard, R. (1961). *Mensonge romantique et vérité Romanesque*. Paris: Grasset.

Girard, R. (1972). *La violence et le sacré*. Paris: Grasset.

Girard, R. (1978). *Des choses cachées depuis la fondation du monde*. Paris: Grasset.

Girard, R. (1982). *Le Bouc émissaire*. Paris: Grasset.

Gracian, B. (1684). *Le Criticon: Maxime CCXCI, Oraculo manual y arte di prudencia*. Paris: Le Seuil, 2008.

Gramsci, A. (1920). Deux révolutions. *L'Ordine Nuovo, 8*: 3 July.

Guillén, N. (1943). *Songoro Cosongo*. La Habana: Editorial Pàginas.

Gutmann, D. (1988). The decline of traditional defenses against anxiety. *Proceedings of the First International Symposium on Group Relations*, Keble College, Oxford. A. K. Rice Institute.

Gutmann, D. (1989). The decline of traditional defences against anxiety. In: F. Gabelnick & A. Wesley Carr (Eds.), *Proceedings of the First International Symposium on Group Relations*, Keble College, Oxford, A. K. Rice Institute.

Gutmann, D. (1993). Reduction in the effectiveness of social systems as a defense against anxiety. Career development worldwide: "How to learn from each other". *Journal of Career Development*, 20(1).

Gutmann, D. (1993). *Vers une nouvelle culture urbaine*. La formation, moteur du développement urbain. Rencontres de Marne-la-Vallée, Altamira.

Gutmann, D., Millat, J.-F., van der Rest, F.-M., Ternier-David, J., & Verrier, C. (2005). *Disillusionment, Dialogue of Lacks*. London: Karnac.

Gutmann, D., Pierre, R., Ternier-David, J., & Verrier, C. (1997). The paths of authority: from the unconscious to the transcendental. Intervention at the Arab University of Jerusalem, *Feelings work in Europe*. Milan: Guerini Studio.

Gutmann, D., Ternier-David, J., & Verrier, C. (1995). *Gruppe og transformation* (Groups and transformation). Copenhagen: Ubevidste Processer.

Gutmann, D., Ternier-David, J., & Verrier, C. (1996). Paradoxer och förvandling i konsultrollen: Från reparation till uppenbarelse (Paradox and transformation in the role of consultant: from reparation to revelation). In: S. B. Boëthius and S. Jern (Eds.), *Den svårfångade organisationen* (pp. 133–160). Stockholm: Natur och Kultur.

Gutmann, D., Ternier-David, J., & Verrier, C. (1997). Transformation et collusion. De la conformation à l'alliance (Transformation and collusion. From conformation to alliance). *Management et Conjoncture Sociale*, 507: 9–23.

Gutmann, D., Ternier-David, J., & Verrier, C. (1999). From envy to desire: witnessing the transformation. In: R. French & R. Vince (Eds.), *Group Relations, Management and Organisation* (pp. 155–172). Oxford: Oxford University Press.

Jullien, F. (1992). *La propension des choses; pour une histoire de l'efficacité en Chine*. Paris: Seuil.

Klein, M. (1946–1963). *Envy and Gratitude and Other Works*. New York: Delacorte Press/S. Lawrence, 1975.

Kohut, H. (1972). thoughts on narcissism and narcissistic rage. In: *The Search for the Self*, Volume 2 (pp. 615–658). New York: International Universities Press.

Lacan, J. (1965). Le stade du miroir comme formateur de la fonction du JE. *Ecrits*. Paris: Le Seuil.

Lacan, J. (1977). *Ecrits: A Selection*. A. Sheridan (Trans.). London: Tavistock.

Laplanche, J., & Pontalis, J.-B. (1992). *Vocabulaire de la psychanalyse*. Paris: PUF.

Lawrence, W. G. (1986). A psycho-analytical perspective on organizational life. In: G. Chattopadhay, Z. H. Gangjee, M. L. Hunt, & W. G. Lawrence (Eds.), *When the Twain Meet: Western Theory and Eastern Insights in Exploring Indian Organisations*. Allahabad: Wheeler.

Massé, P. (1965). *Le plan ou l'anti-hasard*. Paris: Gallimard.

Mendel, G. (1992). *La Société n'est pas une famille, de la psychanalyse à la sociopsychanalyse.* Paris: Editions la découverte.

Mendel, G. (1992). *La société n'est pas une famille,* La découverte.

Menzies Lyth, I. E. P. (1987). *A Psycho-Analytic Perspective on Social Institutions.*

Menzies, L. (1988). *Containing Anxiety in Institutions.* London: Free Association.

Miller, E. J. (1976). *Task and Organization.* London: Wiley.

Moses, R. (1982). The group self and the Arab–Israeli conflict. *The International Review of Psychoanalysis.*

Oldenquist, A. (1986). *The Non-suicidal Society.* Bloomington, IN: Indiana University Press.

Raffel, B. (1983). *The Essential Horace: Odes, Epodes, Satires, and Epistles.* San Francisco, CA: North Point Press.

Robins, R. S., & Post, J. M. (1997). *Political Paranoia: The Psychopolitics of Hatred.* New Haven, CT: Yale University Press.

Rueff, C., & Moreau, J.-F. (1987). *La Démocratie dans l'école.* Paris: Syros.

Schumpeter, J. A. (1939). *Business Cycles: A Theorical, Historical and Statistical Analysis of the Capitalist Process.* New York: MacGraw Hill.

Sibony, D. (1991). *Entre-Deux. L'origine en partage. La couleur des idées.* Paris: Edition du Seuil.

Sturluson, S., & Faulkes, A. (1987). *Edda.* London. Dent.

Tournier, M. (1972). *Vendredi ou les limbes du Pacifique.* Paris: Gallimard.

Volkan, V. D. (1987). *Six Steps in the Treatment of Borderline Personality Organization.* New York: Aronson.

Volkan, V. D. (1988). The need to have enemies and allies: from clinical practice to international relationships. Northvale, NJ: Jason Aronson.

Weber, M. (1904–1917). Essais sur la théorie de la science. Paris: Plon, 1965).

Webster's New World Dictionary of American English (1991). New York: Simon & Schuster.

Winnicott, D. W. (1950). Quelques réflexions sur le sens du mot démocratie. In: *Conversations ordinaires.* Paris: Gallimard.

Winnicott, D. W. (1960). Ego distortion in terms of true and false self. In: *The Maturational Process and the Facilitating Environment: Studies in the Theory of Emotional Development.* New York: International Universities Press, 1965.

Winnicott, D. W. (1965). *The Maturational Process and the Facilitating Environment: Studies in the Theory of Emotional Development.* London: Hogarth.

Winnicott, D. W. (1989). *Human Nature*. New York: Schocken Books.

Winnicott, D. W., Monod, C., & Pontalis, J. B. (1975). *Jeu et réalité: l'espace potentiel*. Paris: Gallimard.

Winnicott, D. W., Winnicott, C., Shepherd, R., & Davis, M. (1987). *Babies and their Mother*. Reading, MA: Addison-Wesley.

INDEX